WHAT LIES BENEATH MATTERS

A WORKBOOK FOR PARENTS OF TWEENS AND TEENS WITH ADHD

**GRACE DA CAMARA | PSYCHOLOGIST
& MADALENA BENNETT | GENERAL PRACTITIONER**

UW
AP

First published in 2023 by

UWA Publishing, Crawley, Western Australia 6009

www.uwap.uwa.edu.au

UWAP is an imprint of UWA Publishing, a division of The University of Western Australia.

THE UNIVERSITY OF WESTERN AUSTRALIA

The information and strategies in this workbook are based on the author's interpretations of the books that she has read, on her experiences as a mother of a child with ADHD and the results of her personal experiences in her clinical work, as a psychologist, working with children and adults with ADHD and their families.

Requests for information should be addressed to: SafeZone Counselling, szcounselling@gmail.com

ISBN: 9781760802172

Editor: Valerie Latimour
Proofreader: Euan Lloyd
Illustrations: Anne-Marie Douse
Cover design: Taloula Press
Printed by Lightning Source

Thank you to my family, especially my son who has ADHD. In your struggles I found the strength to persevere even when challenged by my critical inner voice.

Grace Da Camara & Madalena Bennett

This unique mother/daughter combination brings together the knowledge and experience of a psychologist who specialises in working with children, adolescents, adults and families affected by ADHD; and a general practitioner with a focus on a multidisciplinary approach to treatment.

Grace employs a range of therapeutic approaches, including Cognitive Behaviour Therapy, Rational Emotive Behaviour Therapy, Interpersonal Psychotherapy and Acceptance Commitment Therapy. She adopts an eclectic approach on the basis that each client is unique and has their own particular presentation. Her overriding focus is to help the client develop a better understanding of their challenges and grow in a personally meaningful way.

As a GP, Madalena recognises and acknowledges the need for education on ADHD for mental health professionals, including GPs. She is a member of the RACGP specific-interest ADHD, ASD, and neurodiversity group and has engaged in upskilling for fellow GP colleagues in this area.

Both Grace and Madalena support and endorse the need for greater knowledge and education about the condition, with a focus on interventions targeted to individuals and families living with ADHD.

Contents

The hardest thing about ADHD is that it's "invisible" to outsiders. People just assume that we are not being good parents and that our child is a brat, when they don't have an idea how exhausted we truly are.

Parent

INTRODUCTION

Attention Deficit Hyperactivity Disorder (ADHD) is a prevalent and challenging condition. Contrary to the belief that children will grow out of the disorder, most childhood cases continue to meet the criteria of ADHD during adolescence. Between 50 and 80% of children diagnosed with ADHD will continue to meet the criteria in adulthood.

Parenting is a challenging task at the best of times, and parenting a child with ADHD comes with added challenges – a meltdown, a bad report card, a 10-minute worksheet that turns into an evening-long struggle. Learning to negotiate these challenges is made more difficult by the fact that there are no hard and fast rules. The parent must always be 'on', and this can be exhausting. A parent of a child or children with ADHD needs extra patience, dedication, compassion and knowledge, and the know-how to advocate for their child. The best thing parents and children can do is learn as much as possible about all aspects of ADHD. With this knowledge you can create a family structure that works for you, rather than wasting time and effort trying to fulfil unrealistic expectations about what constitutes the perfect family.

Children with ADHD can be sweet, funny, loving and creative, but it can be difficult to recognise these positive traits during challenging episodes when the child is struggling and acting out. The child's positive aspects become completely buried under power struggles, shame, worry and guilt. Even though parents understand how tiring and challenging their child can be at times, they still hurt and become defensive when others criticise their child, especially when all the attention is focused on the negative aspects of their behaviour.

> *The stigma of ADHD discourages letting people know. School, work and relationships are made difficult due to not feeling comfortable disclosing and yet the right information and understanding would make a massive difference.*
> **Australian National Survey (2020)**

ADHD is in most cases a lifelong condition, and for children to grow and understand their ADHD, they need people with knowledge about the subject area to help them deal with their symptoms and learn how to advocate for themselves. ADHD can cause feelings of shame, fear and self-doubt. As parents we need to recognise when our children are hurting under the strain of ridicule, isolation and frustration, and give them the tools to protect their self-esteem and confidence to build a better life.

'Impact on child's confidence, social skills and emotional wellbeing is so important. Social groups are needed for children to learn how to interact appropriately all the way through schooling.'
Australian National Survey (2020)

Just like so many aspects of parenting, our own temperament and behaviour as parents influence those of our children. Building a healthy relationship with your ADHD strong-willed child is a two-way street and is necessary if we want to survive the challenges they'll present as they find their way through this world. Examining our own temperament is the starting point to building a more effective relationship with our children. This understanding allows us to identify with our child, as we likely share many of the same personality qualities. This self-examination can help develop a strong, positive relationship with your spirited child.

In my clinical work with individuals and groups, as well as parents, I am well aware of how power struggles work with strong-willed children. Think about this for a second: children are always being told what to do by an adult. Almost every part of their lives is being dictated by the adults in their lives. The ADHD strong-willed child is more likely to resist being bossed around and to be more insistent on gaining control of their lives. Their persistence can translate into power struggles when the normal rush of life makes us feel like we don't have time to allow them to make their own decisions.

To avoid power struggles, it's important that we offer choices to our strong-willed children. While the choices we offer may still be within our power, giving options allows children to feel they have some control. It's human nature to crave control.

Stay focused on the long-term goal. Yes, you want your child to learn the skills they need to succeed in life, but you also want to have an intact and interactive loving family, with parents and children who feel good about themselves and each other. Let your child know that you are in their corner and love them no matter what, and that together you will get through the smooth and the rough.

Lastly, remember that you can't be your best at raising your child if you have health problems, emotional distress or general life stress. So, look after yourself first and accept that the rest is largely out of your power to control.

About This Workbook

This parent workbook, part of the 'What Lies Beneath Matters' series, provides parents with strategies to assist their growing children to develop independence and take responsibility for their condition. Its multifaceted approach at times challenges you, the parent, to reflect on your own triggers and analyse your own behaviours as well as your own coping strategies. This increased self-awareness will help you find compassion for your child's struggles, accepting their ADHD symptoms as part of who they are. Sometimes they make your child funny and creative and entertaining, but frequently they lead to dysfunctional responses to the overwhelming requests of the world around them. Learning ways to lessen that overwhelm and provide a positive space for your child to feel accepted can be the first step to inviting not only better behaviours but also a better relationship with your child.

Developed for parents of children with ADHD who understand the need for parent involvement in a multimodal-treatment approach to ADHD this self-help workbook is a great tool for those parents whose children refuse to engage in one-on-one counselling or group programs, or who live remotely where these services are not readily available.

Based on principles of the Cognitive Behavioural Model of ADHD, developed by Safran, Perlman, Sprich & Otto (2005), this workbook has the following objectives:

- provide education to parents about ADHD in their children, including its causes, symptoms and many different presentations.
- improve parents' management skills and competence when dealing with challenging behaviours presented by children with ADHD – including the difficult task of parents managing their own emotions and behaviours.
- increase teen and tween compliance with parental requests, directives and rules.
- create a more harmonious family through the development of positive parenting skills such as consistently providing clear guidance and rules, using fair discipline, and a reliance on values-guided parenting behaviour.
- use collaborative problem-solving strategies and positive communication styles to address struggles in a way that empowers the young person but also ensures the support is there when needed.
- identify and alter unreasonable beliefs or expectations in parents or children that may be hindering the development of positive behaviour.

'I feel there isn't enough support or training for teachers or support staff in schools for ADHD or behaviour and education of the effects of medications. I find children with ADHD quite often get ignored or put in the too-hard basket. Sometimes I feel there needs to be a separate style of learning and school for ADHD. More cross communication between medical professionals is needed and more advice, respite and education for parents struggling are needed.'
Australian National Survey (2020)

How to Use This Workbook

The many activities and self-reflection exercises in this workbook have been developed to help parents understand and manage the most frequently encountered problems related to childhood ADHD. It's important that you take the time to engage in these and do this self-exploration. Your efforts will give you increased insight into the problems and their possible solutions that you may encounter in your parenting role. Only by making sense of it all in a personal way and with the understanding that the job of a parent is not to sculpt your child to fulfil your own expectations but to be a guide, provider, nurturer and protector of their unique gifts and strengths can you learn the strategies in this book and make your efforts pay off. This steering takes place indirectly, through the environment in which you raise your child with ADHD, and the support you provide.

Feel free to skip around between modules. The topics are largely independent of each other and don't need to be read straight through. You may want to start with the topics that are most relevant to your child's needs and go back and read the other topics at a later time. You will need them to form a holistic picture of ADHD and how it impacts your child.

Remember that knowledge has many layers. Each time you revisit a topic, evaluate your situation and apply the strategies to new problems, you'll deepen and strengthen what you know and feel more empowered to bring about change in your parenting and overall family functioning.

I wish people had the information to understand it. Understanding is something that we don't have. Public, professionals, school staff. School staff don't appear to have any basic knowledge of ADHD and often escalate children to point of meltdown.'
Australian National Survey (2020)

A Parent's Gift

Show all children the beauty they have inside.
Let this give them a quiet sense of pride.
Allow this self-awareness to be a safe place from within.
Growth will stem from it and pain can heal.
All the layers will begin to peel.
Teach your teens to dream.
Encourage their imagination to soar.
Let them experience and develop a passion
while embracing themselves
for who they really are;
this will enable them to go very far.
Inner strength will blossom, and a happier life will find;
All they truly need is patience and some extra time.
Your look into their eyes will say, everything will work out just fine!

Kerin Bellak-Adams

Module 1:

Psychoeducation

Topic 1: Understanding Your Child's ADHD

What Exactly is ADHD?

ADHD is a prevalent, long-lasting, treatable disorder. It is characterised by a pattern of developmentally inappropriate behaviours, inattention, hyperactivity/restlessness, and impulsivity that affects approximately 3–7% of school-aged children. A diagnosis of ADHD must meet certain criteria, as detailed in a recognised diagnostic manual. Worldwide, the two preferred manuals are the *Diagnostic and Statistical Manual of Mental Disorders (DSM-5)* and the *ICD-10 Classification of Mental and Behavioural Disorders*. Clinicians use these references for assessment to create a profile of the child in consultation with parents and teachers.

Since ADHD seldom exists in isolation, most clinicians will also include evaluations for additional, co-morbid conditions, such as anxiety, depression, learning disorders (LD) and oppositional defiant disorder (ODD). To meet the diagnostic criteria for ADHD, problem behaviours need to occur in more than one setting/environment, cause impairment in major life activities, and be best explained by ADHD rather than another condition such as intellectual disability; and symptoms must start before the age of 12. Another characteristic that is gaining interest when diagnosing ADHD is the problem with the regulation of emotions. Although not explicitly included in DSM-5, individuals with ADHD have more difficulty in recognising and managing their emotions.

Medication is currently the first-line treatment for ADHD and is the most extensively studied. Although stimulants have been used effectively in the treatment of ADHD for many years, this treatment remains highly debated and does not work for everyone. What we know is that medication can reduce the core symptoms of ADHD – inattention problems, hyperactivity and impulsivity. An effective medication will prepare the brain for better focus, organisation and self-control, but young people will still need to learn strategies and techniques to function effectively in their everyday life.

Furthermore, disruptions to overall quality of life, such as underachievement at school, relationship difficulties and increased conflict at home associated with ADHD, call for treatment that is multimodal in nature. ADHD is not a simple behavioural disorder. It is a complex condition affecting the brain's management system. This system, often called executive function (EF), operates below the surface and coordinates every aspect of our lives. ADHD makes it more difficult for EF to work efficiently.

What parents and educators see is but a fraction of the issue. Like an iceberg, where as much as 90% of its mass sits under the water, many facets of ADHD lie under the surface. The 10% that we see – the core symptoms of ADHD (inattention, impulsivity, and hyperactivity) – are important, but they do not explain the whole picture. From experience as a clinician, what lies beneath the surface is of great importance when attempting to understand the presentation of an individual with ADHD as well as when raising and teaching children with ADHD.

A Brief History of ADHD

In 1798, a Scottish doctor, Sir Alexander Crichton, noticed some people were easily distracted and unable to focus on their activities the way others could. He reported that these symptoms began early in life. That's consistent with what we now call ADHD. In 1902, Sir George Frederic Still spoke about mental conditions in otherwise healthy children of normal intelligence. These children were more impulsive and had problems with attention and self-control. He noted fifteen cases in young boys and five in girls. This is in line with modern-day understanding that males are more likely to be diagnosed with ADHD than females.

The first medication

In 1937, Charles Bradley, the medical director of what is today called Bradley Hospital in Rhode Island, USA, noticed that a stimulant called Benzedrine caused some children to behave better. It also improved their school performance. Benzedrine had been approved by the FDA in 1936, but it was many years before researchers took notice of Bradley's findings. Today, methylphenidate is the stimulant doctors most often prescribe for children with ADHD. It was first made in 1944 and marketed in 1954 as Ritalin. At first, it was used to treat conditions such as chronic fatigue and depression. But it worked best to improve symptoms of ADHD.

ADHD today

In 1994, the American Psychological Association (APA) released a fourth edition of the DSM. It listed three types of ADHD: mostly inattentive; mostly hyperactive and impulsive; and a combined type that includes all three symptoms. This edition of the DSM also recognised that ADHD symptoms in children, in the majority of cases, continue into adulthood.

In the current edition (DSM-5), published in 2013, the APA designated the three types as the three 'presentations' of ADHD – i.e. the ways the disorder may affect people.

More than 5 million children between ages 4 and 17 in the US are now diagnosed with ADHD. Boys make up twice as many cases as girls. In 1997–1999, 7% of all children in this age group in the US were diagnosed with ADHD. By 2012–2014, that had risen to over 10%.

ADHD in Australia today

A national survey conducted by ADHD Australia in 2020, to identify and clarify the key issues faced by people living with ADHD, reported that as many as 7% of children and about 2.5% adults in Australia have ADHD. The following three key areas of concern stood out in the survey results:

- The cost of living with ADHD.
- The need for schools to truly accommodate, empathise with and understand children with ADHD, and to help them meet the unique challenges they face.
- The need for awareness and understanding of the challenges people at all ages with ADHD face in day-to-day aspects of work, social and family life.

Funding is essential to tackling all three of the above: funding for families of children with ADHD and individuals with ADHD; funding school support and resourcing; and funding to raise awareness of ADHD.

For all of the survey participants, the number one difficulty was the everyday challenges of living with ADHD. These included, but were not limited to, living with one or more coexisting condition, dealing with the impact of ADHD in school, employment, and social and relationship matters, and the impact on the family unit. These challenges were exacerbated by a lack of awareness and understanding in the general Australian population about the ADHD community and their needs. The full survey is available on ADHD Australia's website www.adhdaustralia.org.au.

Challenges reported in the survey

Participants were asked to choose the top three things that have been the most difficult for them in regard to ADHD. Below are some of the responses.

- Four in five (79.9%) adults with ADHD selected everyday living challenges with ADHD as their top difficulty. Almost two-thirds (65.2%) chose work being impacted by ADHD and 40.6% chose the financial cost of ADHD.
- More than four in five (84.1%) of young people with ADHD selected everyday living challenges with ADHD as a top difficulty, with about half choosing work being impacted by ADHD (53.6%) and finding the right medications and therapies (49.3%).
- Nearly three quarters (74.4%) of parents of children with ADHD thought schooling a child with ADHD was their most difficult challenge.
- Difficulties for Aboriginal and Torres Strait Islander participants in the survey were consistent with the overall participant cohort, with their top three difficulties being everyday living challenges with ADHD (64.4%), schooling a child with ADHD (60.0%) and finding the right medications and therapies (53.3%).

The following quotes have been adapted from the national survey.

'People not understanding how varied the symptoms are and how they impact every area of life and just how hard things can be.'

'There needs to be awareness that it's not just a childhood issue but follows many people into their adult life.'

'There needs to be more education around ADHD and the various symptoms, how it affects day-to-day living and how it affects education. Because it affects so many more children than autism, it should be legally and socially considered a disability.'

DSM-5 – Diagnostic Criteria for ADHD

A. Persistent pattern of inattention and/or hyperactivity-impulsivity that interferes with functioning or development, as characterised by (1) and/or (2).

Six or more of the following symptoms of inattention, or six or more of the following symptoms of hyperactivity-impulsivity must be present, for at least six (6) months to a degree that is inconsistent with developmental level, and that negatively impacts directly on social and academic/occupational activities.

Note: The symptoms are not solely a manifestation of oppositional behaviour, defiance, hostility, or failure to understand tasks or instructions. For individuals aged 17 and older, at least five symptoms are required.

1. Symptoms of Inattention	2. Symptoms of Hyperactivity-Impulsivity
Often fails to give close attention to details or makes careless mistakes in schoolwork, work, or other activities.	Often fidgets with hands or feet or squirms in seat.
Often has difficulty sustaining attention in tasks or play activities.	Often leaves seat in classroom or in other situations in which remaining seated is expected.
Often does not seem to listen when spoken to directly.	Often runs about or climbs excessively in situations in which it is inappropriate (in adolescents or adults it may be limited to subjective feelings of restlessness).
Often does not follow through on instructions and fails to finish schoolwork, chores, or duties in the workplace (not because of oppositional behaviour or failure to understand instructions).	Often has difficulty playing or engaging in leisure activities quietly.
Often has difficulty organising tasks and activities.	Is often 'on the go' or often acts as if 'driven by motor'.
Often avoids, dislikes, or reluctant to engage in tasks that require sustained mental effort.	Often talks excessively.
Often loses things necessary for tasks or activities.	Often blurts out answers before questions have been completed.
Is often easily distracted by extraneous stimuli.	Often has difficulty awaiting turn.
Is often forgetful in daily activities.	Often interrupts or intrudes on others.

B. Several inattentive or hyperactive-impulsive symptoms were present before the age of 12 years.

C. Several inattentive or hyperactive-impulsive symptoms are present in two or more settings (e.g. at home, school, work, with friends or relatives, and in other activities).

D. There is clear evidence that the symptoms interfere with, or reduce the quality of, social, academic, or occupational functioning.

E. The symptoms do not occur exclusively during the course of schizophrenia or another psychotic disorder, and are not better explained by another mental disorder (e.g. mood disorder, anxiety disorder, dissociative disorder or personality disorder, substance intoxication, or withdrawal).

Prevalence

Population surveys suggest that ADHD occurs in most cultures, in about 5% of children and 2.5% of adults.

Gender-Related Diagnostic Issues

It is estimated that of individuals with ADHD globally, approximately half of them are female. Yet, as children, females are only half as likely to be referred for evaluation and treatment compared to boys.

Indeed, in a recent 2019 report that calculated estimates of ADHD in males and females aged 0 to 14, the authors noted that ADHD is more than twice as prevalent in males than females –5.8% compared to 2.3%, respectively. These statistics highlight the large gender discrepancy in ADHD referral and diagnosis. According to numerous studies, more than 75% of females with ADHD are not formally diagnosed even into adulthood, and those who received a diagnosis in adulthood often reminisce over the signs that were missed in their childhood and wonder how their lives might have been different had they been diagnosed sooner.

Factors contributing to the identification and diagnosis of ADHD in females include biological differences that increase the likelihood of comorbidities in females, symptomatic differences when compared to males, stricter societal expectations for females, as well as an increased ability to utilise masking or compensatory mechanisms that underplay the presence of their ADHD.

What Lies Beneath Your Child's ADHD Iceberg?

Think about your child's ADHD. What are the visible symptoms? Write them above the surface of the iceberg. What do you think is going on under the surface? Write this in too. For more information on what might be hidden below the surface of your child's ADHD iceberg, see the list on the following page.

Hidden Layers of an ADHD Iceberg

To discover what lies beneath the surface of your child's ADHD iceberg, consider the following information. When you look deeper, you begin to understand how the visible symptoms and behaviours your child displays are manifestations of underlying biological and neurological deficits. Check the boxes that apply to your child.

- [ ] **Developmental Delays.** Children with ADHD develop 2–3 years slower than their peers. We see this impact in maturity, social skills, executive functioning, emotional dysregulation and self-regulation.

- [ ] **Executive Functioning Deficits.** Executive function skills help us manage day-to-day planning, organisation, task initiation, emotional regulation and time management. When this group of skills is delayed or impaired, many daily tasks fall apart.

- [ ] **Inflexibility.** Stubborn streaks in our children with ADHD are not wilfulness. Instead, inflexibility is a result of not having the skills to see more than one way, or to manage emotions or cope with change. When children with ADHD are inflexible, they are communicating a deeper struggle.

- [ ] **Intensity.** When a child has lagging skills, emotional awareness, self-regulation and frustration tolerance, it can lead to some extreme emotions. In addition, some individuals with ADHD experience hypersensitivity; they feel their feelings more deeply and intensely.

- [ ] **Emotional Dysregulation.** Children with ADHD struggle to regulate their emotions in a way that's appropriate for the situation and/or their age. They may have a different way of expressing emotion, poor self-regulation skills, or poor communication skills. Whatever the root cause, emotional dysregulation impacts how they function at home, in the family, at school, and in social interactions with peers.

- [ ] **Coexisting Conditions.** It's estimated that 50–60% of individuals with ADHD also have one or more coexisting conditions. These conditions could include a mood disorder, anxiety, autism, learning disabilities, executive functioning deficits, conduct disorder and more. These additional diagnoses can be important because they give us a starting point from which we can understand our children and effectively help them. We resist adding more diagnoses when we already have one or two or five, but when that additional piece of the puzzle helps us understand our child better it can be enormously valuable.

- [ ] **Skill Deficits.** Because ADHD is a developmental disorder resulting from a physiological difference in the brain, skill deficits are common. The most common skill deficits for children with ADHD include time management, frustration tolerance, planning and organisation, emotional regulation, problem solving, social skills and flexible thinking. Some lagging skills can be taught and improved; others, unfortunately, will be a lifelong struggle.

☐ **Time Blindness.** People with ADHD often have a distorted concept of time. For example, your child may not have an innate sense of how long 30 minutes feels. This also affects how your child responds to needing to wait, or they can have the feeling that a simple task will take forever to complete.

☐ **Poor Self-Esteem and Self-Confidence.** Struggling with ADHD can damage anyone's self-esteem.

☐ **Meltdowns.** A meltdown is different to a tantrum. In a meltdown, your child's brain has been hijacked. They are no longer in control of what they are saying and doing. A meltdown can be triggered by a tantrum, or it can be triggered by sensory overload, feeling misunderstood or not feeling heard. In the throes of a meltdown, a child might harm themselves or others. They are not able to consider their actions and rationalise. A meltdown will not stop if the child is offered what they originally wanted.

☐ **School Incompatibility.** Mass education is designed with an expectation of conformity. Students must sit still, be quiet and remain attentive for long periods of time. That's expecting a lot, since it considers none of the weaknesses and challenges common for students with ADHD. It essentially makes them incompatible with Western education.

If you're not going deeper into the mass of the iceberg that's under the surface, it can leave your child feeling misunderstood and a misfit. These hidden layers are all part of ADHD. Others might not see them; you must. Together, they form that beautiful but dangerous iceberg.

1

Personal ADHD Checklist

Below is a list of typical things that children with ADHD report difficulty with. Go through the list and check the ones that apply to your child.

Home

- ☐ Room is a mess
- ☐ Finds it difficult to follow rules
- ☐ Forgets to do things told to do
- ☐ Finds it hard to start homework
- ☐ Often interrupts family members
- ☐ Struggles to get ready for school on time
- ☐ Gets easily distracted
- ☐ Gets angry if not allowed screen time

Friends

- ☐ Often make friends with younger child
- ☐ Does not feel as smart as other children
- ☐ Gets into fights and becomes upset with friends
- ☐ Finds it hard to make friends, or other children don't want to be friends
- ☐ Seldom gets invited to birthdays or get togethers
- ☐ Is often mean to classmates
- ☐ Is bossy in play

School

- ☐ Loses homework and misses deadlines
- ☐ Always wants to finish homework in a rush and ends up making a lot of mistakes
- ☐ Often gets told to calm down or slow down by teachers
- ☐ Blurts things out in the middle of class
- ☐ Struggles to pay attention in class

Add up the checks in each section. Where does your child have the most checks? This will help you determine which area needs attention.

HOME _____ **FRIENDS** _____ **SCHOOL** _____

ADHD Coping Styles

Having ADHD can make relationships, school performance and social settings challenging for some children. However, just like children without ADHD, your child has strengths and weaknesses. Some identified strengths associated with ADHD include a good sense of humour, spontaneity, energy and the ability to hyper-focus and take risks.

Although there is no single ADHD personality, some styles of coping have been identified.

The **poor me** – blames others for their ADHD difficulties.

The **controller** – makes every attempt to manipulate ADHD and the people in their lives. Some cope by getting others to take care of them and their problems. Others cope by withdrawing from life and their problems.

The **aggressor** – uses similar manipulative behaviours as the controller but accompanied by aggression.

The **acceptor** – those who accept their ADHD are less likely to experience shame. They do not hide or deny their ADHD struggles and work hard to bring about change in their lives.

Does your child's behaviour fit any of the ADHD coping styles above?

_____

If so, which one, and what behaviours are indicative of it?

_____

_____

_____

What is one of your child's symptoms/behaviours that is most challenging for you to manage?

_____

_____

_____

What situations make this symptom worse?

_____

_____

_____

In the situations where your child's ADHD symptoms are most problematic, what is one thing that you can do to reduce the symptom?

_____

_____

_____

Who/what can give you respite?

_____

_____

_____

What We Know About ADHD

According to experts, ADHD is a neurodevelopmental (brain based) disorder with strong genetic factors. Twin, family and adoption studies suggest that the genetic contribution of ADHD is in the range of 60–90%. This means that if you have ADHD, there is most probably someone in your family who has it too – maybe undiagnosed. Contrary to many myths, poor parenting and diet do not cause ADHD.

Brain imaging has shown that individuals with ADHD have less dopamine available in the brain's reward networks (Volkow et al., 2011). Because of this, they do not get the same level of satisfaction from doing ordinary tasks. The lack of satisfaction is felt as boredom, and it depletes a person's motivation to persevere or even get started.

Although many questions about ADHD remain unanswered, what we know is that:

- A child with ADHD is four times more likely to have a relative with ADHD.
- There is no cure for ADHD. Treatment only manages symptoms.
- We do not know the exact causes of the disorder.
- The challenges that come with ADHD are different at different life stages, from childhood to teen years to adulthood, so new strategies are needed throughout a person's life.
- Treatment needs be multimodal; in other words, a combination of treatments is needed that may or may not include medication.
- Parents need be active in the child's treatment.
- ADHD delays executive functioning (EF) development.
- ADHD impacts on emotions.
- ADHD impacts on motivation.
- ADHD seldom exists in isolation.

Knowing this, we can work on addressing the issues over which we have some control. The rest of this module provides information on the concepts of EF development, emotions and motivation, comorbidities, and the options for multimodal treatment.

Topic 2: Executive Functioning and ADHD

In many ways, ADHD and executive functioning (EF) issues go hand in hand. That's because most of the symptoms of ADHD are actually due to delays in EF. The signs of ADHD and EF issues are similar: the one big difference is that ADHD is an official diagnosis, whereas EF impairment is not.

EF impairment refers to weaknesses in the brain's self-management system. Trouble with executive function isn't just a problem for children with ADHD; many children with learning differences struggle with one or more of these key skills. You can think of EF as the top-level 'boss' in a company. A company usually has different departments (e.g. accounting, marketing and IT) just as the brain has different skill areas (e.g. language, movement and spatial perception). Individual areas may be functioning well, but unless there is a 'boss' to ensure smooth coordination, a complex task is unlikely to be completed effectively.

The following table shows the differences between ADHD and EF issues in children:

Definitions			
ADHD	**Executive Functioning Issues**		
A neurobiological (brain-based) condition that makes it hard for children to concentrate, use working memory, organise and manage themselves. They may also be impulsive or hyperactive. These are all issues with executive function.	Weaknesses in key mental skills that are responsible for attention, memory, organisation and time management, and flexible thinking. Children with ADHD struggle with these skills. But so do some children with learning differences who don't have ADHD.		
Observable Signs			
Symptom		**ADHD**	**EF**
Has a hard time paying attention		✓	✓
Has difficulty with self-control		✓	✓
Has difficulty holding information in working memory		✓	✓
Has trouble switching easily from one activity to another		✓	✓
Has trouble getting started on tasks		✓	✓
Has problems organising their time or materials		✓	✓

Has trouble keeping track of what they're doing	✓	✓
Has difficulty completing long-term projects	✓	✓
Has trouble thinking before acting	✓	✓
Is easily distracted and often forgetful	✓	✓
Has trouble waiting their turn	✓	✓
Fidgets, interrupts or talks excessively	✓	
Acts as if they are 'driven by a motor'	✓	
Has problems remembering what they've been asked to do		✓

Social and Emotional Challenges		
Symptom	**ADHD**	**EF**
Impulsivity and trouble managing emotions may cause difficulty with making and keeping friends	✓	
Poor self-control, self-monitoring and remembering what they've been asked to do can cause problems with friends		✓
Frequent negative feedback can impact self-esteem and motivation, resulting in children feeling 'bad' or 'no good'	✓	
Not thinking flexibly can make it hard to be flexible with others		✓

Professionals who can help		
	ADHD	**EF**
Paediatricians and Psychiatrists		
Can diagnose ADHD and prescribe medication	✓	
Can look for other issues like anxiety or sleep problems	✓	
May refer patients to psychologists (or neuropsychologists) for more complete evaluations	✓	
Psychologists		
Can diagnose ADHD and co-existing mental-health issues such as anxiety	✓	
May evaluate for learning differences	✓	✓
May provide cognitive behavioural therapy to teach children to manage their actions and interactions as well as help with emotional issues	✓	✓

1

Paediatric neuropsychologists		
Can evaluate for learning differences using tests that involve executive function	✓	✓
May evaluate for ADHD and common mental-health issues that co-exist	✓	✓
What you can do at home		
	ADHD	**EF**
Create daily routines and rituals to provide structure	✓	✓
Practice self-regulation skills	✓	✓
Model appropriate social behaviour	✓	✓
Set rules and stick to them	✓	
Break tasks into smaller chunks	✓	
Allow for frequent breaks	✓	
Have clear expectations for behaviour and prepare them in advance for new experiences	✓	
Give frequent feedback	✓	
Provide positive reinforcement for positive behaviour	✓	
Teach time-management skills		✓
Give advance warning of upcoming transitions		✓
Have them talk through difficult tasks. Model thinking aloud during planning and problem solving situations		✓
Improve monitoring skills by asking them to evaluate their performance		✓
What the school can provide		
Accommodations under an Individualised Education Plan (IEP)	**ADHD**	**EF**
Eligible for IEP under 'other health impairment' category	✓	
Eligible for IEP if a learning difference or ADHD are also present		✓
Tutoring or coaching for EFs	✓	✓
Help with organisation skills	✓	✓
Extra time on tests	✓	✓
Preferential seating	✓	✓
Opportunities for the student to repeat and rephrase important information	✓	
Additional structure to the day with routines, transitions and expectations	✓	
Tasks broken down into smaller components	✓	

Multisensory teaching techniques	✓	
Specific academic skill strategies (e.g. strategies for reading or summarising and organising thoughts)		✓
Positive reinforcement to increase confidence		✓
Structured teaching of complex skills with detailed steps		✓

1

Delays in Executive Functioning

Delays in executive functioning are always observed in children with ADHD. These delays can cause major challenges across different parts of a child's life. EF challenges fall under three main areas.

Working memory: the ability to keep information in mind and then use it as needed. For example, a student might use this to learn a formula in maths, hold unto the information and then apply it when needed.

Flexible thinking: the ability to think about something in more than one way and adapt when an initial idea is ineffective. For example, a student may use this to take different perspectives and find relationships between different concepts.

Inhibitory control/self-control: the ability to ignore distractions and resist temptation. For example, a child might use this to stop themselves blurting out an answer in class. It helps children regulate their emotions and keep from acting impulsively.

The following EF skills fit under the above-mentioned areas:

- managing time, organising, prioritising and planning
- paying attention
- starting tasks and staying focused on them
- managing emotions
- keeping track of what you're doing
- adjusting when an initial strategy is ineffective
- making decisions by considering multiple options.

Deficits in these skills can impact a child at home, at school and in social situations. Other skills that might be hard for people who struggle with EF include:

Reflection: a process that allows an individual to stop and think before they respond to something. This skill is key for solving problems. The more often children practice reflection, the better they get at it.

Processing speed: Children need to go through the reflection process quickly to solve problems on time. That's where processing speed comes in. Some experts view this skill as the engine that drives how well people use EF skills to solve problems and achieve goals. Unfortunately, children with ADHD often struggle with timed tasks.

How EF Affects Learning

Below is a list of the performance challenges related to ADHD and EF. Please tick the ones that are true for your child.

- ☐ Keeping track of time
- ☐ Getting started and finishing classwork (procrastination)
- ☐ Keeping track of more than one thing at a time
- ☐ Remembering, completing and submitting homework
- ☐ Engaging in group dynamics
- ☐ Reflecting on work and evaluating ideas
- ☐ Losing homework
- ☐ Getting organised
- ☐ Keeping cool in the face of challenges or upsets
- ☐ Asking for help
- ☐ Impulsivity
- ☐ Distractibility
- ☐ Changing classes or activities
- ☐ Following instructions
- ☐ Planning ahead
- ☐ Controlling emotions
- ☐ Solving problems flexibly
- ☐ Making decisions by weighing up the options

What follows are strategies to help your child better manage their challenging EF issues.

Strategies to Help Your Child Manage EF Impairment

Every new school year presents new challenges for your child. The general assumption that basic skills have been learned and good study skills have been formed, may not be the case for children with anxiety, EF or attention issues or learning differences. Your child may be struggling with gaps in basic skills, or experiencing problems with speed of performance. When this gap in basic skills leads to lower performance and/or causes missed deadlines, it can become challenging for your child and you. Work with your child collaboratively to implement some of the solutions below.

Understand where their skill gaps lie

Solution: You need to know what knowledge or skills your child is missing in order to help them acquire them. Perhaps the content is hard, involving abstract ideas and their corresponding details. Your child should revisit concepts until they're clear. If you move on without gaining mastery of a skill, you will need to relearn or review it every time you have to perform related tasks. Use flash cards to build or retain maths facts or vocabulary words. If reading is the problem, a good program for building word fluency could help.

Do things differently

Solution: If boredom is your child's problem, change things up. It's not always possible to find a new teacher or class, but changing the way they do things can make a difference. Can they do homework in a new place, like the library at school? Or with a buddy? Is there a new twist that your teacher could add to repetitive work? Is there a new hobby that they could engage in? Or a new sport?

Form habits

Solution: Practice makes perfect, but practising the wrong thing creates mess. If your child is struggling, it might be time to review those good habits that were set at the beginning of the school year. Are they misplacing their planner? Are they forgetting to chunk big tasks into smaller ones? Have homework routines been shelved?

Get back to routines

Solution: Re-establishing good habits and routines – planner use, homework structure, or breaking large assignments into smaller ones – can increase the capacity of working memory and help us manage complexity. Making something a habit or routine that you stick to consistently allows you to do tasks without having to tap into working memory. Having more working memory left over for your tasks enables higher-level thinking and increases performance and speed – we work smarter, not harder!

Tackle burnout

Solution: School can wear down students with EF challenges. Imagine having to show up for track practice five days a week, eight hours a day with a bad knee. It's the same feeling for those with learning problems who are in an intense learning environment. To others, especially teachers and parents, burnout may look like laziness, irritability, or work avoidance. At home it can mean that after a long day at school the child has very little self-control left, and so minor stresses and upsets are harder to cope with. Try to build in downtime for your child by rethinking your family schedule. Taking a look at your calendar might show that you're all overloaded! While it may include many worthwhile activities, doing all of them can take a toll. Maybe you can reduce the number of obligations you take on as a family, or let your child skip some once in a while.

Boost the brain

Solution: Research suggests that even 20 minutes of green time – exposure to nature – 'resets' our attention and helps us to refocus. Nature seems to give the right level of brain input to better access EF and self-regulation, especially if there is some light exercise built in. This effect seems to last well beyond the time spent in nature.

Get started

Solution: Decide which of these challenges is most affecting your child. If you'd like to create change, take out a calendar and make a plan to start this week. Ask yourself, 'What can I start doing today?' Turn those plans into habits through repetition, and you will be in a better position to help your child through the many transitions that are part of this phase of life. Provide scaffolding and support to bridge the gap when there are skill deficits; and then after the skills have started to improve, the scaffolding can be scaled back.

Would you like to share any strategies that your child has used, or is using, that are not mentioned above?

_____

_____

_____

_____

Let's look at a Day in the Life of a Year 7 Child With EF Impairments

Meet Tristan, a seventh grader with ADHD and EF delays. These delays cause many challenges in Tristan's day but do not mean that he isn't smart. It means that his brain's management system has trouble getting organised and getting started on tasks. Look at a typical day in Tristan's life.

8:15 Tristan's mother is already in the car waiting for Tristan. He opens the door of the car, drops his backpack and runs back inside. He's forgotten something. He gets his sports bag but it happens again, and he ends up leaving his lunch on the kitchen counter.

EF impaired: Organisation, working memory

10:30 Tristan's teacher asks the children to open their homework and leave it on their desks as she goes from desk to desk, checking it. Tristan anxiously fidgets, hoping that the bell will go before she gets to his desk. He didn't write the homework in his diary and has no idea what he was supposed to have done.

EF impaired: Organisation, focus

12:30 The best part of the school day for Tristan: lunch! But Tristan has no food. His cousin who goes to the same school kindly shares his sandwich with Tristan. His friends start talking about games and soon Tristan takes over the conversation. He gets excited and cannot stop talking about the new game that he got for his birthday. He does not notice his friends' annoyance.

EF impaired: Self-control, self-awareness

15:00 In water polo he is so focused on getting the ball that he doesn't keep in mind which direction he's supposed to swim once he gets it. He quickly heads for the nearest goal and throws the ball into his own team's net.

EF impaired: Shifting focus, thinking flexibly

18:00 Tristan isn't happy when his mum tells him to turn off the Xbox and set the table. Frustrated that he has to stop playing, he yells at his mother and tells her that his sister can do it.

EF impaired: Managing frustration, keeping information in check

19:00 After lots of reminders from his mum, Tristan sits down to do his homework. But he doesn't know where to start and feels overwhelmed. Instead of doing the 400-word English essay due the next day, he surfs the web to find information on

World War II for a more interesting project that is due in a week. Then he goes back on his Xbox because his friend messaged him to say they have just logged in online.

EF impaired: Setting priorities, starting tasks

22:00 Tristan is supposed to be in bed by now. He has not finished the essay and his mind is racing. He can't figure out what to write and only gets one sentence down on paper before he gives up for the night. He thinks that he will get up early and try to complete it then – even though he's never managed any work in the morning before and is often tired due to problems getting to sleep.

EF impaired: Paying attention, staying on task, organisation

Most children who learn and think differently have trouble with executive function. All children with ADHD struggle with it. These difficulties don't mean that the child isn't smart, but that the brain differences make it hard for them to focus, set goals, stay calm, get started on and complete homework, manage temptations and stick to daily routines.

These struggles are often misunderstood, and people might label the child as just being lazy and not trying hard enough. Although challenging, with the right support children with executive functioning issues can thrive.

Does your child struggle with EF impairment? If so, which issues are most problematic and in which areas of your child's life are those issues a problem?

_____

_____

_____

Do you think that your child would relate to how Tristan experienced his day? If so, how?

_____

_____

_____

Topic 3: ADHD and Emotions

Children with ADHD don't have different emotions from their peers. They feel hurt, anger, sadness, discouragement, laziness, and worry, just like everyone else does. What is different for many children with ADHD is that these feelings seem to be more frequent and intense. They also seem to last longer. And they get in the way of everyday life.
Thomas E. Brown

We all experience a mixture of positive and negative emotions daily. For some people, these emotions – particularly negative emotions like anger, frustration, sadness and guilt – can be overwhelming. Emotional regulation is a term generally used to describe a person's ability to manage and respond to an emotional experience in an adaptive way. Emotional regulation is essential for social and emotional wellbeing.

Managing emotions is particularly challenging for children, who often experience high levels of conflict with parents and peers. This is especially true for adolescents with ADHD, who Russell Barkley describes as having 'low frustration tolerance, impatience, and being quick to anger'.

Although teens with ADHD have significant difficulty managing negative emotions, many also have difficulty managing positive emotions. Specifically, when happy or excited, adolescents with ADHD often display age-inappropriate levels of enthusiasm or exuberance. They may yell, jump up and down, and invade others' personal space when they receive good news. As a result, parents, teachers and peers often view these teenagers as immature and boisterous.

Recent evidence suggests that the extreme changes from day to day in positive and negative emotions among adolescents with ADHD is linked to less peer acceptance, more internalising symptoms (anxiety, depression), and more externalising symptoms (oppositionality, defiance, conduct problems). Overall, poor emotional regulation may contribute to many of the negative outcomes they experience, such as engagement in risky behaviours including verbal and physical aggression, peer rejection, relationship difficulties, family conflict and substance abuse.

Is Emotional Dysregulation Part of ADHD?

There is ongoing debate in the medical field as to the role of ADHD in symptoms of emotional dysregulation. Emotional dysregulation used to be considered a core part of ADHD and was always included in descriptions of ADHD. There have been many name changes to ADHD, with medical literature from the 19th and 20th centuries referring to 'minimal brain dysfunction', 'defect in moral control', 'mental restlessness', 'hyperactive child syndrome' and 'hyperkinetic impulse disorder' before the term ADHD was adopted. In all of these early conceptualisations, emotional dysregulation was considered a key part of ADHD, and physicians sought to treat patients and mediate the impact emotional dysregulation had on someone's life.

In the 1970s, ADHD research became more formalised so that it could be incorporated into the DSM (Diagnostic and Statistical Manual – a psychiatric diagnostic tool that contains descriptions of symptoms and other criteria necessary for diagnosing mental health disorders). Emotional dysregulation was repeatedly reported clinically and observed during research, but researchers chose to focus on inattention, hyperactivity and impulsivity since these traits were far easier to measure and develop treatments for in a laboratory or clinical setting. Measuring emotional dysregulation was more challenging and, as such, it was phased out of medical descriptions of ADHD.

What is known about emotional dysregulation and ADHD today?

Emotional dysregulation is increasingly recognised as a core feature of ADHD. Studies show that 70–80% of children with ADHD struggle with emotional dysregulation. Inappropriate responses may be both internalised (e.g., the individual may be withdrawn, moody or sad) or externalised (e.g., they may be emotionally volatile, aggressive and combative).

For very young children, emotional regulation is largely managed extrinsically, by the parents. As children grow older, they need to develop their own regulatory processes. For children with ADHD, this may not be learned at age-appropriate times, and they may also have poor attention distribution and impulse control. This can result in the child disengaging from the cognitive process – they stop thinking – leading to issues such as:

- emotional reactions that seem out of proportion to the cause
- an inability to calm down once an emotion takes hold
- being insensitive to, or unaware of, the emotions of others.

According to Barkley (2015) ADHD-related emotional dysregulation is thought to result from poor EF control, which contributes to an individual having the following problems:

Highly volatile emotional trigger sensitivity and emotional impulsivity due to poor self-control. Emotional impulsivity contributes to ADHD symptoms such as impatience and low frustration tolerance, quickness to anger, reactive aggression or temper outbursts, and emotional liability.

Problems self-regulating their primary emotional response. Individuals with ADHD can experience such intense, overwhelming primary emotional reactions that they find it difficult to inhibit the expression of this emotion or to moderate the emotion and replace it with a secondary emotional reaction.

Problems refocusing their attention away from strong emotions. An inability to refocus attention away from strong emotions can make it difficult to reduce or moderate a primary emotional response. Refocusing problems can also contribute to thought rumination.

Difficulties self-soothing in order to moderate their primary emotional response due to poor working memory (i.e., reduced ability to use self-speech and visual imagery).

Difficulties organising and executing an appropriate secondary response due to difficulties appraising, flexibly manipulating and organising information; generating and appraising alternative responses and their possible outcomes; and planning an appropriate response.

How Parents Can Help Emotional Regulation Development

Parents play an important role in adolescent emotional development through their use of emotional socialisation practices. Parental emotional socialisation is an umbrella term used to describe emotion-focused parenting behaviours. It includes modelling of emotions and regulating emotions, discussing emotions, and responding to emotional displays in others, particularly their children.

When parents model helpful ways of dealing with negative emotions, such as talking to someone or taking space to calm down, and respond to their child's negative emotions by validating, coaching problem solving, and providing comfort, adolescents show better emotional regulation, more prosocial behaviours, and lower levels of anxiety, depression and aggression. In contrast, when parents model anger; engage in arguments or violence; and punish, minimise or escalate their teen's negative emotions, it may further exacerbate emotional regulation difficulties.

As a result of emotional dysregulation, children with ADHD are more likely to:

- become overly excited
- focus on the more negative aspects of a task or situation
- avoid and procrastinate
- express frustration or anger and become verbally or physically aggressive
- experience problems in social relationships including social rejection, bullying and isolation
- have difficulties achieving academic goals/requirements, receive a school suspension or expulsion, lose their job or fail to be promoted

- report increased psychological distress from their emotional experience
- develop anxiety and/or depression
- be involved in road rage and car accidents in adulthood
- have conduct problems, be involved in crime and be institutionalised in teen and adult years.

Do any of these issues affect your child? If so, which ones?

_____

_____

_____

In what settings (home, school, social etc) does your child struggle to regulate the most?

_____

_____

_____

1

Scenario

Joseph is a 12-year-old boy with ADHD who has been suspended from school. His mother stays at home with him but insists that Joseph does a number of homework exercises. He understands the necessity and is doing the work but becomes increasingly frustrated by the amount of work. Joseph thinks he is doing the last exercise when his mother tells him that there is one more page of maths to do. Joseph's heart starts to beat a little faster and he feels agitated. Just then the telephone rings; it is the school psychologist wishing to speak to Joseph's mother about the suspension and reintegration process. Joseph can hear only a little of the conversation but, already agitated, he becomes increasingly angry. His face turns red, and he begins to throw things around the house. He yells and screams, disrupting the telephone call, and strikes his mother with the remote control in desperation. Finally, he goes to his bedroom, destroying things along the way and slamming the door shut.

His mother hangs up the phone and goes into her room where she sobs uncontrollably. She applies make up to her cheek to hide the bruise left by the remote, so that Joseph's father won't see the bruise.

Imagine Joseph's mother is your friend, and she confides in you about her struggles with Joseph. What would you tell her?

_____

_____

_____

What do you think is the function or payoff of Joseph's behaviour? Do you think there may be some benefits to Joseph's behaviour, including some he may not even be aware of?

_____

_____

_____

Joseph is clearly angry, but what other feeling might he be experiencing and why?

_____

_____

_____

The Connection Between ADHD and Anger

The children who need the most love will ask for it in the most unloving of ways.
Unknown

Of all the emotions, anger is the one that gets children into most trouble. Suspension, expulsion, exclusion from peer groups, family conflict and, in extreme cases, trouble with the law, are reported.

For many people, anger is used to mask other feelings. Like an iceberg, the anger is but the tip above the water surface – what people see and judge. Beneath the surface lies what really matters and what needs to be addressed – sadness, helplessness, hurt, guilt, shame, rejection, loneliness, feeling overwhelmed, humiliation, or lack of understanding of self and others. People need to understand what feelings and issues underlie their anger in order to manage and cope better. Anger is a cover-up emotion. It covers up a 'real' emotion. In fact, it is often referred to as a 'secondary emotion' because it is a defence mechanism and is used to cover true feelings.

How are ADHD and anger linked?

One of the most significant emotional difficulties is anger regulation, as this can have the most profound effects on social relationships and educational and vocational advancement.

ADHD children have problems with emotional control, which can affect their peer relationships as they are often disruptive or annoying. These children are often teased or provoked, and when they respond with extreme anger and aggression, they are less likely to be accepted by their peers.

This tendency towards anger also affects adults with ADHD, as they have more explosive outbursts and can become chronically angry or easily provoked. At home, this leads to more spousal conflict and relationship stress, and at work, this can lead to suspension or termination.

Although some adults with ADHD attempt to maintain emotional control as they understand the consequences of their emotional volatility, others cannot self-reflect and are oblivious to the connection between their anger and their damaged relationships.

What do you see your child do when they are angry?

_____

_____

_____

What do you think is the function or payoff of that behaviour?

_____

_____

_____

How does your family manage anger?

_____

_____

_____

Anger is often misdirected and is taken out on those people around us now, even though it stems from unfair criticisms or events in the past. Is this statement true or false for your child's behaviour? Give a reason for your answer.

_____

_____

_____

It is often very hard for children to access their deeper feelings while they are feeling very angry, and the focus for parents at that time is often more on containment and safety rather than processing the emotion. How could you come back to a situation later to talk about what may have been going on more deeply for your child?

_____

_____

_____

Things done or said in anger often lead to hurt feelings, damaged relationships, or even damaged property or missed opportunities. Once your child has calmed down, how can you help them take ownership of this and perhaps make amends for something that has been lost or damaged?

_____

_____

_____

What Does Your Anger Iceberg Look Like? What Lies Beneath

Think about times when you have been angry. What was visible on the surface? What other factors lay beneath the surface? Write them in on the iceberg.

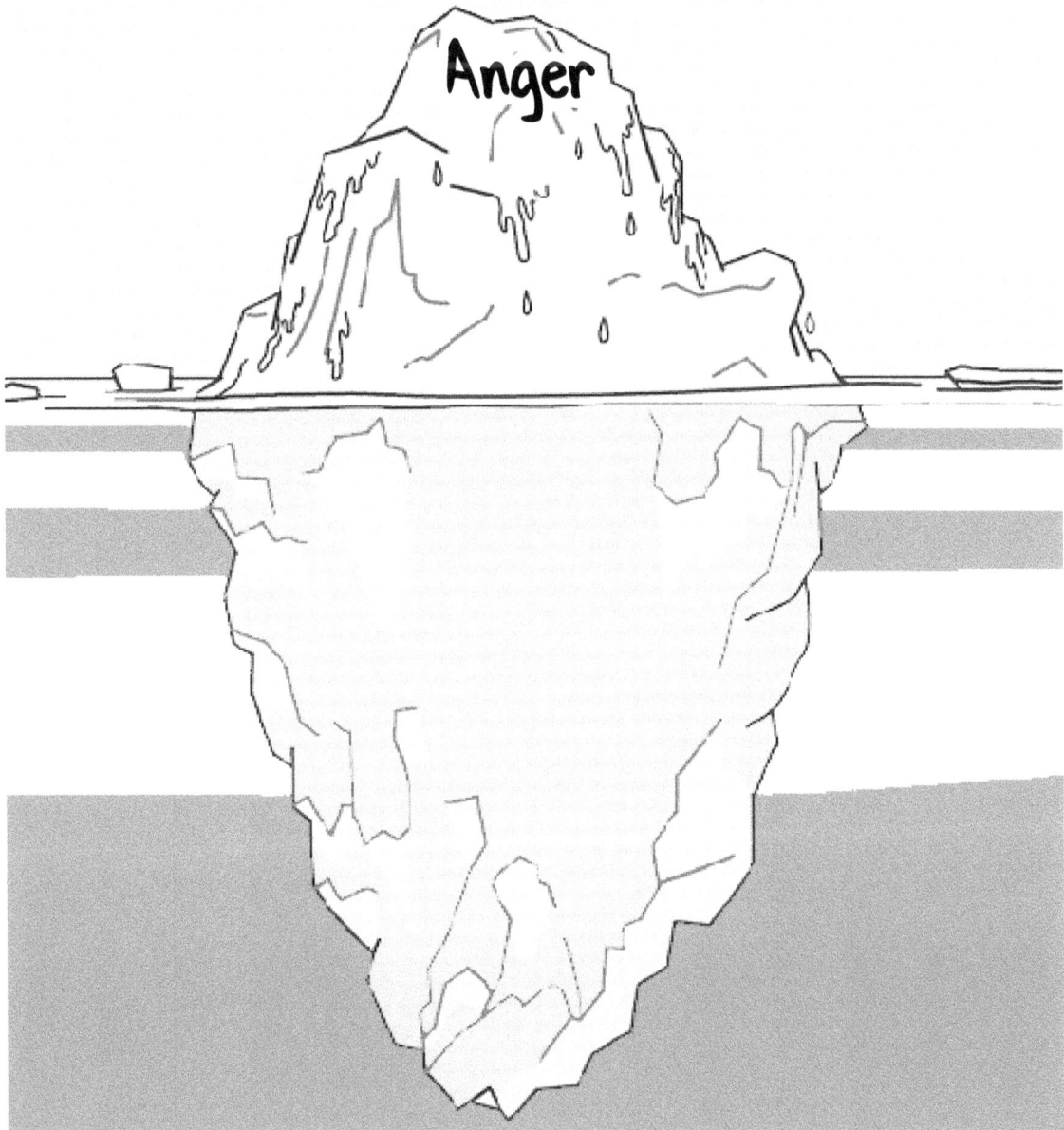

What Does Your Child's Anger Iceberg Look Like?

Now that you have explored your anger iceberg, how well do you know what contributes to your child's anger? Circle the things that apply to your child.

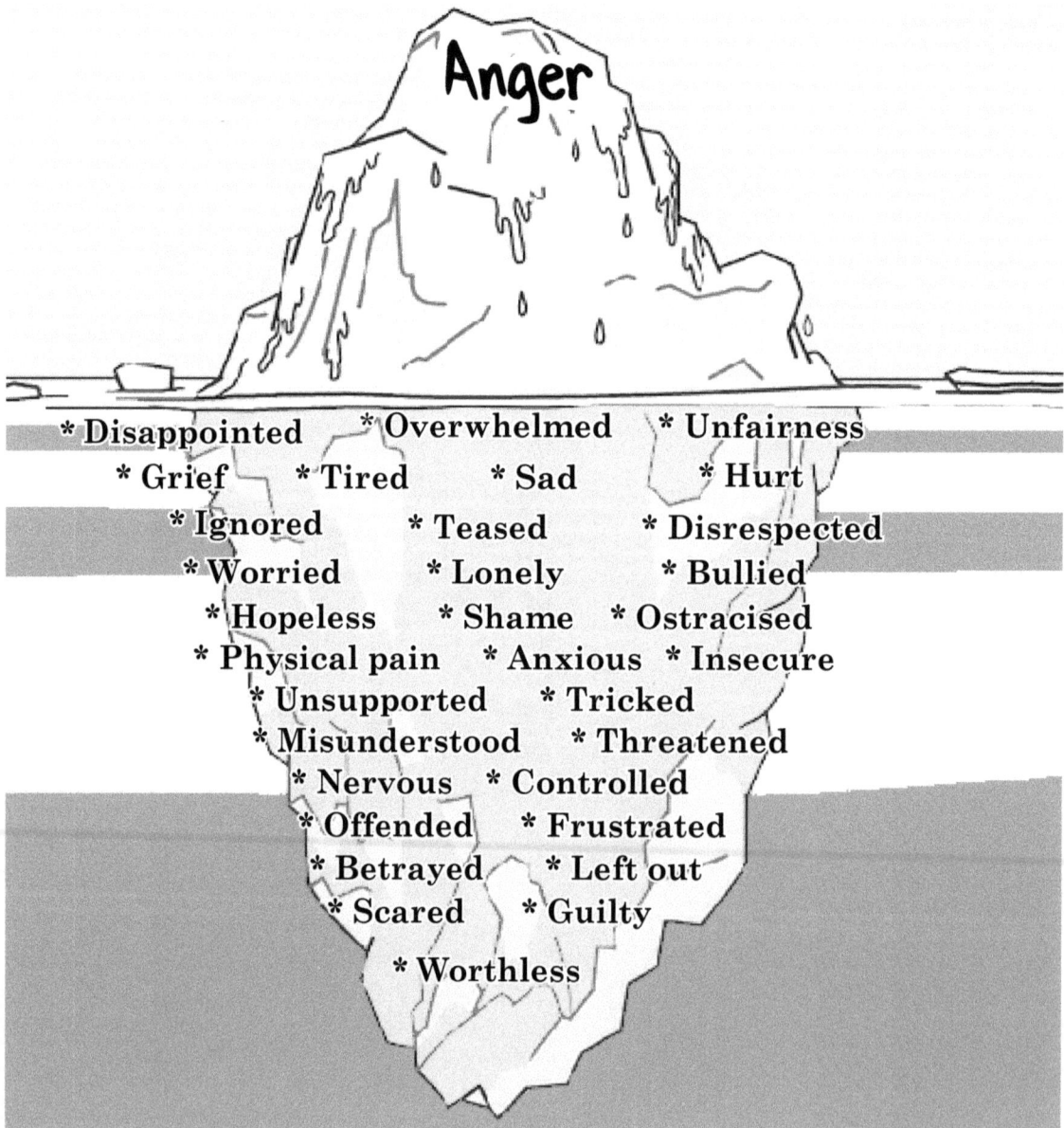

* Disappointed   * Overwhelmed   * Unfairness
* Grief   * Tired   * Sad   * Hurt
* Ignored   * Teased   * Disrespected
* Worried   * Lonely   * Bullied
* Hopeless   * Shame   * Ostracised
* Physical pain   * Anxious   * Insecure
* Unsupported   * Tricked
* Misunderstood   * Threatened
* Nervous   * Controlled
* Offended   * Frustrated
* Betrayed   * Left out
* Scared   * Guilty
* Worthless

The diagrams below show the difference between showing respect and disrespect in relationships with family members. The respect diagram behaviours acknowledge other people's values, and are behaviours we should strive to engage in.

Abuse of Family Members

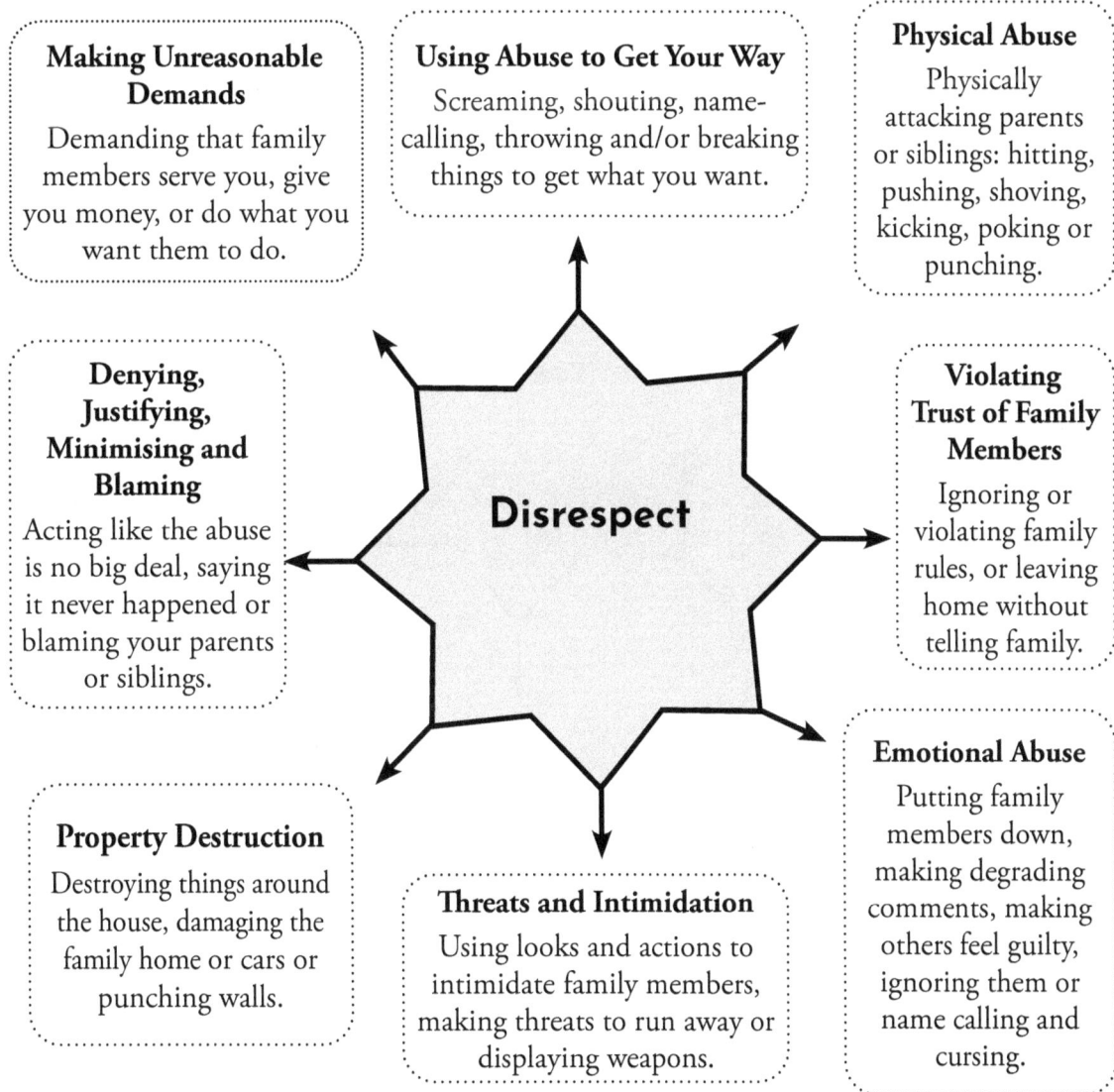

Making Unreasonable Demands

Demanding that family members serve you, give you money, or do what you want them to do.

Using Abuse to Get Your Way

Screaming, shouting, name-calling, throwing and/or breaking things to get what you want.

Physical Abuse

Physically attacking parents or siblings: hitting, pushing, shoving, kicking, poking or punching.

Denying, Justifying, Minimising and Blaming

Acting like the abuse is no big deal, saying it never happened or blaming your parents or siblings.

Disrespect

Violating Trust of Family Members

Ignoring or violating family rules, or leaving home without telling family.

Property Destruction

Destroying things around the house, damaging the family home or cars or punching walls.

Threats and Intimidation

Using looks and actions to intimidate family members, making threats to run away or displaying weapons.

Emotional Abuse

Putting family members down, making degrading comments, making others feel guilty, ignoring them or name calling and cursing.

Mutual Respect

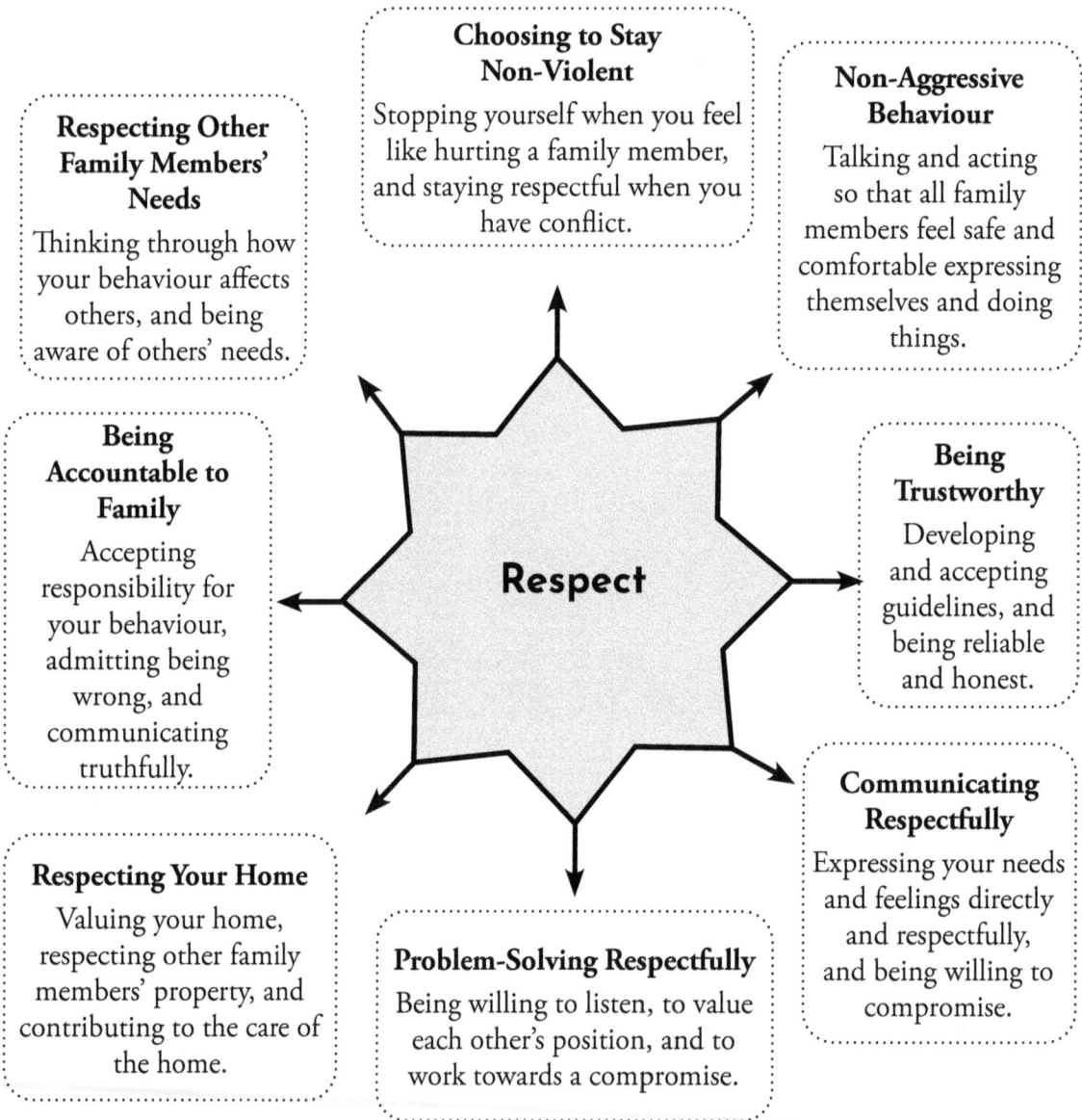

Choosing to Stay Non-Violent

Stopping yourself when you feel like hurting a family member, and staying respectful when you have conflict.

Non-Aggressive Behaviour

Talking and acting so that all family members feel safe and comfortable expressing themselves and doing things.

Respecting Other Family Members' Needs

Thinking through how your behaviour affects others, and being aware of others' needs.

Being Accountable to Family

Accepting responsibility for your behaviour, admitting being wrong, and communicating truthfully.

Respect

Being Trustworthy

Developing and accepting guidelines, and being reliable and honest.

Communicating Respectfully

Expressing your needs and feelings directly and respectfully, and being willing to compromise.

Respecting Your Home

Valuing your home, respecting other family members' property, and contributing to the care of the home.

Problem-Solving Respectfully

Being willing to listen, to value each other's position, and to work towards a compromise.

Look at the Respect and Disrespect diagrams and write down any behaviours your child engaged in over the past week in the appropriate columns.

Disrespectful	Respectful

If your child engaged in a behaviour on the Disrespect diagram, what could they have done differently so that they stayed on the Respect diagram?

_____

_____

_____

How can you help your child stay respectful?

_____

_____

_____

Anger Warning Signs

Anger signs are clues that our body uses to let us know our anger is increasing. These clues start to appear while our anger is still manageable. If we notice them in time, we can hit the brakes and take control of our anger before we 'flip our lids' and get ourselves into trouble. We all have our own anger stop signs.

Help your child identify their anger warning signs, so that they can spot them before it gets out of control.

Do you recognise any of the anger signs below in your child? Check the ones that ring true to your child. Add any others you have noticed.

Common anger warning signs

- ☐ Flushed face
- ☐ Starts to shake
- ☐ Raises their voice
- ☐ Goes quiet
- ☐ Eyes become watery
- ☐ Tries to bother people
- ☐ Does not think straight
- ☐ Feels annoyed and lashes out
- ☐ Feels like they are going to explode
- ☐ Wants to run away or escape
- ☐ _____
- ☐ _____
- ☐ _____

Managing Anger Challenges

The interventions will very much depend on the child's developmental stage. For children, a clinical intervention has three parts.

First, parents can benefit from counselling to help them not get caught up in negative or angry exchanges with their child. Research shows that those dynamics, while understandable, seem to contribute to perpetuating the problem. In other situations, parents have fallen into a habit of giving additional attention or another unintended reward that is maintaining the child's tantrum habit. In either situation, counselling can help identify alternative ways of handling a child's tantrums so they can be phased out.

Second, counselling of the child (if they are willing) will help them to do less over-interpreting of situations that lead to needless anger. Often, they are misinterpreting the meaning of a situation. With counselling, they can decrease that. Children can also develop more-mature ways of coping with frustration – their usual anger trigger – when they don't get what they want.

Third, stimulant medications for ADHD are often not very effective in helping with anger problems. (If the dose is wrong, stimulants can even make the problem worse.) Studies have indicated that in some cases, when stimulants alone are not working, children with severe anger problems may benefit from adding a type of antidepressant called an SSRI (selective serotonin reuptake inhibitor).

For adults, typical ADHD medications are also only partially helpful. Even when they help the ADHD, they don't help anger or emotional coping as much. However, CBT has proven quite beneficial. This type of counselling helps with attributions ('maybe that guy is tailing me because he has a medical emergency and not because he's an idiot, so I'll just relax and move over to the other lane so that he can pass'), and with developing other coping skills like anticipating situations and planning around them. Including mindfulness principles, like learning to observe emotions in ourselves before we react, can sometimes bring additional benefit.

The jury is still out on newer tools like meditation, omega-3 fatty acid supplementation, or therapeutic vitamin and mineral supplementation. These all appear promising and are safe, so you can try them. However, they do not yet have an expert consensus behind them. Other treatments, such as hypnosis, neurofeedback, or learning about emotions without doing skill-building practice, have not been shown to be effective.

As always, for children and adults, a healthy lifestyle – plenty of exercise, making sure sleep is adequate, eating fresh and healthy food, mitigating stress, and, for adults, avoiding alcohol or drugs – is going to help soften the edges around any emotional struggle.

The best intervention options for children with ADHD who experience severe tantrums include:

- Evaluation to rule out depression or other causes
- Parenting counselling to add skills to your toolkit
- Child skill-building counselling to help them learn how to cope with frustration
- Adjusting ADHD medication and possibly adding an SSRI
- Good nutrition and omega-3 supplementation

Most importantly, take care of your own wellbeing. Attend to your own mental and physical health, believe the best, and go easy on each other during these challenging times.

STOP Worksheet

When anger or another emotion is overwhelming your child, it can be useful to try the **'STOP'** technique to manage their reaction and move forward in a more constructive way. The aim is for the child to develop awareness of their anger warning signs so that it can be managed before it gets out of control.

Help them notice when their anger is getting the better of them, and try this strategy:

S = Stop

T = Take a Breath

O = Observe – name your thoughts and feelings, and what is happening around you. Take perspective and look at the bigger picture.

P = Proceed – what is the best thing to do in this situation?

Have you used the **STOP** technique before? If so, was it helpful?

_____

_____

_____

When the Anger Overpowers Reason

Your child needs to express their anger. It is healthy. 'But the emotion should be like a sneeze: it clears the passageways and is over', says Dr Ned Hallowell. Below are anger-management strategies for children who feel intensely and sometimes spiral out of control and 'flip their lids'. Of all the emotions that can get a child into trouble, anger leads the list. While sadness or anxiety causes misery, it is anger that leads to trouble – punishment, suspension, expulsion, and a host of other outcomes we don't wish our children to suffer. It is important that a child expresses their anger, for a child who cannot get angry is in as much danger as a child who cannot control their anger. Here are Dr Hallowell's tips for managing anger.

Exercise away hostility: One of the best tonics for the brain is physical exercise. In his book *Spark: The revolutionary new science of exercise and the brain*, Dr John Ratey showed that exercise is helpful in promoting healthy brain function, including the ability to control aggression.

Learn to put feelings into words: One of the more common reasons a child loses control is that they are unable to articulate their frustration. Saying, 'I'm really angry' can prevent anger from morphing into violence.

Curb the electronics: Not only does staring at a screen all day numb the mind, it also precludes more useful exercise and face-to-face social interactions, which can help with anger management. Some electronics use is fine, even desirable. But too much, more than two hours a day, should be avoided.

Teach that anger is a signal, not an outcome: When your child gets angry, they should learn to stop and ask, 'Why am I angry?' If they can put that into words, it will be easier to control that feeling. Furthermore, if they are angry because they are being mistreated or are in danger, they can ask for help.

Practice compromise and negotiation: In his book, *The Explosive Child*, Ross W. Greene, Ph.D., introduces a method he calls collaborative problem solving. It is based on negotiation, not giving orders or commands. Learn the technique – it works wonders for most children. (See www.livesinthebalance.com)

Check for any underlying problems: Various conditions, including ADHD, conduct disorder, seizure disorders, thyroid dysfunction or brain tumours, can manifest themselves as uncontrollable anger.

Keep notes: If your child has a problem with anger, take a few minutes every day to document what they have done. After a month, read through the entries. You may see a pattern that will suggest effective interventions.

Skip physical punishment: Families run best if they have a shared agreement: 'We never put hands on each other in anger.' The days of spanking should be long gone. It will worsen a child's anger.

Be the boss: That does not mean you should run your family as if it were the Army. But children manage anger better when they know that their parents are in charge.

Final Message

Get support. If none of the above suggestions help, talk to people you trust or find a support group of ADHD parents. Most children who have anger challenges can learn to control their anger. It may take some time and perseverance, but solutions can be found. Never worry alone.

Topic 4: ADHD and Motivation

We can motivate by fear or by reward. But both these methods are only temporary. The only lasting thing is self-motivation
Homer Rice

What Makes Your Child Act the Way They Do?

Feeling unmotivated is a big obstacle for children and adults with ADHD. In fact, inconsistency in motivation and performance is one of the most puzzling aspects of ADHD. Teachers and parents struggle to understand why children show strong motivation and focus well for some tasks and not for other tasks that they consider as important. This inconsistency can appear as a lack of willpower or pure defiance. 'If you can do this, why can't you do the same for other things that are even more important?' parents may ask. The reality is that ADHD behaviours are not a matter of willpower. It is a problem with the dynamics of the chemistry in the brain.

When individuals with ADHD are faced with a task that is interesting to them – not because someone told them that it ought to be interesting, but because it is attractive to them at that moment – that perception, conscious or unconscious, changes the chemistry of the brain instantly. This process is not under voluntary control.

Intrinsic Vs. Extrinsic Motivation: Why We Do what We Do

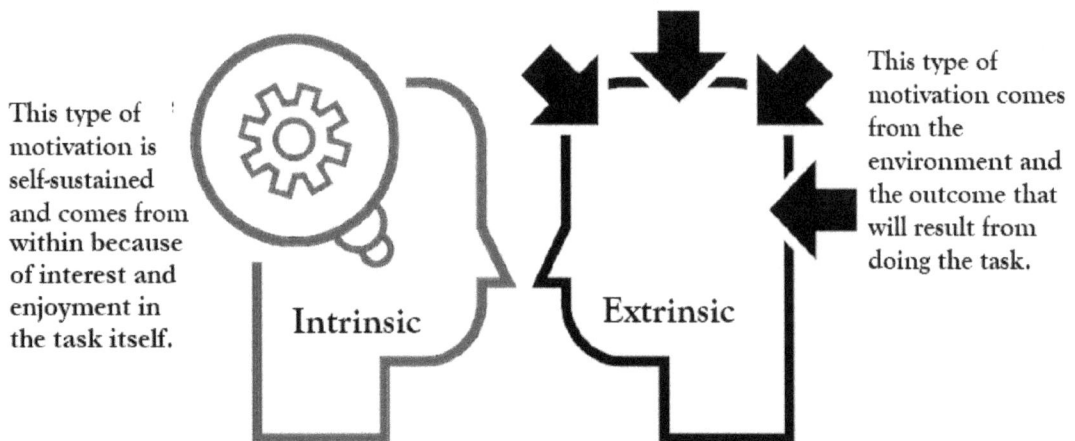

This type of motivation is self-sustained and comes from within because of interest and enjoyment in the task itself.

This type of motivation comes from the environment and the outcome that will result from doing the task.

Intrinsic

Extrinsic

Adapted from Ryan & Deci 2000

In psychology, motivation can be intrinsic or extrinsic. Intrinsic refers to something coming from within. It is the inner drive that propels a person to pursue an activity, not for external rewards but because the action itself is enjoyable. In other words, a person is motivated by the fun, challenge or satisfaction involved with an activity, not for an outside outcome, pressure or reward. Extrinsic motivation, as the word suggests, refers to doing an activity to attain some separable outcome, such as earning a reward or avoiding punishment.

What do You Think Makes Your Child Act the Way They Do?

See how well you know your child. Read the questions below and circle A or B for the option that your child would most likely choose.

1. **They are offered two roles in the school play. Which one will they choose?**
   A. The lead role, which is glamorous and gets them a lot of attention
   B. Another part that's less glamorous but lets them use more of their acting skills

2. **They are offered two jobs. Which one will they choose?**
   A. The one that pays very good money
   B. The one they'd really love doing, even though the pay isn't very good

3. **They are choosing between two classes. Which one will they choose?**
   A. The easier one
   B. The more interesting and challenging one

4. **They need to read at least one book this semester. Which one will they choose?**
   A. One book from the list the teacher has given them
   B. Five books of their choosing that are just as long

5. **Two people have invited your child out. Which one will they choose?**
   A. The person who is fashionable to be seen with
   B. The more interesting but less popular person

6. **Which do you think your child learns more from?**
   A. Studying for a class so they can get an A
   B. Studying for a class because they're interested in it

7. **In deciding between two sports, which one will your child choose?**
   A. The one that gives trophies to the best players at the end of the season
   B. The one that is the most fun

8. **Which do you think feels better for your child?**
   A. Cleaning their room so that they will get their allowance
   B. Cleaning their room because they want to

Topic 4: ADHD and Motivation

We can motivate by fear or by reward. But both these methods are only temporary.
The only lasting thing is self-motivation
Homer Rice

What Makes Your Child Act the Way They Do?

Feeling unmotivated is a big obstacle for children and adults with ADHD. In fact, inconsistency in motivation and performance is one of the most puzzling aspects of ADHD. Teachers and parents struggle to understand why children show strong motivation and focus well for some tasks and not for other tasks that they consider as important. This inconsistency can appear as a lack of willpower or pure defiance. 'If you can do this, why can't you do the same for other things that are even more important?' parents may ask. The reality is that ADHD behaviours are not a matter of willpower. It is a problem with the dynamics of the chemistry in the brain.

When individuals with ADHD are faced with a task that is interesting to them – not because someone told them that it ought to be interesting, but because it is attractive to them at that moment – that perception, conscious or unconscious, changes the chemistry of the brain instantly. This process is not under voluntary control.

Intrinsic Vs. Extrinsic Motivation: Why We Do what We Do

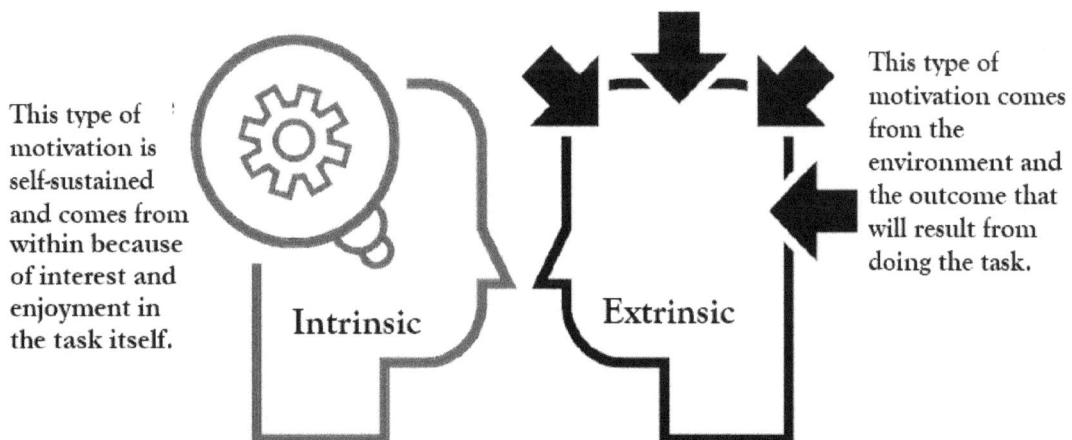

This type of motivation is self-sustained and comes from within because of interest and enjoyment in the task itself.

Intrinsic

Extrinsic

This type of motivation comes from the environment and the outcome that will result from doing the task.

Adapted from Ryan & Deci 2000

In psychology, motivation can be intrinsic or extrinsic. Intrinsic refers to something coming from within. It is the inner drive that propels a person to pursue an activity, not for external rewards but because the action itself is enjoyable. In other words, a person is motivated by the fun, challenge or satisfaction involved with an activity, not for an outside outcome, pressure or reward. Extrinsic motivation, as the word suggests, refers to doing an activity to attain some separable outcome, such as earning a reward or avoiding punishment.

What do You Think Makes Your Child Act the Way They Do?

See how well you know your child. Read the questions below and circle A or B for the option that your child would most likely choose.

1. **They are offered two roles in the school play. Which one will they choose?**
    A. The lead role, which is glamorous and gets them a lot of attention
    B. Another part that's less glamorous but lets them use more of their acting skills

2. **They are offered two jobs. Which one will they choose?**
    A. The one that pays very good money
    B. The one they'd really love doing, even though the pay isn't very good

3. **They are choosing between two classes. Which one will they choose?**
    A. The easier one
    B. The more interesting and challenging one

4. **They need to read at least one book this semester. Which one will they choose?**
    A. One book from the list the teacher has given them
    B. Five books of their choosing that are just as long

5. **Two people have invited your child out. Which one will they choose?**
    A. The person who is fashionable to be seen with
    B. The more interesting but less popular person

6. **Which do you think your child learns more from?**
    A. Studying for a class so they can get an A
    B. Studying for a class because they're interested in it

7. **In deciding between two sports, which one will your child choose?**
    A. The one that gives trophies to the best players at the end of the season
    B. The one that is the most fun

8. **Which do you think feels better for your child?**
    A. Cleaning their room so that they will get their allowance
    B. Cleaning their room because they want to

9. **In general, which is more important to your child's decision-making?**
    A. Appearances
    B. Meaning

10. **In general, which is your child more interested in?**
    A. Quantity
    B. Quality

Total your As and Bs: A __ B __

If you scored 8 or more As, your child is probably motivated from the outside. They cares a lot about what people think of them.

If you score 8 or more Bs, your child is probably motivated from the inside. They care more about their own opinion than the opinions of others.

Sometimes it helps to be motivated from both inside and outside. For example, you can care about what others think but still be true to yourself.

1

How to Motivate Children with ADHD

Help your child tap into their innate, but often untapped, motivation by understanding what they really want (besides video games and clothes), and use those desires to help them set goals. Below are some tips on how to help motivate your tween/teen.

What tweens and teens want!

Tweens, and especially Teens, want the same four things:

1. to make their own choices and decisions
2. to have their opinions valued
3. to decide what rules apply and how
4. to be able to do what adults do.

The challenge, of course, is using these central desires wisely when working to motivate a teenager to move toward adulthood and become more independent.

Set the Tone. It's important to ensure that your child understands that you want to help them accomplish something that benefits them. Together, focus on something that your child wants and work together to find a way to make it possible. They are more likely to participate and feel motivated to act if they feel like they are a partner in the process instead of simply following orders.

Let Teens Choose the Goal. Emphasise your child's goals, not your own. The first goal your child chooses might not be a school related one. It can be easier to start with your child's interests. Ask, 'What makes you happy? What would you like to become an expert in?' Then say, 'I wonder if there is a goal we could relate to that.'

Ask Questions. Help your teen set a specific, realistic goal, and create an outline of how they will spend their time to get there by asking questions or requesting more information. Parents can say:

- What's your plan?
- Do you have a strategy for that?
- What's your schedule?
- When do you plan on starting?
- How will you remember all the details?
- How will you measure progress?

This puts the responsibility of thinking about how to reach a goal on your teen instead of relying on you to manage things. If your child answers, 'I don't know', or looks at you blankly, say, 'Well, here are a couple of options for starting. Which do you think might work?' or 'Do you have another idea?'

Focus on Independence. Home in on how the desired change or goal will boost your teen's independence. For example, you can say, 'Once you've done X, Y and Z, that means that you've shown me you're responsible, and you'll get to do [insert a thing your child wants].' If you are worried that a goal or part of the plan is unrealistic, present that in a respectful way. Say, 'Here's my concern about what you've said. Here's what I want to see happen. Is that what you want to see happen? Can you go over your goal again?'

Work Together. Create a To Do list with them. Teens with ADHD and EF deficits often think their working memory is better than it is. They think, 'I won't forget to do it.' Start by making a To Do list for them. Once that is working well, make the To Do list as a team. Then, have children independently make a list for themselves. Work toward providing the minimum support necessary for your child to be successful.

Create Rewards. Set up an incentive system that supports the goal. Many experts and parents have mixed feelings about using rewards. If your child's goal is to do better in school, create a points system that will allow them to feel like they are making progress. They could accumulate points for getting a grade of B- or above on tests, for handing in homework on time, or for writing down assignments in a planner. If the goal is to do two chores a day, then children can choose from a menu of chores where some are harder than others and worth different point values. Then, the accumulated points can be traded in for something they value.

Be Fair. If you decide to use rewards, make sure it is a fair system. Typically, when incentives fail, it is because parents ask for too much for too little payoff. For example, offering payment for getting As on a report card doesn't usually work well because it is a long-term goal that children can't easily visualise. Instead, create rewards for daily behaviour that moves them toward a goal. A fair reward is one that children can earn 70% of the time.

Build Persistence. Focus on building goal-directed persistence. This is a late-developing executive skill that means working to achieve a task without getting distracted by other interests or giving up when the going gets tough. A teen may not really appreciate that how they perform in school will affect what university they get into in four years. Parents need to help teens understand that, and bolster skills to work toward a goal. They can also help by modelling. Children notice when you persist over time – especially once they move beyond high school. Help them set up and achieve little goals that don't take very long but add up over time. Praise effort rather than traits or results. Say, 'Wow, you stuck with it. You figured it out. I can't believe how hard you worked for that.'

Help Your Child Develop A Growth Mindset

Growth mindsets must be translated into action,
usually outside of the comfort zone.
Unknown

Leaving Your Comfort Zone

People with a growth mindset believe that their abilities can improve over time, that things can always get better and that problems are challenges that can help them improve. A small change in thinking can mean big changes in your child's life. Encourage your child to move outside their comfort zone – for that is where growth happens.

Instead Of...	Try Thinking...
This is too hard.	This may take some time and effort.
I can't make this any better.	I can always improve so I will keep trying.
I will never be that smart.	I will learn how to do this.
I give up.	I will use some of the strategies that I have learned.
My friend can do it.	I will watch how they do it, so that I can try it.
I just can't do this.	I need help understanding this.
I am not good at this.	What am I missing?
It's good enough.	Is this really my best work?
I made a mistake.	Mistakes are opportunities to learn.
Plan A didn't work.	There is always plan B.
This task is too big.	I can tackle anything I put my mind to.
I don't understand this.	I don't understand this *yet*.

Does your child have a growth mindset? Give reasons for your answer.

_____

_____

_____

How important is it for children to develop a growth mindset and how can this help them manage their ADHD?

_____

_____

_____

A mind is like a parachute. It doesn't work if it is not open.
Frank Zappa

1

Topic 5: When ADHD is Not the Only Problem

You may encounter many defeats, but you must not be defeated. In fact, it may be necessary to encounter the defeats, so you can know who you are, what you can rise from, how you can still come out of it.
Maya Angelou

ADHD by itself can be challenging, but when your child has other coexisting conditions it can make it more difficult. A landmark study by the National Institute of Mental Health (NIMH) showed that up to two thirds of children with ADHD also had one or more other conditions. Sometimes these conditions are secondary, meaning that they came about as a result of dealing with the daily challenges of ADHD. When this is the case, once ADHD is managed, the symptoms of the secondary condition may resolve themselves. In other cases, these conditions are separate and need to be treated separately from ADHD. Since many childhood problems can look like symptoms of ADHD, it is very important that a child who appears to have ADHD be evaluated for other conditions.

For example, sadness that stems from a daily life of not fitting in at school, being bullied, teased or rejected by peers, failing to achieve academically and being in conflict with parents can slowly develop into depression. These struggles can lead some children with ADHD to have low self-esteem and periods of unhappiness. Adding to their sadness may be a sense of hopelessness that comes from their inability to control their ADHD symptoms and the many negative messages that they receive daily.

The following are the most common conditions that can co-exist with ADHD:

- Learning Disabilities (LD) and developmental coordination disorder
- Depression
- Anxiety disorders including Generalised Anxiety Disorder (GAD)
- Obsessive Compulsive Disorder (OCD)
- Oppositional Defiant Disorder (ODD)
- Autism Spectrum Disorder
- Tourette Syndrome

Was your child diagnosed with one or more of the above conditions as well as ADHD? If so, which one?

_____

_____

_____

Do you sometimes question whether a behaviour is a result of ADHD or has another cause? If so, give an example.

_____

_____

_____

1

Stress and Worry

The only thing you sometimes have control over is your perspective. You don't have control over your situation. But you have a choice about how you view it.
Chris Pine

Just as symptoms of ADHD can cause ongoing stress, stress can exacerbate core symptoms of ADHD – inattention, impulsivity and distractibility. Not completing homework, leaving homework at home, forgetting the time of an exam, not meeting assignment deadlines, and social and family relationship difficulties are all sources of stress. A person who has ADHD struggles to focus and filter out excess stimuli, which increases stress levels. Anxiety, which can stem from approaching deadlines, procrastination and the inability to focus on the work at hand, can increase stress levels even more.

Monitor your child's periods of excess stress, for example, when they fail to meet a deadline – are they more hyperactive than usual? What about their concentration level? What negative self-talk do they engage in?

Ways to Help Your Child Manage Worry and Stress

Find out what's on their minds. Be available and take an interest in what's happening at school, on the team, and with your child's friends. Take casual opportunities to ask how it's going. As you listen to stories of the day's events, be sure to ask what your child thinks and feels about what happened. Encourage your child to put what's bothering them into words. Ask for key details and listen.

Show you care and understand. Being interested in your child's concerns shows they're important to you and helps them feel supported and understood. Reassuring comments can help – but usually only after you've heard your child out. Say that you understand your child's feelings and the problem.

Guide your child to solutions. You can help reduce worries by helping your child learn to deal with challenging situations. When your child tells you about a problem, offer to help come up with a solution together. If your child is worried about an upcoming maths test, ask them how you can help.

In most situations, resist the urge to jump in and fix a problem for your child – instead, think it through and come up with possible solutions together. Problem-solve with your child, rather than for your child. By taking an active role, children learn how to tackle problems on their own.

Keep things in perspective. Without minimising a child's feelings, point out that many problems are temporary and solvable, and that there will be better days and other opportunities to try again. Teaching children to keep problems in perspective can lessen their worry and help build strength, resilience and the optimism to try again. Remind your children that whatever happens, things will be OK.

Make a difference. Sometimes children worry about big stuff – war, climate change, pandemics – that they hear about at school or on the news. Parents can help by discussing these issues, offering accurate information, and correcting any misconceptions the child may have. Try to reassure the child by talking about what adults are doing to tackle the problem to keep them safe. Be aware that your own reaction to global events affects your child too. If you express anger and stress about a world event that's beyond your control, children are likely to react that way too. You can also look for things you can do with your child to help you all feel like you're making a positive difference. You can't stop a war, for example, but your family can contribute to an organisation that works for peace or helps children in war-torn countries. Or your family might perform community service to give your children the experience of volunteering.

Offer reassurance and comfort. Sometimes when children are worried, what they need most is a parent's reassurance and comfort. It might come in the form of a hug, some heartfelt words, or time spent together. It helps children to know that, whatever happens, parents will be there with love and support.

Highlight the positive. Ask your child what they enjoyed about their day and listen when they tell you about what goes great for them or what they had fun doing. Give plenty of airtime to the good things that happen. Let them tell you what they think and feel about their successes, achievements, and positive experiences – and what they did to help things turn out so well. Daily doses of positive emotions and experiences – like enjoyment, gratitude, love, amusement, relaxation, fun and interest – offset stress and help children do well.

Be a good role model. The most powerful lessons we teach our children are the ones we demonstrate. Your response to your own worries, stress and frustrations can go a long way toward teaching your children how to deal with everyday challenges. If you're rattled or angry when dealing with a To Do list that's too long, your children will learn that as the appropriate response to stress. Set a good example with your reactions to problems and setbacks. Responding with optimism and confidence teaches children that problems are temporary and tomorrow's another day. Bouncing back with a can-do attitude will help your child do the same.

When you find your child worrying about something that they have no control over, encourage them to take a step back by asking them the following questions:

- Is this your issue or problem to solve?
- Is it under your control?
- What is the worry or stress costing you?

Encourage them to practise some of the following techniques:

- Use deep breathing exercises and relaxation techniques as often as possible throughout the day.
- Take a walk. Being in nature has a calming effect. Thirty minutes of exercise per day is shown to help clear the mind and improve concentration levels.
- Vent to someone – a friend, or someone from their circle of support. Don't give advice, just be their sounding board.
- Suggest they keep a stress-relief object with them. This can be a stress ball, something attached invisibly to their clothing or to the bottom of their chair, or a photo of a pet or a family member that has a calming effect on them.
- Suggest they move around whenever possible and do stretching exercises for a few minutes.
- Monitor their sleep, diet and use of technology.
- Practice assertiveness communication with your child.

Reflect:

- What do you think causes most stress or worry in your child's life?
- What strategies does your child use to manage their stress or worry? Have they worked long-term?
- What negative self-talk does your child engage in?

Topic 6: Multimodal Treatment Plan

We know that when managing ADHD, no treatment is sufficient on its own. A multimodal approach – a variety of interventions that target the individual's needs – has shown to be the most effective. Because ADHD is a condition that impacts the child in most areas of their lives, interventions need to be designed for home and school. For example:

At home	School
Morning routine	Classroom
Afterschool routine	Playground
Homework routine	Recess
Chores	Team activities
Dinner	Sport events
Bath	Excursions
Bedtime	Assembly

Intervention options include:

- Medication
- Behaviour modification
- Cognitive behaviour therapy – individual and family therapy
- Parenting courses
- Special education
- Tutoring
- Coaching or mentoring
- OT or physio and speech therapy

Although not treatments for ADHD per se, we cannot disregard the importance of healthy eating, physical exercise, adequate sleep and proper hygiene in keeping a healthy mind and a healthy body.

What treatments or interventions do you find work best for your child?

_____

_____

_____

Neurotransmitters Involved in ADHD

If you understand how your own unique brain wiring works, you won't suffer, you will learn how to thrive.
ADD Coach Academy

In order for your child to be more open to taking medication or engaging in other interventions, it helps for them to have a good understanding of how ADHD is impacting their life, and a little about the ADHD brain and the nervous system.

Our body moves in response to messages from our brain. These messages are carried from neurons in the brain to the central nervous system by chemical messengers called neurotransmitters. Thoughts and feelings also rely on neurotransmitter activity.

The synapse, as shown in the diagram, is where neurotransmitters cross from one nerve's axon (called the pre-synaptic side) to the next nerve's dendrite. The other side of the synapse is called the post-synaptic or receiving cell, where the neurotransmitters latch onto the receptors of the next neuron. When enough neurotransmitters attach to the post-synaptic neuron, the nerve fires and it releases neurotransmitters at its own pre-synaptic end. This process keeps on repeating.

The neurotransmitters implicated in ADHD include:

Dopamine – this chemical has to do with controlling impulsivity, paying attention and memory. Dopamine is an excitatory chemical, which means that it helps the nerve cells fire off impulses to communicate with one another.

Norepinephrine/Noradrenaline – helps with paying attention.

Serotonin – is involved with sleep and mood. If you don't have enough of this chemical, you may have sleeping problems and get depressed more easily.

The primary role of ADHD medication is to treat ADHD symptoms by balancing neurotransmitter availability in the brain. However, finding the best

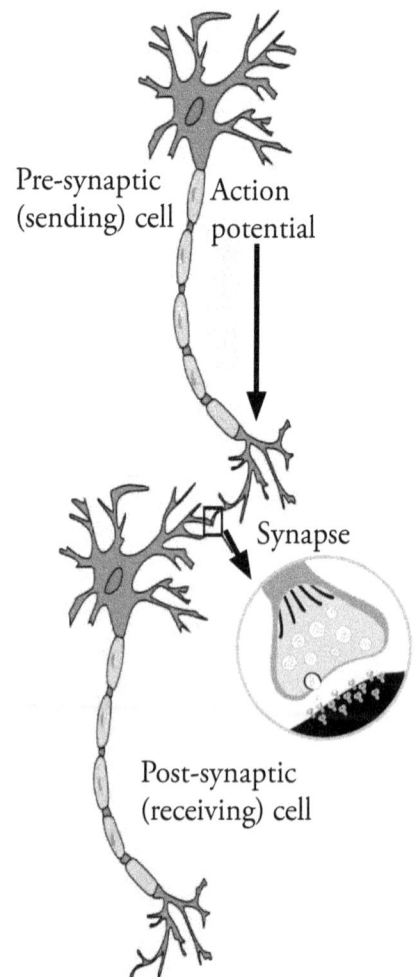

Pre-synaptic (sending) cell

Action potential

Synapse

Post-synaptic (receiving) cell

medication and dose is not always easy and you have to be willing to persevere, because when you finally do get it right, it can be life changing.

There is a fine balance between not taking a high enough dose (and therefore not having enough of a treatment effect) and taking too high of a dose (and therefore experiencing some side-effects). There is often a process of fine-tuning required.

When your child starts a new medication, it is a good idea to keep track of how the medication is working by keeping a medication side-effect rating scale. Take the results to the doctor for a discussion on whether this medication is giving the best outcome, and whether it needs some adjusting in terms of the dosage or type. There may also be ways of managing side-effects, such as dietary and sleep changes, so the young person is able to continue with a medication without other important areas being affected.

1

Medication Response Form

Below is a list of some side effects that may result from taking ADHD medication. Logging this information will help your child's doctor identify what problems were present before ADHD medication was started and what problems may have developed after the treatment started. If there are experiencing other issues you would like to monitor, you can add them in the blank spaces.

Problem	Time on Medication				
	Before	1st week	2nd week	3rd week	4th week
Reduced appetite					
Weight gain					
Insomnia					
Nausea					
Dry mouth					
Headaches					
Tiredness					
Tics					
Mood swings					
Anxiety					

Important Points to Remember About ADHD

ADHD is not:

- a learned behaviour
- a spoiled child
- 'the easy way out'
- an inability to willingly control oneself
- a discipline problem
- a temper tantrum
- a willpower issue

ADHD is:

- a medical condition
- a war between brain and body
- a struggle to develop relationships
- a battle to maintain self-esteem and self-confidence
- a big deal to those who suffer with it
- a chemical imbalance
- a struggle to fit in

ADHD Is a Real Condition!

Topc 7: Going Solo to the Doctor

Be strong enough to stand alone. Smart enough to know when you need help,
and brave enough to ask for it.
Unknown

By Dr Bennett

Adolescence is a time of increased independence. This may include wanting to see a general practitioner (GP) or a mental health professional privately. Although some parents may find this difficult, it should be encouraged as it helps adolescents gain confidence to assume responsibility for their health and general wellbeing.

The age at which a young person can consent to simple health-care treatments without a parent or guardian present varies, but can be as young as fourteen.

It is always important to be honest with your child about their medical conditions and to use age-appropriate, correct terminology, especially in relation to health-related concerns.

The most common reported concerns that teens talk to their GP about include:

- general worry
- bullying at school
- family conflict
- relationships
- substance abuse.

The GP can offer guidance on things like sexual health, sleep, hygiene, fitness, healthy eating habits and overall mental wellbeing. If your child is not comfortable about going to the same GP as the rest of the family, have a discussion about important aspects of your family's health history – for example allergies, mental-health issues, asthma or diabetes.

You can also help them choose a new GP. The most important thing should be that they are talking to someone who can guide and – obviously with the child's consent – involve you, the parent, where needed.

Reasons reported by teens for wanting a different GP include:

- not feeling comfortable with their family GP any longer
- wanting to see a GP who does not know their parents

- wanting to manage their own health and start a new doctor–patient relationship
- Nnot trusting the family GP with confidential information
- wanting to talk more openly about issues like relationships, including sexual matters, and substance use.

Has your child expressed the need to see a health professional on their own?

_____

Does your child readily ask for help? If not, what do your think is the obstacle to seeking help for them?

_____

_____

_____

Does your child sit back and wait for someone to make the first move and offer help?

_____

_____

_____

Topic 8: Circle of Support

Don't be afraid to ask questions. Don't be afraid to ask for help when you need it. I do that every day. Asking for help isn't a sign of weakness, it's a sign of strength. It shows you have the courage to admit when you don't know something, and to learn something new.
Barack Obama

A Circle of Support is based on an understanding of the importance of relationships in our life and the need for strong support networks. This is especially important for someone who might be vulnerable because of a mental-health illness or a physical condition. Many of us have friends or informal networks that we rely on when we need advice, when we are in a crisis, and when we want to celebrate successes. These relationships are important. Do you know who is in your child's Circle of Support? Try to complete their Circle of Support on the next page – and prepare to be surprised when you compare yours to theirs. If your child has any names that are unfamiliar to you, ask them about it in a non-threatening way while showing interest.

Are you concerned about any of the names or positioning of the names on your child's Circle of Support?

_____

_____

_____

Is there anything you can do for your child – for example encourage them to see positive peers more often? Do you need to get to know some of the people who are important to your child? Is there any way you could discuss your concerns about a person or group that you think may be less helpful for your child?

_____

_____

_____

Who is in Your Child's Circle of Support?

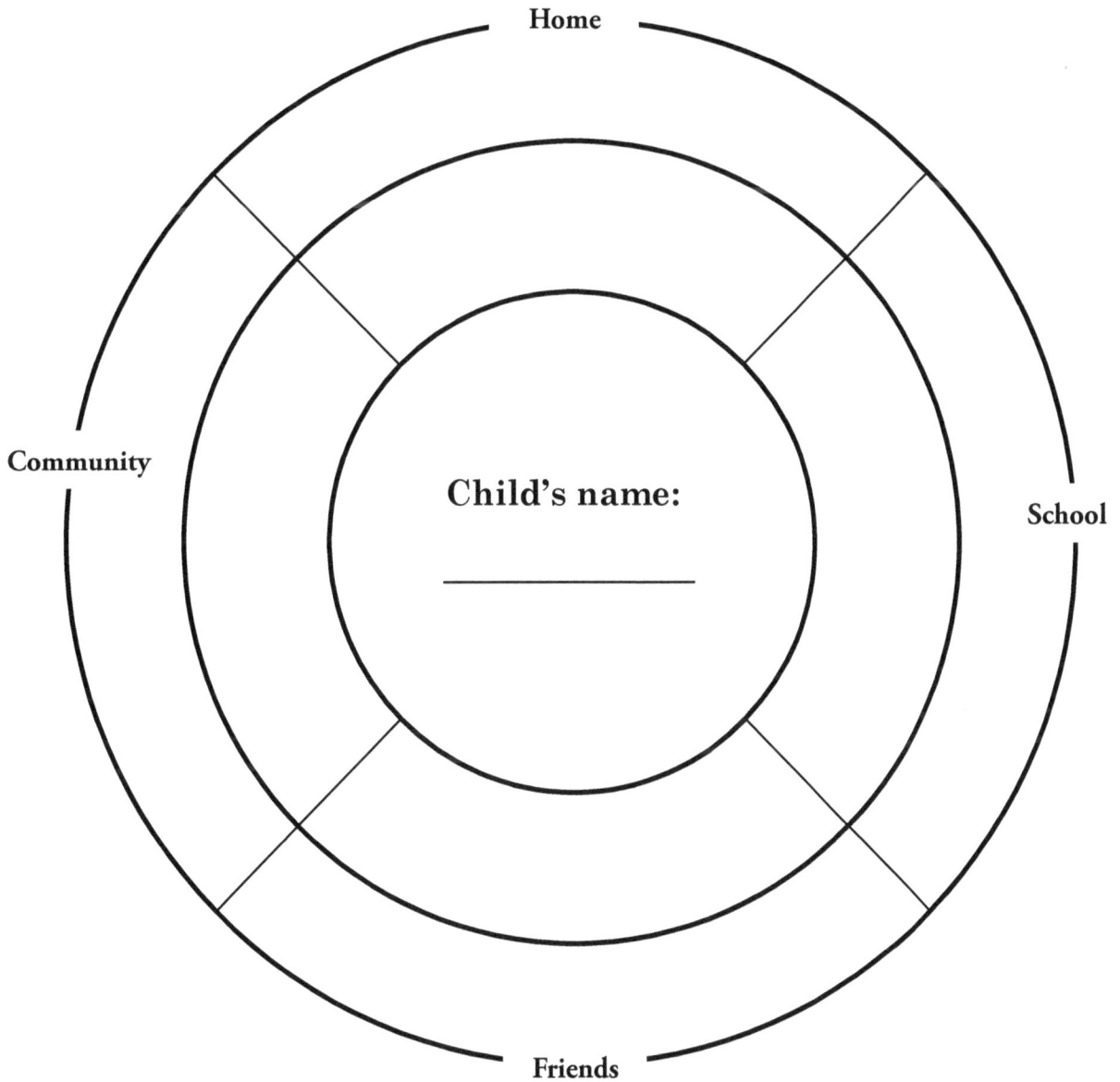

Home

Community

Child's name:

_____

School

Friends

Topic 9: Disclosing that Your Child Has ADHD

Having a child with ADHD is nothing to be ashamed of. This being said, many parents worry about disclosing the diagnosis to family members or friends. This is understandable, as even the people who love you can react negatively. Family members may unfairly blame the situation on your parenting.

Before telling someone that your child has ADHD, ask yourself whether you really want this person to know, and how it will make a difference. You have the choice to tell people if you want to, and if it would help them understand your child and family dynamic better.

If you decide to tell someone, rather than simply saying, 'My child has ADHD', try asking the person a question to find out how much they know about ADHD. For example, 'What do you know about ADHD?' or 'Do you know someone who has ADHD?' Listen carefully to their reply.

Asking an open question like this will let you know two things: their attitude towards ADHD and their factual knowledge about it.

Attitude towards ADHD

Attitude is everything! As they are replying to your question, you will quickly know if they are anti-ADHD, or open-minded and compassionate about it. There are still a lot of people who don't believe it exists, or that it's something people use as an excuse for being lazy.

Factual knowledge about ADHD

There are still many misconceptions about ADHD. For example, some people still think that ADHD is a childhood disorder and that adults don't have it. Others know about hyperactive ADHD and not inattentive ADHD. Some people know a person with ADHD, so they base their knowledge on how it affects that person without realising it is different for everyone.

Once you know the person's attitude to and knowledge of ADHD, you can decide if you want to disclose. This method does take a little more time; however, it is worth it as it results in a positive experience for both you and your child.

Have you had to explain your child's diagnosis to friends or family? If so, what was that like for you?

_____

_____

_____

If you haven't had to explain it yet, or if you would like to try a different way next time, what different options could you tap into?

_____

_____

_____

1

Topic 10: Introducing Your Child to Their New Teacher

Many children struggle with change, especially all of the changes associated with a new classroom and a new teacher. Many also report feeling insecure about their condition and worried that the teacher does not understand them or their issues. At the beginning of the school year, you might want to help your child introduce themself to their new teacher in writing. Ideally, do this within the first two weeks of the school term. Below are some ideas to of what to include:

- Name (and what they prefer to be called)
- What they like doing in their spare time
- Activities they enjoy
- The subjects they enjoy the most
- Subjects they find most challenging
- What they want to be when they grow up.

Situations when your child is most productive and studies the best:

- Time of day?
- Alone or with someone?
- Where – e.g., floor, desk?
- Conditions – e.g., kneeling at a desk, in a quiet area, wearing headphones?
- They need a study breaks – e.g., every 20 minutes
- They work better sitting – in the front, at the back of the classroom etc.

Strategies that help them stay organised and complete their work:

- Write down assignments
- E-mail assignments to parents
- Keep an extra textbook at home
- Work with a buddy to stay organised
- Estimate how long an assignment will take
- Colour code subjects
- Break down assignments into chunks with different due dates
- Send home a reminder of due dates for the final project

What helps them learn and remember information?

- Write things down
- Use mind maps
- Use a computer for writing
- Read out loud
- Make or build something
- Use songs and rhymes
- Use flash cards
- Listen to a recording of the lesson
- Talk about the information with a buddy
- Use associations and mnemonics
- Fidget
- Doodle

What else would your child like their teacher to know?

_____

_____

_____

Discovering Your Child's Hidden Strengths
Help your child re-frame their thinking about ADHD

Easily distracted
Forgetful
Can't stay on point
Hyperactive
Impulsive
Disorganised
Stubborn
Inconsistent

Curious
Engaged in the moment
Sees things others miss
Energetic
Creative
Spontaneous
Persistent
Has flashes of brilliance

Topic 11: Help Your Child Find Their Passion

Strength does not come from winning. Your struggles develop your strengths. When you go through hardships and decide not to surrender, that is strength.
Arnold Schwarzenegger

People with ADHD, just like those without it, have unique sets of interests and skills that they are passionate about. Remind your child that they are unique with many good qualities and a one-of-a-kind personality. Help them discover their passion and purpose by exploring two things:

1. what they love to do

2. what comes easily to them.

For example, JP did work experience in the fitness industry in Year 10. During this time, he discovered his true passion for this industry. He decided that he wanted to become a personal trainer and work towards owning his own gym one day. He was so excited by this idea that he started researching alternative ways of following his passion and opted to go to TAFE at the end of Year 11 to gain his fitness certification.

Write two things that you know that your child is good at and loves to do.

1. _____

2. _____

List two jobs that match one (or both) of the things you listed above.

1. _____

2. _____

Repeat this exercise with your child. Help them find someone who works in one of the areas identified. If possible, set up a time to meet with that person. Help your child prepare questions to ask during the meeting.

Possible questions include:

- What do I need to do to prepare for a career in this field?
- What sort of volunteering would help me to determine if this career is a good fit for me?
- What specific interests and talents would I need to succeed in this field?

ADHD Does Not Discriminate

ADHD is recognised in countries across the world. The condition affects many populations, with little difference in rates regardless of ethnicity or social standing. While some of those affected will outgrow symptoms, the majority will experience symptoms through adolescence and into adulthood.

While this may seem discouraging, it is important to realise that many people with ADHD go on to lead happy, successful lives. Adults with ADHD can have successful careers and fulfilling family lives, even reaching the top of their field, achieving fame and fortune.

You may recognise some of these famous people who have experienced ADHD challenges.

Michael Phelps

Howie Mandel

Adam Levine

Paris Hilton

Jamie Oliver

Emma Watson

Ryan Gosling

Jim Carrey

Solange Knowles

These celebrities and many others show that you can live a full, happy life, regardless of your diagnosis. The key is understanding your condition, finding a treatment plan that helps you manage your symptoms, and sticking to it.

Take Away Message

As a parent to a child with ADHD, you are an essential part of your child's treatment, and you play a huge role in helping them overcome their challenges and succeed in life. Parenting practices can improve ADHD challenges or make them worse. My message to you is to hang in there and keep doing your best. The following strategies will help you on your journey.

Education is vital. The more you know, the better you can help your child. Learn everything you can about: ADHD in general and the way it affects your child; your medical team; and the medications your child is on, including any side effects. Stay informed about new developments in ADHD research and treatment. Investigate whether you might also have ADHD. The condition is often inherited, and parents or other relatives of children with ADHD might not know they have it too. When parents with ADHD get diagnosed and treated, it helps them be at their best as parents.

Learning to be realistic will save both you and your family from much heartache. Know what your child's challenges are, and set realistic expectations based on what they can currently do. Similarly, be aware of the effects of medication, so you can expect realistic results from them. Observe your child's behaviour, noting how it changes when medication is administered and as it wears off.

Get the team onboard and working together. Follow all recommendations for medication and other therapies. Work together with the school and your child's teacher to give your child their best chance at success. The school environment can be overwhelming for children with ADHD. This can be mitigated by advocating for your child and, where necessary, educating teachers regarding the condition. Empower your child with the tools to advocate for themselves where possible. Ask whether an (IEP) would benefit your child.

Remember to look after yourself as well. Connect with others to find support and advice. There are many online and in-person support groups that can connect you with others going through the same struggles and triumphs.

Module 2:
Adaptive Thinking

Section 1:
Helping Your Child Learn to Cope Inside Out

Topic 1: Adaptive Thinking

An important component of parenting is to foster adaptive thinking in children. The aim of this section is to help your child learn to cope inside out. I often talk about helping the child to till the soil before you plant. This is achieved by using cognitive behavioural therapy (CBT) principles to help your child understand that it is not what happens to us but rather how we interpret it that drives behaviour. The way you think about situations affects how you feel and what behaviours or actions you engage in. Negative thoughts increase stress levels and worsen mood. This can interfere with starting and completing tasks. Learning to think adaptively can help you be more aware of negative thoughts, find strategies to keep your thoughts in check, and find ways to reduce your symptoms.

Important to note is that although ADHD is not caused by negative automatic thoughts, living with ADHD, especially if untreated, can cause frustration and underachievement in various aspects of life, such as school, family and social relationships. This can erode away the pillars of self-esteem and confidence that we need in order to feel competent in our approach to tasks in general.

The following example will help you understand how this relationship works.

Two children experiencing the same event can respond very differently. Let's see how.

Situation: Emily and Olivia have ADHD. They both fail a science test.	
Emily	**Olivia**
Thought: If I didn't have ADHD, I would be smarter, and would have passed the test. I'm so stupid.	**Thought:** I must've underestimated this test. I didn't study hard enough.
Emotion/Feeling: Depressed and negative about her ability to do well in future tests.	**Emotion/Feeling:** Disappointed, but confident about the next test.
Behaviour: Emily develops a negative opinion of herself and doesn't adjust her test preparation, because she believes she is the problem.	**Behaviour:** Olivia isn't happy about her test score, but it doesn't affect her self-esteem. She plans on using different strategies and being better prepared.

Topic 2: Unhelpful Thinking Styles and Thinking Errors

A man is but the product of his thoughts. What he thinks he becomes.
Mohandas Gandhi

We all fall into the trap of unhelpful thinking at some point in life. However, when you are struggling with a condition like ADHD, extremes in thinking can become the norm. Personalisation, blaming, comparing, and jumping to conclusions are just a few of the many unhelpful thinking traps that you can fall into. Identify your own thinking errors below.

Do you know which thinking traps your child engages in the most? Help them identify their thinking traps and teach them the importance of challenging these thoughts and exercising self-compassion. See mistakes as opportunities for learning. Even when something has gone wrong, they can still make the choice to ask positive questions and look for alternative ways of understanding the situation. For example, 'What really went wrong?', 'What have I learned?' or 'What can I do differently next time?' Help your child learn to use their energy to focus on bringing about positive change rather than beating themselves up.

Unhelpful Thinking Styles

The following thinking styles can be subtle yet very powerful in causing us to experience needless emotional distress. Interestingly, the more distressed we become, the more our thinking can become narrowed and focused, making it difficult to think in balanced ways. Many times, simply identifying which thinking styles we are using can be very liberating, allowing us to break free from narrowed, unhealthy thinking patterns.

Can you relate to any of the thinking errors in the list below? Please check the relevant ones.

- ☐ **All-Or-Nothing:** Events are only good or only bad. They are black or white, with no grey areas between the extremes. If something falls short of perfection, then it is seen as a complete failure. 'My work today was a total waste of time.' This can reduce the ability to see 'shades of grey', and in turn reduces the range of problem-solving options.

- ☐ **Overgeneralisation:** You draw general conclusions based on one event or a single piece of evidence. If something bad happens one time, you see it as an unending cycle of defeat. 'People are always mean to me.' This can lead to the sense that things will always be this way, or that things are worse than they are.

☐ **Personalisation:** Blaming yourself for something that wasn't completely your fault or blaming other people for something that was your fault. 'He didn't greet me; I must have done something wrong.' This can lead to feelings of worry or guilt if you believe everything is your fault, or anger if you are frequently blaming others.

☐ **Mind Reading:** Even though they have not told you so, you believe you know what people think and feel about you, as well as why they behave the way they do towards you. 'He thinks I'm stupid.' Often the conclusions you draw from mind-reading are influenced by your fears, rather than from the reality of the situation.

☐ **Catastrophising:** You expect things to turn out badly. 'If I ask my teacher for an extension on my assignment, she is going to tell me off.' The conclusion is often based on the 'worst case scenario', which is often not how things turn out.

☐ **What Ifs:** You ask questions about bad or fearful things that could possibly happen in the future, while being unsatisfied with any answers. 'What if something happens to Dad?' It can result in becoming 'fixated' on worry thoughts, unable to move on because you can't be 100% sure the negative event won't happen.

☐ **Filtering:** You magnify or dwell on the negative details of a situation while ignoring all the positive ones. 'Look at all the things I have done badly.' Focusing only on unfavourable details has a negative impact on mood.

☐ **Jumping to Conclusions:** You make illogical leaps in believing that 'A causes B' without enough evidence or information to support your conclusions. 'My boyfriend was late in picking me up. He doesn't really want to go out with me tonight.'

☐ **Emotional Reasoning:** You automatically believe that what you feel is true for you or the world around you. If you feel strange, boring, stupid, etc., then you believe you are these things or that something is wrong with the situation because you feel that way. For example, 'I feel worried so the test must have gone badly.'

☐ **Being Right:** You are always trying to prove that your opinions and behaviours are the right ones. You cannot accept that you might be wrong or inaccurate, and you will go to great lengths to prove that you are right or others are wrong. 'You don't know what you're talking about. We have to do it my way or it won't work.' This can make it harder to accept feedback or consider other ways of behaving.

☐ **Reward Fallacy:** You expect to receive rewards or payoffs as a result of your own deeds or sacrifices, as if someone is keeping score. You feel angry or resentful if your actions do not reap rewards. 'I spent all that time fixing a nice dinner and no one appreciated it.' It can lead to feelings of anger and resentment, or the sense of being 'owed' something for a good deed.

☐ **Fairness Fallacy:** You believe you know what is fair, but since others don't agree with you (or don't follow the rules that you have decided upon), you feel resentful or angry. 'I deserve to have more screen time since I got an 'A' for my maths test.'

Choose two or three of your most typical unhelpful thinking styles, and think about how these would influence how you feel and how you behave. Do any of them influence your parenting style in ways you're less than pleased about?

Now that you have identified your unhelpful thinking styles, please list the ones that ring true to your child. How would these thinking styles be influencing your child's feelings and behaviour?

_____

_____

_____

Help Your Child Challenge Their Unhelpful Thinking

The questions below are focused on testing thinking traps. Help your child challenge their thinking styles by questioning their thinking.

Trap 1 – Generalising from negatives (applies to personalisation and over-generalisation)

Ask yourself the following questions to challenge the tendency to generalise from negatives:

- Am I allowing one or two negative aspects to become an overall view? Have I exaggerated the negative?
- Have I allowed something in this situation to trigger a general, negative label about myself (e.g. 'I'm such an idiot'), the situation (e.g. 'it's terrible') or someone else (e.g. 'she's useless')?

Trap 2 – Anticipating the worst (applies to catastrophising, 'what if', jumping to conclusions and emotional reasoning)

- Have I confused what I know to be the case with what I fear will happen?
- Have I made an assumption here?

2

- If it turns out to be as bad as I fear, how would that be? Could I bear that?
- Is it inevitable that the worst will happen? It is possible that things will turn out differently to what I'm picturing? Have I over-reacted and made too big a deal of something?

Trap 3 – Discounting positives (applies to filtering)

Ask yourself the following questions to challenge a tendency to discount positives:

- Have I underplayed the positives here? Have I missed aspects or glossed over them?
- Have I been too self-critical? Would I have made the same assessment if the same thing happened to someone else?
- Have I been genuinely open to more positive views about myself or others?

Trap 4 – All or nothing (applies to all or nothing and being right)

Questions you can use to challenge all or nothing thinking:

- Have I artificially polarised my options into one extreme or another?
- Does this situation have to be so black and white? Could there be some shades of grey?
- Are there alternative ways of thinking that I haven't considered?

Trap 5 – Mind reading

Questions you can use to challenge mind reading:

- How do I know that they think or feel like this?
- Have I jumped to any conclusions here?
- What do I actually know about what's going on here for anyone else involved? What are they actually saying and doing?

Trap 6 – Martyrdom (applies to reward fallacy)

Questions that you can use to test for martyrdom:

- How do I know that this is down to me?
- What was my part in this?
- What was actually within my influence and control?
- Who or what else might account for things being like this?

Exercise: Thought Record Diary

Use this chart to identify and challenge your negative thinking and to help your child identify and challenge theirs.

Situation (something happens)	Automatic thoughts (the meaning we give to the situation)	Feelings (how do you feel and where in your body do you feel it?)	Behaviour (what did you do in response to your thoughts and feelings)	Did it work for you?	What could you have done differently?
Getting ready for a friend's party	Will I know anyone there? What if they don't talk to me? Am I going to look stupid?	Nervous. Sick in my stomach. Hands shaking.	Told my friend I was sick. Stayed home.	Not really. Felt sad and lonely, angry at myself, felt like a coward.	Told my friend I was feeling nervous, asked her to make sure I had someone to talk to.

2

FACT or OPINION

FACT	OPINION
■ Evidence to support its truth	■ Based upon a belief or personal view
■ Indisputable	■ Arguable
■ Driven by rational thought	■ Driven by and reinforced by emotion
■ Head	■ Heart

At stressful times, we tend to be driven by our emotions and opinions, which create a vicious cycle by fuelling each other.

This leads to impulsive acts and unhelpful longer-term consequences, which help to maintain the overall problem. Realising that many thoughts are opinion rather than fact makes it less likely that we'll be distressed by them, and we're more able to make wise and calm decisions about the best action to take.

It is helpful to ask ourselves whether our thoughts are FACT or OPINION.

- If OPINION, then we can look at the facts – what we do know about the situation.
- If FACT, then we can make choices about the best thing to do.

Reflect:

- Think about a time when your child treated an opinion as fact.
- How did you acknowledge their opinion?
- How could you suggest that there are other opinions available?

Topic 3: Core Beliefs

A belief is something we consider to be a fact. It is anything that we assume to be true. Some beliefs are very commonly held to be true (e.g., grass is green) whereas others are more up for debate (e.g., meetings are boring).

Once formed, these beliefs become ingrained in us. We take them for granted, and we also assume our beliefs to be factual, whether they are true or not. Our beliefs influence how we consider something or someone to be good or bad, right or wrong, beautiful or ugly, desirable or undesirable, safe or dangerous, worthy or unworthy, or acceptable or unacceptable. Our beliefs also dictate what we consider to be possible or achievable, and how we view ourselves.

Most of our core beliefs are formed during childhood. When we are born, we enter this world with a clean slate and without preconceived beliefs. We are impressionable and look for meaning in almost everything because we are naturally inquisitive. Of course, we come into the world with certain temperament factors and traits, but our parents and environment play a big part in shaping our beliefs from a young age. Our school environment and our friends also play an important part.

Your core beliefs are like a filter that each thought must pass through. If someone has the core belief that they are unlovable, each of their thoughts will have to make sense in the context of that belief. Thoughts and events that are consistent with that belief are more likely to be noticed and processed, whereas thoughts and events that are inconsistent with the belief may not be noticed or may be reshaped or discarded.

Before you can challenge your core beliefs, you first need to identify what they are and where they stem from. Here are some common examples:

| I'm unlovable | I'm stupid | I'm boring | I'm a useless person |
| I'm a failure | I'm broken | I'm worthless | I'm not good enough |

Can you identify one of your child's core beliefs from the table above?

What does your child say or do that suggests to you that they have this belief?

_____

_____

_____

2

Can you name two pieces of evidence contrary to your child's core beliefs that they may not have noticed or processed accurately?

_____

_____

_____

Consequences of Negative Core Beliefs

Beliefs about oneself:

- Often has negative beliefs about oneself
- Takes events personally
- Beliefs about oneself often too generalised
- Unmotivated to try new things

Interpersonal:

- Doesn't trust others
- Feels inadequate in relationships
- Jealousy
- Confrontational or aggressive
- Puts others' needs above one's own needs

Mental health problems:

- Depression
- Anxiety
- Difficulty managing stress
- Low self-esteem
- Unhealthy substance use

Facts About Core Beliefs:

- People are not born with a set of core beliefs. Core beliefs are learned.
- Core beliefs usually develop during childhood, or during stressful or traumatic periods in adulthood.
- Information that contradicts our core beliefs is often ignored, or is distorted to make sense in the context of our belief.
- Negative core beliefs are not necessarily true even if they feel true.
- Core beliefs tend to be rigid and difficult to change, but not impossible.

Topic 4: Triggers, Functions and Payoffs of Behaviour

Understanding the triggers and functions of your child's behaviour is vital in parenting. Tantrums, refusing to give in, self-pity, yelling – all have payoffs (e.g., an outlet for an uncomfortable feeling, avoiding something difficult, or gaining access to something enjoyable). Let me explain, and you may find a little bit of your child in this explanation.

When your child is faced with a challenge or conflict, they are likely to have an emotional response. They are also likely to have thoughts that reflect their values. These thoughts and emotions will lead to a reaction. It may be aggression, tantrums, avoidance, procrastination or any number of other reactions or behaviours. Some examples are below.

Behaviours of concern that often occur in a classroom setting: humming loudly, telling an inappropriate joke, putting their head on their desk, refusing to participate, throwing books on the floor, yelling, swearing, threatening, pushing, hitting, punching, or running out of the classroom.

Behaviour payoffs: escape, attention, avoidance, power, control or tangible gain.

Date	Time	What happened before behaviour occurred	Behaviour	Consequence	Possible payoffs/ Function
30/07	10:15	Teacher asks the class to take out their maths homework	Brad gets up and kicks his chair	Class disrupted, Brad sent to the office	Avoided having to explain why homework was not done and avoided feeling embarrassed in front of his peers
20/8	9:30	Teacher announces that it is time for reading	Brad tells inappropriate joke	Peers laugh, class disrupted	Escape and attention

Behaviours of concern that often happen at home: refusing to do homework, refusing to do chores, refusing to participate in family activities, throwing books on the floor, yelling, swearing, threatening, pushing, hitting, punching, locking themself in the bedroom, running away from home, stealing.

Behaviour payoffs: escape, attention, avoidance, power or control.

2

In the example below, we can see that the intention of the behaviour is to escape frustration and boredom. For this child, the payoff is a big one; no wonder the playing of computer games continues. We can say that the consequences of the behaviour are highly reinforcing.

Triggers (situation, thoughts and feelings that happen before the behaviour)	Behaviour (something that a person does)	Function/Payoffs (outcomes of the behaviour that keep it going)
Situation: studying for maths test, does not understand material **Thoughts:** I don't like maths This is a waste of time. I don't understand this **Feelings:** Frustrated, overwhelmed and has an urge to play games	Packs books away and plays computer games against others	**Short-term payoff:** Scores the most points, feels happy, socially connected and relaxed

During a parent–child conflict, behaviour payoffs can reinforce negative actions. A child may respond to overly strict discipline or demands for compliance with disobedience or defiance. The parent and child enter a cycle of coercion and aversion that escalates into aggression. The cycle continues until one of the participants wins. If the child finally gives in, the parent wins and coercive parenting is reinforced. If the parent disengages, the child wins, reinforcing the aggressive behaviour. This coercion cycle is illustrated on the following page.

Can you identify a behaviour and its payoff that your child exhibits?

_____

_____

Having identified the payoffs, how can you help your child discover more effective ways to help them meet their needs?

_____

_____

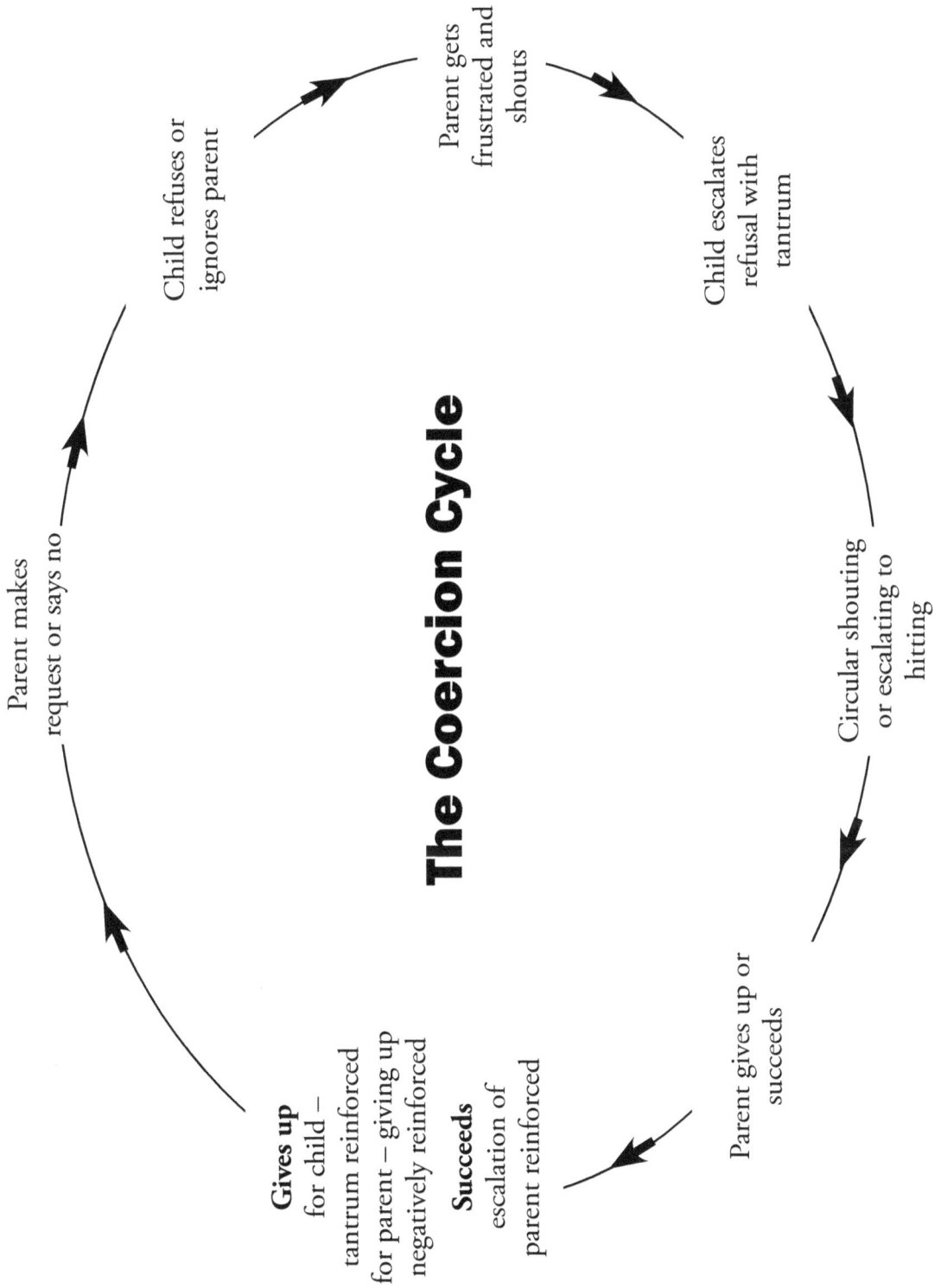

The Coercion Cycle

Parent makes request or says no

Child refuses or ignores parent

Parent gets frustrated and shouts

Child escalates refusal with tantrum

Circular shouting or escalating to hitting

Parent gives up or succeeds

Gives up for child – tantrum reinforced for parent – giving up negatively reinforced

Succeeds escalation of parent reinforced

2

Module 2:
Adaptive Thinking

Section 2:

Mindfulness - Mind and Body

Topic 1: Mindfulness

Children must be taught how to think, not what to think.
Relax Child

Research is increasingly showing that mindfulness can help increase focus, calm busy brains, and reduce symptoms of inattention and impulsivity in children with ADHD. The challenge is that not many children jump at the idea of practicing mindfulness, often because of a lack of understanding of what it entails. The key is to tailor activities to your child's maturity and interests and to be realistic about your expectations – not to expect that mindfulness will be a cure-all for your child's ADHD symptoms. Keep an open mind and encourage your child to try the activities that they like that help them relax – ideally strengthening self-awareness and finding their happiest self along the way.

For example, if your child is feeling anxious, simply noticing and saying, 'I notice that I am feeling anxious' and accepting it for what it is – just a thought, or a feeling – and not fighting it is a great start. The more they fight it, the bigger the struggle will be. Mindfulness breathing can stop a cascade of inner events that cause anxiety and stress – states that challenge your child's ability to concentrate and pay attention.

The way we breathe is strongly linked to the way we feel. When we are relaxed, we breathe slowly, and when we are anxious, we breathe more quickly.

Let's look at three different patterns of breathing:

Normal breathing: when we breathe, we take in oxygen that is used by the body. This process creates carbon dioxide, a waste product that we breathe out. When our breathing is relaxed, the levels of carbon dioxide and oxygen are balanced, allowing our body to function efficiently.

Exercise breathing: when we exercise, our body uses more oxygen to fuel our muscles and therefore produces more carbon dioxide. Since our breathing rate increases during exercise, we breathe in extra oxygen and breathe out the extra carbon dioxide. This means that the balance between oxygen and carbon dioxide levels is maintained.

Anxious breathing: When we are anxious, our breathing rate increases: we take in more oxygen and breathe out more carbon dioxide than usual. Because we are not exercising, our body is not using up the extra oxygen, and so it is not producing any extra carbon dioxide. Because carbon dioxide is being expelled faster than it is being produced, the levels of carbon dioxide in the blood go down, leading to a temporary change in the pH of the blood. This can lead us to feeling unpleasantly light-headed, tingly in our fingers and toes, and clammy and sweaty.

When our breathing returns to its usual rate, the levels of carbon dioxide return to normal, and the symptoms resolve. You can deliberately relax your breathing to feel better.

Relaxed breathing instructions:

1. Sit or lie down comfortably. Close your eyes if you so wish.

2. Breathe in slowly and steadily through your nose for the count of four.

3. Hold your breath for a count of four.

4. Breathe out slowly and steadily through your mouth to the count of four, pursing your lips as if you are blowing through a straw. Repeat for a few minutes as many times as you need throughout the day.

Like any new skill, the more your child practises, the better they will get at it. But do not wait until the storm hits to secure your belongings. The idea is that we equip ourselves and our children so that when life throws curve balls at us, we know what to do – do you run and catch it, or duck and dive to avoid it? Be prepared!

Topic 2: Physical Activity

In every walk with nature, one receives more than he seeks.
John Muir

Several studies have shown that spending time in nature can improve concentration. Similarly, time outdoors allows your mind to wander and roam without being constantly vigilant. In fact, recent research shows that time in nature has measurable and specific benefits for those with ADHD, including improved concentration, increased ability to follow directions, and decreased disruptive behaviour. There's less research with children, but it seems to point in the same way. There are many activities that you and your child can do in nature. Add your own ideas to the ones below:

- Walking in the park
- Walking your dog
- Hiking
- Biking on a nature trail
- Walking in the rain
- Sleeping outdoors
- Bird watching
- Fishing
- Lying back watching the shapes of the clouds
- Camping
- Climbing a mountain
- Swimming outdoors
- Photography
- _____
- _____

Does your child engage in any of the activities above? If so, do you notice any changes in their mood and ability to focus and concentrate afterwards?

_____

_____

Benefits Of Exercise On Mental Health

> *The best six doctors anywhere, and no one can deny it,*
> *are sunshine, water, rest, air, exercise and diet.*
> **Wayne Fields**

Exercise helps manage ADHD symptoms. Exercise is often said to be the body's natural antidepressant. Physiologically, it contributes to better sleep, increases the release of chemicals such as serotonin and endorphins in the brain, and increases blood flow, which improves neural functioning. Psychological benefits are many, and include heightened self-esteem, interruption to negative thoughts, and an increase in social contact. Recent studies have also shown how as little as 30 minutes of exercise per day can increase the ability to concentrate and improve general executive functioning. The key is to make exercise part of your family's lifestyle and part of an ADHD management plan. Exercise is also beneficial for conditions that can co-exist with ADHD, such as:

- Depression
- Substance abuse
- Sleep difficulties
- Low energy
- Anxiety
- Oppositional defiant disorder
- Stress
- Low self-esteem

Additional benefits of physical exercise

Physical health – The more your child moves, the better their movement skills will be. Physical activity helps build healthy bones, muscles, heart and lungs. For maximum benefit, aim for activity that gets them breathing a bit harder and sweating a bit!

Brain functioning – Being active develops the brain and improves mental functions. Exercise leads to improved motor skills, better thinking and problem-solving, stronger attention skills and increased learning. Even the simple act of playing outside with friends can help your child do better on tests and assignments.

Emotional and mental health – If your child is feeling depressed or anxious, or just having an off day, exercise might seem too hard. But if they can get started, physical activity releases feel-good chemicals, or endorphins, in the brain. These help to improve mood, energy levels and even sleep. These positive effects will flow on into things like self-confidence, resilience and learning.

Reduced anxiety – By focusing on the demands of physical activity, an anxious child can distract from anxiety-inducing issues, developing new skills and achieving a sense of accomplishment.

2

Improved relationships – Exercising and playing team sport can increase your child's sense of belonging and companionship. Focusing on the sport can help relieve social anxiety over being in a group situation. The positive effects of sharing experiences, developing a rapport and working towards common goals help develop confidence and foster friendships in school if the activities are school based.

Improved body image (self-esteem, self-worth and self-confidence) – When your child sees how much fun it is to be able to dance, jump, walk, run, stretch and play, they are more likely to want to continue enjoying being active throughout their life. Seeing and appreciating what their body can do, rather than how it looks, is a great way for them to build a positive body image and self-esteem. As they develop this awareness, it becomes part of their lifestyle.

Topic 3: The Role of Nutrition in Managing ADHD

A substantial amount of research has examined how nutrition affects ADHD. While there's no evidence that diet causes ADHD, research suggests that for some people, dietary changes can help to improve symptoms.

Nutrition and behaviour

The science behind how food affects behaviour is still new and developing. However, certain foods do affect behaviour – caffeine can increase alertness, chocolate can affect mood, and alcohol can reduce inhibitions and exaggerate emotional reactions. Nutritional deficiencies can also affect behaviour. One study concluded that taking a supplement of essential fatty acids, vitamins and minerals led to a significant reduction in antisocial behaviour, compared with a placebo. Studies suggest vitamin and mineral supplements can also reduce antisocial behaviour in children, and polyunsaturated fatty acids have been shown to decrease violent behaviour. Since foods and supplements may influence behaviour, it seems plausible that they could also affect ADHD symptoms, which are largely behavioural.

For this reason, a certain amount of effort has been put into research on the effects of foods and supplements on ADHD. Studies performed are usually either supplement studies, which focus on supplementing with one or more nutrients, and elimination studies, which focus on eliminating one or more ingredients from the diet.

Supplements examined by nutrition studies for their effects on ADHD symptoms include amino acids, vitamins and minerals, and omega-3 fatty acids. While several studies show promise, the results are mixed, and more work needs to be done.

Elimination studies

People with ADHD are more likely to have adverse reactions to food, causing speculation that eliminating problematic foods might help to improve symptoms. Studies have examined the effects of eliminating many ingredients, including food additives, preservatives, sweeteners and allergenic foods.

Eliminating salicylates and food additives

In the 1970s, patients following a diet prescribed by an allergist named Dr Feingold to eliminate foods that caused reactions noted an improvement in their behavioural problems. Soon after, Feingold started recruiting children diagnosed with hyperactivity

2

for dietary experiments. He claimed that 30–50% of them improved on the diet. Although subsequent reviews concluded the Feingold diet was not an effective intervention for hyperactivity, it stimulated further research into the effects of food and additive elimination on ADHD. The diet was free of salicylates, which are compounds found in many foods, medications, and food additives.

Eliminating artificial colours and preservatives

After the Feingold diet was no longer considered effective, researchers narrowed their focus to look at artificial food colours (AFCs) and preservatives. These substances seem to affect the behaviour of children, regardless of whether or not they have ADHD.

One study followed 800 children suspected of hyperactivity. Of the group, 75% of them improved while on an AFC-free diet but relapsed once given AFCs again.

Even though overall studies indicate that AFCs can increase hyperactivity, many people claim the evidence is not strong enough. In Australia, food additives in most packaged food must be listed in the statement of ingredients on the label. Most food additives must be listed by their class name followed by the name of the food additive or the food additive number, for example, Colour (Caramel I) or Colour (150a). Enzymes and most flavourings (or flavour) do not need to be named or identified by a food additive number and can be labelled by their class name only.

Eliminating sugar and artificial sweeteners

Soft drinks have been linked to increased hyperactivity, and low blood sugar is also common in those with ADHD. Some observational studies have found sugar intake to be related to ADHD symptoms in children and adolescents. While, overall, sugar and artificial sweeteners have not been shown to directly affect ADHD, they may have indirect effects.

The Few Foods Elimination Diet is a method that tests how people with ADHD respond to foods. It works by:

Elimination. This step involves following a very restricted diet of low-allergen foods that are unlikely to cause adverse effects. If symptoms get better, the next phase is entered.

Reintroduction. Foods suspected of causing adverse effects are reintroduced every 3–7 days. If symptoms return, the food is identified as 'sensitising'.

Managing nutrition in children with ADHD can be complicated by sensory issues causing food avoidance or over-eating, as well as the possibility of medication-related appetite loss.

A small percentage of children who take stimulant medication for their ADHD, may experience loss of appetite, which may result in weight loss. For some, this decreased appetite is often only delayed appetite. They may eat very little during the day while the medication is most active but will get hungry late in the afternoon and into the evening, when the medication starts to wear off. If they can be encouraged to eat when they feel hungry, possibly having a second dinner before bedtime, appetite difficulties usually become less problematic. Some children seem to adjust to the medication, and their appetite returns.

Even though there are clear links between children's diet and their behaviour, the recommendation is that all children just stick to a healthy diet. Ideally what we want is for them to eat a typically healthy diet from the five food groups, spreading it out during the day, if possible.

Whatever your nutrition difficulties with your ADHD child, it is essential to work together with your medical team to ensure that you have the most up-to-date information and strategies. Taking advantage of support groups and comparing notes with other parents can also be helpful.

Topic 4: The Importance of Sleep

I want to sleep but my brain won't stop talking to itself.
Credit needed

Having good sleep hygiene is vital for good functioning, better school performance and general wellbeing. Although many mechanisms of the brain remain a mystery, there is no doubt that the brain requires a lot of energy to function as the body's management system. In addition to food, water and oxygen, the brain clearly needs sleep. A good night's sleep is exactly what the doctor will order to prepare us for the many things that we have to do in any given day. In essence, no sleep equals no energy in the brain to help us recover from the day and recharge our minds for the adventures of the next day.

If, after using the sleeping tips below, your child is still struggling to get a good night's rest, speak to your family doctor or paediatrician. Sleeping medications are an alternative but should be avoided, as these tend to be only effective in the short term. Long-term use may lead to dependence, and may prolong your child's sleep difficulties.

Generally, pre-schoolers (ages 3–5 years) need 10–13 hours of sleep per night and school-age children (ages 6–13 years) need 9–11 hours of sleep per night.

Guidelines to Improve Sleep

Routine: Have a bedtime routine and a set bedtime. A routine can start well before bedtime and include activities to help you wind down, such as a warm bath or shower, or practising mindfulness. Staying up late on weekends can throw off a child's sleep schedule for several days. Stick to the same bedtime and wake time every day, even on weekends. Children sleep better when they have the same routine every day.

Caffeine: Good sleep hygiene begins in the day, with the consideration of food and drink intake. Caffeine is a stimulant that prevents sleep and is present not only in tea and coffee, but also in chocolate and cola and energy drinks. If your child drinks these, try to limit their intake and avoid them altogether after lunchtime.

Food: Eating a large meal before bedtime can prevent sleep. Consider the best time to eat your dinner meal and plan an earlier dinner for your child on school nights. You can still all have family meals at weekends and during holiday periods. A glass of warm milk can help you fall asleep.

Exercise: Children may have difficulty in falling asleep if they have been inactive throughout the day. Encourage your child to engage in sports and play outside. This will help them to burn off energy and feel tired at the end of the day. Even if they are not very sporty, just going for a walk in the fresh air can be helpful. However, avoid exercising directly before bedtime, as the heat created in the muscles by exercise can prevent them from falling asleep.

Environment: Encourage your child to use their bed only for sleeping. Lying on a bed and doing other activities (e.g., homework, watching TV, or using a tablet or computer) makes it hard for the brain to associate bed with sleep. The sleep environment should be a place to feel safe and secure, and not associated with play. There are several ways your child can adjust their sleep environment. Have them consider whether they prefer a night light or total darkness. What about the temperature and noise level of the room? Clear their room of things that distract them from sleeping.

Technology: Using electronic devices (such as televisions, mobile phones and tablet computers) close to bedtime can prevent your child from settling to sleep. These devices produce light that suppresses natural hormones in the brain that cause sleepiness. Ideally, these devices should not be used for at least an hour before bed and should not be in your child's room overnight. If they use these devices to help them fall asleep, suggest replacing this routine with reading or listening to soothing music. Avoid using devices during nighttime awakening as well.

Alarm clocks are for waking up: Children who tend to stare at the clock, waiting and hoping to fall asleep, should have the clock turned away from them.

Start the day off right with exercise: Exercising earlier in the day can help children feel more energetic and awake during the day, have an easier time focusing, and even help with falling asleep and staying asleep later on that evening.

Don't toss and turn: Some parents give the child the following option: 'If you can't sleep, get out of bed.' If a child is tossing and turning in bed, have them get out of bed and do something that isn't too stimulating, such as read a book. They can return to bed once they are sleepy again. If they are still awake after 20–30 minutes, they can repeat the process and get out of bed for another 20 minutes before returning. Doing this prevents the bed from being associated with sleeplessness.

Put children to sleep drowsy, but awake: The ideal time for a child to go to bed is when they are drowsy, but still awake. Allowing them to fall asleep in places other than their bed teaches them to associate sleep with other places than their bed.

Use a sleep diary: A sleep diary can be a useful way of making sure you have the right facts about your child's sleep, rather than making assumptions. Help your child keep a sleep diary to track naps, bedtimes, wake times and behaviours to find patterns and work on particular problems when things are not going well.

Sleep Diary

Date	Example 30/3/21					
What time did you go to bed?	9:00 pm					
What time did you fall asleep?	11:00 pm					
What time did you wake up?	6:00 am					
How many times did you wake up during the night?	4 times					
How many hours of sleep did you get during the night?	5 hours					
What was the total time that you were awake during the night?	2 hours					
Reasons for waking up during the night	Mind racing Over tired Worried about not sleeping					
How rested do you feel in the morning? Score from 0 to 10 (10 is most rested)	5					

Work through the sleep diary with your child if they are not able to fill it out for themself.

Module 2:
Adaptive Thinking

Section 3:
Values
and
Goals

Topic 1: Knowing Your Values

Values are like fingerprints, nobody's are the same,
but you leave them allover everything you do.
Elvis Presley

The aim of this sections is to help you reflect on those principles and beliefs that keep you on track and give you meaning, things you believe are most important for you – your values. Values help to determine your priorities in life and heavily influence decision-making. For example, a person who values wealth might prioritise their career, whereas a person who values family might try to spend more time at home. When a person's actions do not match their values (e.g., valuing family, but working a lot), they may become discontent. The main benefit of knowing your values is that you will gain greater clarity and focus on what really matters to you, and use this newfound clarity to make decisions, set goals and take committed action. Values signify what is important and worthwhile in our lives.

Different people have different values, and that is okay. Values help us prioritise how to best spend our time, right here and now. This is important because, firstly, time is our most limited resource – it does not renew itself, and once we spend a day, it's gone forever. If we don't prioritise and we waste that day on actions that don't produce the results we want, that loss is permanent. Secondly, priorities matter because we humans tend to be inconsistent in how we invest our time and energy. We are easily distracted and fall into the trap of living by different priorities every day. One day we are consistent with our rules; the next day we slack off. One day we work productively; the next we procrastinate and lack motivation. If we don't consciously use our priorities to stick to a consistent course, we'll naturally drift off course and shift all over the place. Like a ship without a radar, in the middle of the ocean, who knows where it will dock? Before you can set a course for your ship, you must first determine the port at which you want to dock – your values.

Where Can I Apply Values in My Life?

Although you already apply your values to your decision process every day, you probably haven't put a lot of thought into it, so it might not result in the best possible decisions, for you or your future. Let's look at an example:

If you strongly value honesty, will you easily tell a lie? Not unless you also have a belief or value that says in certain circumstances it's alright to lie. Fortunately, unlike real fingerprints, our values fingerprints can be changed. Since you're leaving your prints on everything you touch, and on every life you come in contact with, make them something you are proud of. They are your choices and your values – it's your life.

Identifying Your Values

If you don't know where you are going, any road will get you there.
Lewis Carrol

Review the list of life values below, and choose the top 10 values to identify what you consider to be most important in your life – what gives you direction. Put them in order of importance, where 1 is the most important. Ask your spouse or partner to do the same.

Achievement	Assertiveness	Beauty
Caring	Challenging Work	Cleanliness
Compassion	Confidence	Courage
Courtesy/Consideration	Creativity	Detachment
Determination	Enthusiasm	Excellence
Faith in oneself	Faith	Faithfulness
Flexibility	Forgiveness	Friendship
Generosity	Gentleness	Health
Helpfulness	Honesty/Truthfulness	Honour
Humility	Idealism	Independence
Integrity	Joyfulness	Justice
Kindness/Empathy	Knowledge	Love
Loyalty	Mercy	Moderation
Modesty	Morality	Obedience
Orderliness	Patience	Peacefulness
Personal Growth	Pleasure	Power
Purposefulness	Recognition	Reliability
Religion	Respect for self and others	Responsibility
Security	Self-Discipline	Self-Esteem
Service	Steadfastness	Tact
Thankfulness/Gratitude	Tolerance	Trust
Trustworthiness	Wealth	Wisdom

List your (and your spouse or partner's) top ten values below

1. _____
2. _____
3. _____
4. _____
5. _____
6. _____
7. _____
8. _____
9. _____
10. _____

Children's Traits

Now that you and your spouse or partner have identified your values, let's see how well you know your child.

Exercise: Below is a list of behaviours common in children. Pick the five that you admire the most and the five that you admire the least about your child. You can have your spouse or partner do this exercise separately and then compare and discuss your lists.

1. **Energetic**: very active, always on the go

2. **Aggressive**: takes whatever they want without consideration

3. **Sporty**: can throw and catch a ball very well

4. **Attractive**: is a very beautiful child

5. **Cheerful**: has a smile for everyone

6. **Clean**: doesn't want to be dirty or messy

7. **Coordinated**: can do physical things easily (e.g. run, climb, ride a trike)

8. **Courageous**: faces unpleasant situations (e.g. injections) without flinching

9. **Curious**: asks questions about everything

10. **Flexible**: can do things a variety of ways

11. **Frugal**: always turns out lights when leaving a room

12. **Generous**: gives toys away to anyone who asks

13. **Helpful to others**: sees what needs to be done and helps without being asked

14. **Honest**: tells the truth even when it is to their disadvantage

15. **Independent**: always wants to do things by themself

16. **Intelligent**: is tested as academically gifted

17. **Obedient**: does what anyone says

18. **Passive**: lets another child bite them

19. **Persistent**: doesn't like activities being interrupted

20. **Polite**: always thanks people

21. **Popular**: is always sought out by playmates

22. **Religious**: says prayers every night

23. **Self-controlled**: can be trusted to leave tempting items alone

24. **Sensitive**: comforts a sad child at school

25. **Self-reliant**: gets own snack whenever hungry

Ranking children's traits

Rank the traits that you chose in order of preference, where 1 is the trait you most or least admire.

Traits most admired

1. _____
2. _____
3. _____
4. _____
5. _____

Traits least admired

1. _____
2. _____
3. _____
4. _____
5. _____

Exercise: Re-read the quote by Elvis at the start of this section (p.106) and see if you can identify your child's top five values, based on the traits that you've identified above and what they say and do. Rank these values, where 1 is the most important.

1. _____
2. _____
3. _____
4. _____
5. _____

How consistently is your child living by these values?

_____

_____

_____

What actions does your child engage in that demonstrate how important these values are for them?

_____

_____

_____

How important is it for you that your children share your values?

_____

_____

_____

What happens when your child's behaviour is not aligned with your values?

_____

_____

_____

When your child's behaviours are not consistent with their chosen values, how can you help them reflect on this inconsistency?

_____

_____

_____

Values are often passed down by your family and the society you live in. Who taught you the values that you identified above? Think about the values of the people who surround and influence you.

My mother's values:	My father's values:
1	1
2	2
The values of a person I respect:	**The values of the society I live in:**
1	1
2	2
The values I would like to live by:	**The values I actually live by:**
1	1
2	2
3	3
4	4

Have you at some point in your life questioned your personal values? If so, what was going on in your life and what was the outcome?

_____

_____

_____

_____

_____

What behaviours are indicative of how consistently you are living your top five values?

_____

_____

_____

How open is your family to discussing the importance of personal and family values in everyday life?

_____

_____

_____

Could you encourage your spouse and family members to explore and identify their own values?

_____

_____

_____

Do you think that living consistently with your identified values makes parenting easier? If so, what behaviours would be indicative of this?

_____

_____

_____

Would you have chosen the same values 5 years ago?

_____

_____

_____

Complete the Bullseye

Look at your listed values above, then make an X in each area of the dartboard below to represent how well your life currently reflects these values.

The closer you are to the Bullseye, the more consistently you are living your values. The further you are from the Bullseye, the more inconsistently you are living your values.

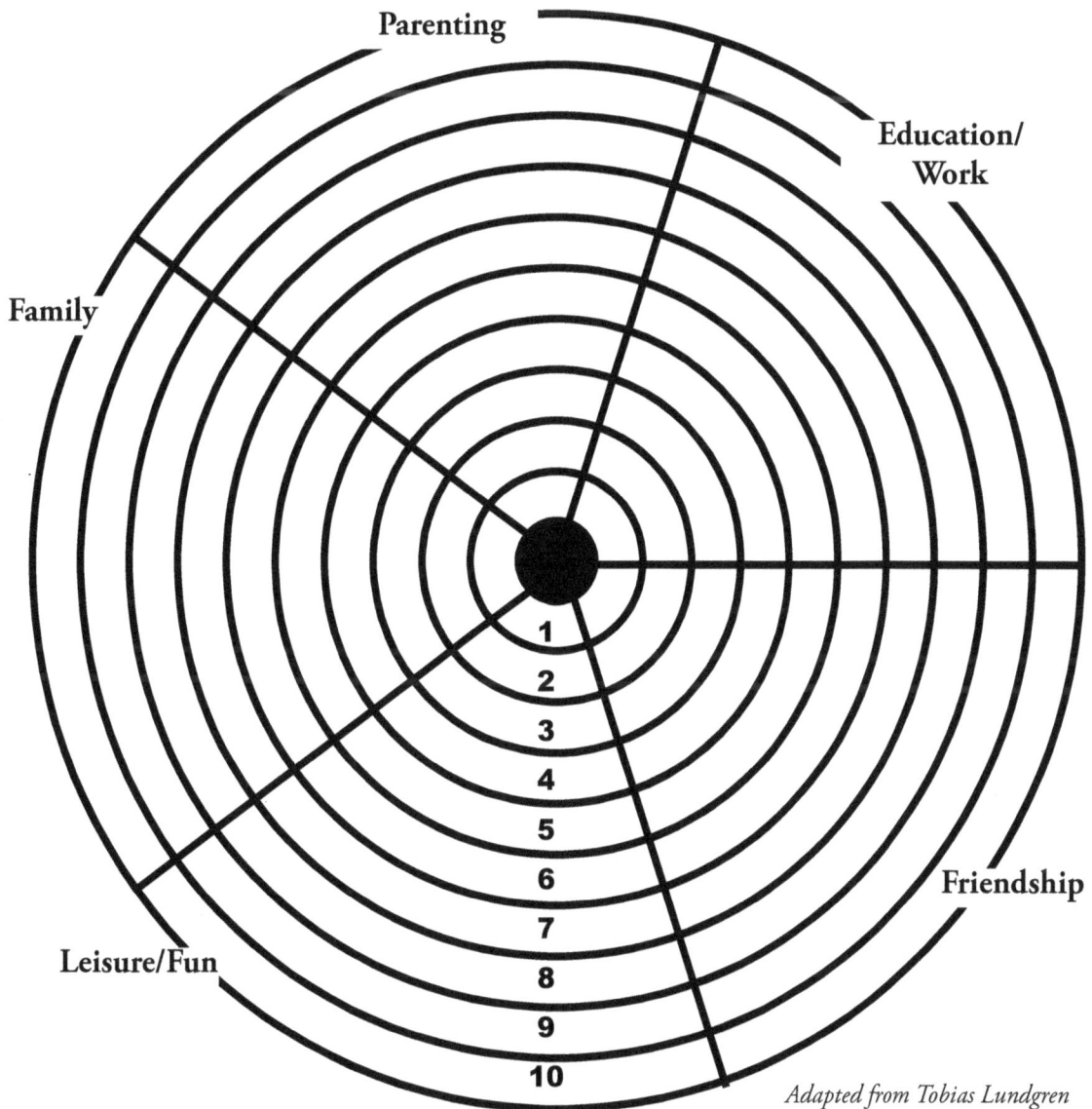

Parenting

Education/
Work

Family

1
2
3
4
5
6
7
8
9
10

Friendship

Leisure/Fun

Adapted from Tobias Lundgren

How happy are you with how your Bullseye looks?

_____

_____

Establishing Rules

Now that you have determined your values (with your spouse or partner if applicable), and have attempted to identify your child's top values, you are ready to begin setting or evaluating the rules of your home.

Rules should be determined in accordance with your values. It is confusing and frustrating for everyone when you expect your children to adhere to rules that are not a reflection of values. For younger children, it may have been sufficient to explain that they had to do something because Mum or Dad said so. However, as children move into their teens, this answer becomes less appropriate and more likely to cause arguments and disobedience. It is important for their development that they understand the reason and rationale behind rules, even when they may not agree.

Thus, it is important for you to explain to your child what the rules are and why. Before you can do that, you have to be prepared by understanding the rules yourself.

Behind every great rule there is typically one or two main themes. These themes are usually safety and respect. Virtually every rule is (or should be) designed to teach a child how to respect others and themselves. Even rules based on safety revolve around the concept of respecting oneself. For religious families, respecting your faith may also be an important value. Consider the following examples:

- **No bad attitudes or talking back to Mum or Dad.** At its heart, this rule is clearly designed for the child to treat their parents with respect.
- **Call if you are going to be home late.** This rule may help a child show respect to their parents by not making them worry needlessly; it may also help them respect others' time such as in instances where they may be late for dinner or a family function.

Sometimes your child may not understand that some of your rules are for their own benefit and may not see it as a matter of respect. For example, requiring adherence to a curfew may not be understood as a respectful thing by a teenager. To most teens, it is not disrespectful to stay out all night unless their parent does not trust them. Rather than simply arguing about it, talk to them about the kinds of things that happen late at night or in the early hours of morning that may involve needless danger or threaten their wellbeing. Help them understand that you are concerned for their safety and should not be expected to stay up until 3 am just so they can watch another movie at their friend's house. Chances are, they will continue to disagree with the rule, but you have demonstrated to them that you have a reason for the rules that they are expected to live by.

114

You do not need to (and really should not) engage in an argument. Sharing your reasons for the rules they live by is important but should not be confused with you having to defend yourself, or your teen believing that they have to agree with the rules to be expected to live by them.

Individual considerations

When you have determined your values and the role that they play in making the rules in your home, it is time to consider your individual child.

However, some rules are perfectly appropriate to be universal and do not need to consider the individual personality and habits of each child.

However, not all children are the same, and as a parent, your job is to meet the needs of your child. In fact, if you have more than one child or teenager, it is completely acceptable to have rules that change based on the child. If you make rules that are more restrictive for one child because of past behaviour, their sibling should not be expected to pay for their mistakes. This requires the parent to determine honestly whether or not the rule was a good one in the first place.

Likewise, if you have a rule that your child has been following but you determine that you are no longer comfortable with that rule for whatever reason, you have the right to change the rules. The most important thing is to collaborate with your child and keep the lines of communication open. Let your child know the reason for the rule change and, where possible, invite brainstorming of possible ideas.

Establishing consequences

Obviously, rules are pointless without consequences. As a parent, one of the most important things you can do to prevent bad behaviour is to have already determined the consequences for breaking any rules, and communicated those consequences to your child.

Consequences should make sense. If your rules are based on values, your consequences should reflect that as well. Whenever possible, use the concept of natural consequences. Natural consequences tend to be situations where the consequence is related directly to the rule breaking.

For example, if your teen goes overboard with data use and when your bill arrives it is three times the normal rate, a natural consequence may involve your child helping pay the bill and/or losing phone privileges for a period.

Not allowing your child to go to the birthday party of a friend would not be a natural consequence. Although there are some situations where natural consequences may not be sufficient, they typically can work surprisingly well. Rationally speaking, if your child valued whatever they did (or did not do) over following your rules, it naturally follows that a loss relating to what they did is likely to have a significant impact, as they have shown that it is important to them.

It may be difficult to remember, but many of the things you make available to your child are privileges; your teen does not have any right to a number of things they enjoy. Mobile phones, tablets, game consoles, laptops, e-readers, cars and money and so on are all privileges that you may (or may not) allow your child to have. If your child is violating your rules regarding any of these things, respond appropriately. Their world will not shut down if they lose their mobile phone privileges, regardless of how much they may say it will.

Sometimes, the actions taken by your child may be wildly inappropriate and require harsher penalties. Nevertheless, there are some methods of punishment that are never appropriate.

Physical abuse is not an appropriate disciplinary technique

Physical abuse is usually interpreted as any time that a child may be struck with anything other than an open hand, on any place other than their buttocks, and should not ever result in visible bruises or welts. If the actions taken by your teen are so inappropriate that you find yourself struggling not to hit them, remove yourself from the situation until you are in better control of your emotions. Unlike a three-year-old, your teenager will still understand why they are in trouble even if they have to wait an hour before you respond.

Emotional abuse is likewise inappropriate

Calling names and making sweeping judgments such as 'You always make the stupidest decision possible!' are both ineffective and highly damaging to your child's psychological development. Over the past few years there has been an increase in incidents of shaming children, such as forcing a 12-year-old to stand on a busy street corner holding up a sign stating that they stole something or broke a rule. However, shaming a child in such a way has the potential to do far more harm than good, especially if you have a sensitive child.

While minor bouts of shame and guilt may have an important role to play in your child's development, they should be naturally occurring and do not need to be public. If your child has hurt someone with their behaviour, apologising to that person is appropriate and the embarrassment that is likely to accompany such an apology is a natural consequence. Making your child an object of ridicule for the general public, no matter how grievous their rule breaking, is far more likely to do harm than good.

When parents disagree over values

Parents may disagree about what is important and which traits to encourage in their children. For example, one parent may want their child to be assertive and outspoken, while the other parent prefers a child who is obedient, gets along with others and defers to the parent's decisions. This can cause conflict in the parent dynamic.

When parents with different values live in different households, it is easier for teens to adopt the values of their primary caregiver, but confusion and disruption may occur when the child prefers one set of values over another. In a two-parent household where there is a significant difference in values between parents, this can present an extremely challenging and frustrating environment for the teenager as well as for the parents.

It is very important for parents to determine their values, especially the values regarding parenthood and those they want to impart to their children in early childhood. If you have not done so, or situations arise where parents are not sure that they agree on a topic, do your child a favour and discuss it privately, especially if the discussion is likely to be heated. This applies whether or not the parents are married or live in two separate households. Once a decision has been made between the parents, it can then be presented to the child. At this point, it may be helpful for each parent to share their perspective with the teen to promote critical thinking; do not do this with your child until or unless both parents have reached a conclusion as to how you will proceed or what value will determine the rules.

Some people worry that having different values or ideas to their partner – on important issues like parenting, politics or morality – means it's likely they're going to run into problems further down the line.

While it's true that having opposing opinions on big subjects, like parenting, can create friction, it's by no means a sign that you can't work as a couple.

The values component in this workbook tries to help parents understand that different values within a family aren't usually the problem. It's how you deal with them that matters.

2

Topic 2: Goal Setting

*When it is obvious that the goals cannot be reached,
don't drop the goal adjust the action steps.*
Confucius

Helping Your Child To Set Goals

Aside from helping children believe in themselves, feel more in control and setting them up for success in school, SMART goal setting also:

- Provides direction, which most youths are seeking
- Helps children to clarify their values and what is important to them, and to focus on it
- Facilitates more effective decision-making through better self-awareness, self-esteem and direction
- Allows children to take a more active role in building their own future
- Acts as a powerful motivator by giving children something to hope for and aspire to
- Gives children a positive experience of achievement and personal satisfaction when they reach a goal
- Assists children in finding a sense of purpose in life

When your child wants to give up on a goal because it's too hard, help them:

- Remember the value underpinning the goal.
- Review their action plan.
- Discuss the obstacles and how they can be solved.
- Reward effort, determination and persistence.
- Practice positive self-talk.
- Take small steps.

Goals exercise

Write a goal you want to accomplish, and two obstacles you might encounter along your way. Then write three steps you could take to overcome those obstacles. Where possible, identify the values underpinning this goal. For example:

Goal: To lose 10 kg in the next 5 months

Values: Health/fitness

Obstacles: I don't like to exercise, and I have a sweet tooth.

To overcome these obstacles, I can:

- ask myself, 'In service of what value am I willing to go to the gym and limit my sugar intake?'
- use my diary to allocate blocks of time to go to the gym or take walks in nature.
- limit my sugar intake by only having sweet things on weekends.

What can I start doing today to work toward my goals?

_____

_____

_____

Who can help me and how?

_____

_____

_____

Use the SMART goal planning tool on the next page to help you set and achieve your goals.

2

SMART Goal Planning

Set your goals high enough to inspire you and low enough to encourage you.
Unknown

Goal: _____

S Specific

_____
_____
_____

M Measurable

_____
_____
_____

A Achievable

_____
_____
_____

R Relevant

_____
_____
_____

T Timely

_____
_____

Topic 3: Problem-Solving

We cannot solve our problems with the same thinkingwe used when we created them.
Albert Einstein

One of the core symptoms of ADHD is impulsivity. This means children often act on impulse, repeat the same problems over and over, and rush into dealing with a problem without thinking it through.

Systematic problem-solving doesn't come naturally to children with ADHD, but this skill can be taught. Learning to tackle challenges on their own and using the solutions that they come up with boosts their self-esteem and confidence. Help your child learn these easy five steps to problem-solve.

Overcoming Obstacles

Having ADHD can make it difficult to get on task and reach your goals, which can cause stress. Problem-solving is a technique you can use when you are overwhelmed and under stress.

Follow the these steps. You can also use the sheet on page 124 to help you.

Step 1: Identify the problem (obstacles).

The first step is to identify what the obstacle is. It's important to be specific and clear.

Step 2: Think of solutions to the problem.

You have just taken the first step towards overcoming these obstacles. The following study was conducted with several classrooms of school children. Some of the children were shown a picture of a young man in a wheelchair and asked if the young man could drive. The answer was overwhelmingly 'no'. In other classrooms, they asked the children how the man could drive. Those children came up with many ideas. The moral of the story is that we should ask ourselves *how* we can do something and not whether we can.

Now think of as many solutions as possible to the obstacle. Just brainstorm ideas, and do not overthink whether a solution is good or not. The following table lists possible solutions to different obstacles:

2

Obstacles	Example Solutions
I have no time	Learn to plan, organise and prioritise. Use a diary.
I tried the activity and did not like it	Try it one more time, and reward yourself. Chunk the activity so that you don't spend too much time on it.
I have no energy do anything	How is your sleep and diet? What time of day are you most productive?
Too much schoolwork and sport commitments	Speak to your parents and your teacher. The rule of thumb is to spend at least 10 minutes on schoolwork per grade per day (i.e., grade 6 = 60 minutes).
Intrusive thoughts	Practice mindful breathing and relaxation exercises.
Negative self-talk	Challenge your negative self-talk, exercise self-compassion.
Planned a lot of activities and felt overwhelmed	Learn to be assertive and how to say no.
Don't think that I'll enjoy a new activity	Try it anyway – you might surprise yourself.
No transport	Ride your bicycle to school, get a ride with a friend or ride the bus. Use your problem-solving skills.
My teacher does not like me	Keep the lines of communication open, tell your teacher what you are struggling with and learn to manage your anger so that you don't become aggressive or disruptive in class. Use 'I' statements when stating your feelings, needs and wants.
My parents are always on my case	See things from your parents' perspective, keep lines of communication open, keep your cool and remain respectful. Excuse yourself from the table if you start feeling angry. Show your parents that you are responsible by your actions. Use 'I' statements when stating your feelings, needs and wants.
I don't like being told what to do	Have a To Do list so that you remember what needs to be done. Don't wait to be reminded.
I have no friends	Learn social skills and try to identify things that you might be doing that are contributing to not having friends. Are you bossy? Or very talkative? How much of the conversation pie are you having?
I am very forgetful	Use reminders and a diary every day. Keep your routine even on weekends if possible.

Step 3. Choose the solution that makes the most sense.

Now that you have identified the problem and brainstormed all the possible solutions, it is time to choose one or two solutions and try them. Work on one problem at a time.

Step 4. Try the solution and see if it works.

Implement the solution that you feel will give you the best outcome.

Step 5. Evaluate. If the solution did not work, try a different solution.

Sometimes multiple solutions may look equally workable; however, you have to make a choice. The good thing about this process is that if the option that you chose is not giving you the result that you expected, you can always go back and try another option. Don't give up!

2

Problem-Solving Sheet

Identify the Problem _____

_____

Possible solutions:

1. _____

2. _____

3. _____

4. _____

5. _____

Solutions	Pros	Cons
1		
2		
3		
4		
5		

Best Solution:

How to implement it:

Evaluate:

Module 2:
Adaptive Thinking

Section 4:

ADHD and
Relationships

Topic 1: Importance of Family

ADHD is a neurological and behavioural disorder that affects not only the person with it, but the entire family, including parents and the extended family of parental siblings and grandparents. It tests the limits of the family's ability to be supportive, understanding and loving.
Dresher Larry

ADHD can be a gift to family life, lending a spontaneity that is sometimes absent in other families. However, in most cases families with a child with ADHD are enmeshed in a battle of wills. This contest of wills sets child against parent, and parent against parent. It can last for years, and the whole family suffers. The battle of wills often starts when a child does not do their chores or schoolwork, ignores family rules and schedules, and generally fails to live up to their parents' expectations. In response, parents' set tougher limits on their behaviour, and penalties for failing to toe the line.

Unfortunately, the outcome of this battle of wills is an angrier and more defiant child. They come across as a child with a bad attitude rather than what they are: a child with a neurological problem who is wired to be a free spirit.

In this struggle, neither the parents nor the child is entirely right or wrong. The parents feel that they have the duty to 'straighten out' their child – who, in turn, feels as if they are in a war fighting for freedom and independence. This is clearly a lose–lose battle. It only gets resolved when everybody works together in a collaborative manner to create an environment in which behaviour patterns are encouraged to change. For this to happen the whole family must be educated on ADHD and expectations changed where needed.

No matter what happens, it is important not to blame each other for the struggles that the family is facing. It comes with the territory of ADHD. The important thing is to change the family dynamics that maintain the struggle. This can be challenging to do but it's always worth the effort!

The following exercise will help you examine how relationships and spheres of influence within the family affect your child's behaviour, and how this understanding can help improve family dynamics.

Family Relationships

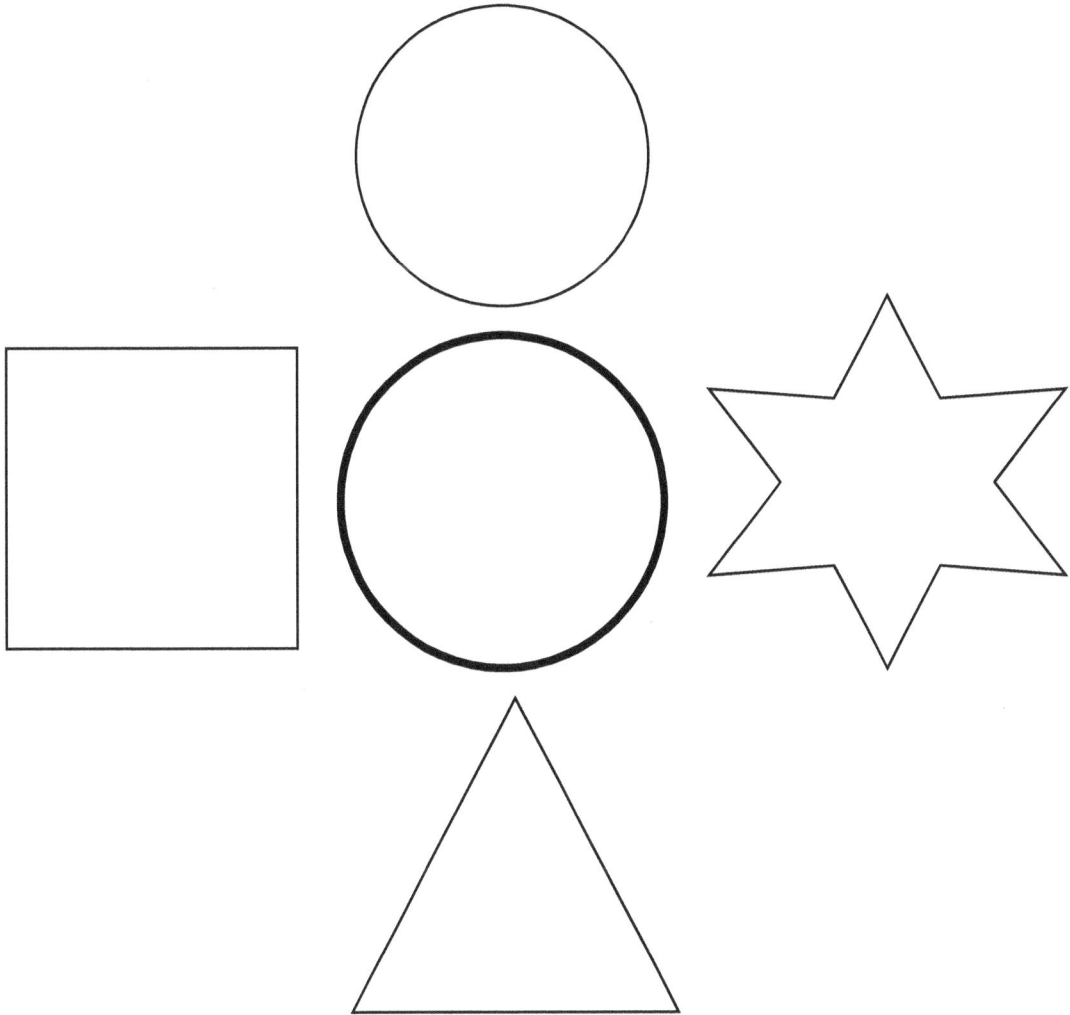

Write your child's name in the middle circle.

Now, write the name of the family member that you think they are the closest to in the outer circle.

What, in your opinion, does this person do that makes your child close to them?

_____

_____

_____

Next, write the name of the family member with whom your child has the most conflict in the square. What is the conflict usually about?

_____

_____

_____

In the triangle, write the name of the family member that you think your child admires the most. What does this person do that makes your child admire them?

_____

_____

Lastly, in your opinion who does your child respect the most? Write the name of that person in the star. What does this person do that warrants your child's respect?

_____

_____

Think of one thing that your child can do to improve the relationship with the person that they are in conflict with.

_____

_____

Do you have family meetings, or have you had them in the past?

_____

If you had family meetings in the past, why did this stop?

_____

_____

_____

If you've never had a family meeting and feel that it could work to solve some of your family conflicts, how could you go about it?

_____

_____

_____

How the Family Can Help the Child with ADHD

Because of EF deficits, children with ADHD have difficulty keeping their attention on the task at hand, shifting from one thing to another, and thinking through the consequences following an action. These difficulties create delays in the child's ability to manage their own behaviour.

Parents and carers can help by setting up clear expectations and routines. Children learn skills for self-management when they have a structure to guide their behaviour. Discipline strategies that work with other children also work with children who have ADHD, but they need to be put in place more strictly and over a longer time span until the child's self-management has developed. If you find yourself irritated by your child's behaviour, try to remember that they may be struggling more than other children to learn how to respond as expected. Try the strategies below:

- **Be consistent**. Set up rules and daily routines to provide a structure for children with ADHD. Be consistent with your expectations. This helps children to remember what is expected of them so that they can learn to regulate their own behaviour.

- **Give clear instructions**. Make instructions brief and to the point. If necessary, ask your child to look at you and repeat the instructions back to you to ensure they have focused and are ready to hear and understand what you mean.

- **Give prompt feedback**. Feedback and consequences work better when given straight away.

- **Avoid the negatives**. Try to ignore minor misbehaviours. It is best to try to stay out of power struggles with your child. Try to also remain positive and avoid strong criticism.

- **Incentives before punishment**. Use praise and reward to increase motivation and build cooperation. Program yourself to see the achievements rather than the mistakes. Look for reasons why the child has not done as expected and use consequences sparingly.

- **Less talking, more action**. Showing children as well as telling them what is wanted ensures the message is understood. Follow through on what you have asked your child to do and help them to finish what they have started if required so that they can experience successes.

- **Teach skills**. It can be very helpful for parents and carers to teach problem-solving skills, time management skills, and good work habits. Remember to spell out what is involved in easy steps. Provide lots of support and praise until your child becomes more independent with these skills over time.

- **Plan ahead**. Help your child make plans to organise what they have to do. Create lists and display them as reminders for your child.
- **Be a coach**. Encourage rule following, monitor progress and increase motivation.
- **Look after yourself**. Having a child with extra needs can be stressful. Be sure to take care of your own needs too.

How Does Your Child Handle Conflict?

Tick the column that best shows how your child typically handles conflict

Response	Usually	Sometimes	Never
Raise their voice or yell			
Ignore			
Walk away			
Apologise			
Suggest solutions			
Complain			
Forgive			
Threaten			
Look for a win–win			
Call people names			
Understand all points of view			
Get upset			
Ask for help from an adult			
Use humour			
Cry			
Let others have their way			
Assign blame			
Work toward agreement			
Make a deal (compromise)			
Work it out fairly			

Are you happy with the way that your child handles conflict? If not, what can you start doing today to help them make changes?

_____

_____

_____

Stop and Think

Use this worksheet when you want to help your child reflect on their not-so-good choices.

1. What rule did I break?

_____

_____

_____

2. What are the consequences of my actions?

_____

_____

_____

3. Why did I break this rule?

_____

_____

_____

4. What will I do differently next time?

_____

_____

_____

Child: _____ Parent: _____

Behaviour Contract

Behaviour contracts have proven to work in behaviour modification. If you think this may resonate with your child, adapt this template to any behaviour that you would like to modify – for example screen time, curfew, chores or respect (visit kidpointz.com for ideas on contracts and much more). Including a witness introduces an outside point of view which can help minimise conflict between parent and child over the meaning of the contract.

I _____ agree to make the following changes:

_____

_____

When I successfully complete this contract, I will be rewarded by:

_____

_____

If I don't follow through with this contract, the consequence will be:

_____

_____

This contract will be reviewed on this date: _____

Outcome: _____

_____

_____

2

Child's name: _____ Date _____

Signature:_____

Parent's name: _____ Date: _____

Signature _____

Witness's name: _____ Date: _____

Signature_____

Topic 2: Stop Blaming and Take Responsibility

You are free to choose but you are not free from the consequences of your choices.
Unknown

'It wasn't my fault' and 'he made me do it' are phrases that children often repeat. Learning to take responsibility and stop shifting blame for your actions in childhood is very important, both because it's right and because it helps the child learn cause and effect. A lesson that will serve them well for life.

Although it's human nature to test boundaries and try new things, even if those are forbidden, it's also human nature to not want to get into trouble and to take the path of least resistance. However, a measure of maturity is in the child's ability to own up to their mistakes and be the master of their own responses without shifting blame.

For example, if one child takes something off another and the response is a kick, there are two things happening. One, a child took a possession. Two, a child responded with a kick. Both have a level of responsibility, and I believe it's important that both parties shoulder the responsibility for their own choices. Excusing bad behaviour (in response to another's bad behaviour) just says, 'Sure you can hit/slap/scream if someone does something unpleasant to you.'

Blame shifting:

- encourages passivity
- discourages ownership
- increases pride and decreases the capacity for humility.

Help your child stop blame shifting by teaching them to:

- be accountable for their actions, regardless of who 'started it'
- notice when they are not taking responsibility for their actions and gently encourage them to remind themselves where the responsibility lies
- ensure that they follow through with what they started
- take ownership of their chores and accept the consequences if they go undone
- learn to problem-solve and ask questions when they feel powerless
- not engage in self-pity and think outside of themselves.

Why do you think it's easier to blame others for our problems than to accept responsibility?

_____

_____

_____

Next time you find your child either blaming or being blamed, what can you do to help manage their emotions?

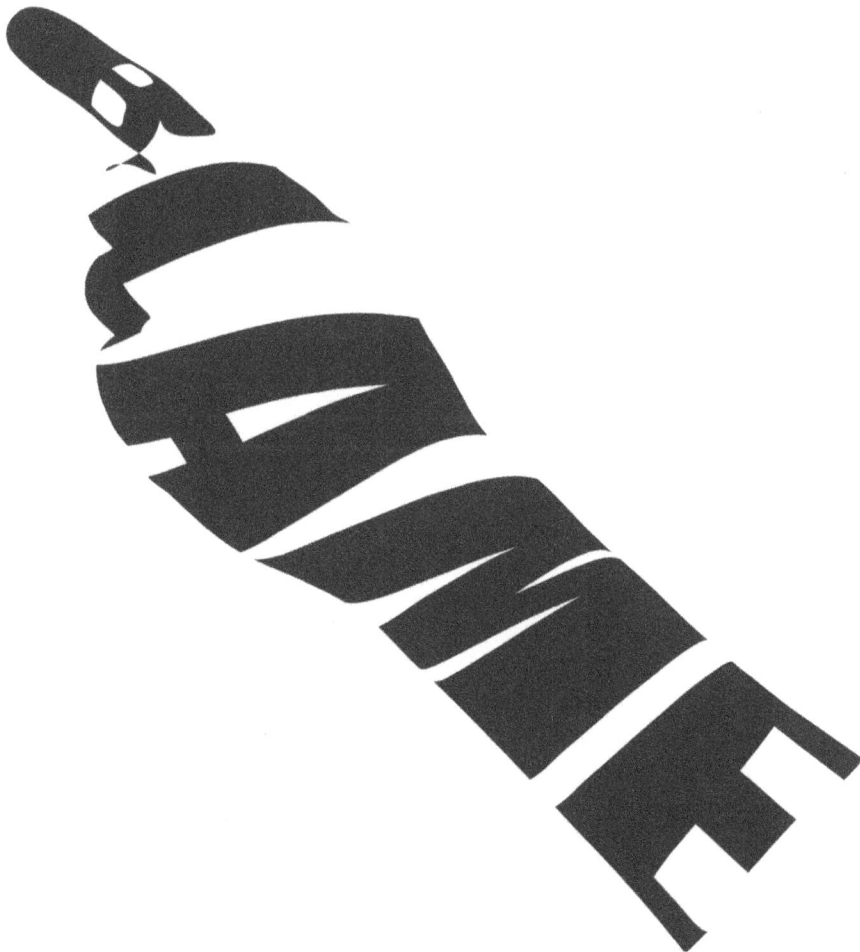

_____

_____

_____

Responsibility Pie

Name a problem that you are currently dealing with:

_____

_____

1. Make a list of the people or events you think caused the problem.
2. Think of the amount of responsibility each person or event has.
3. Fill in the pie chart by figuring out how many pieces of the pie each person or event gets. Fill in the whole pie.

1. _____

2. _____

3. _____

4. _____

5. _____

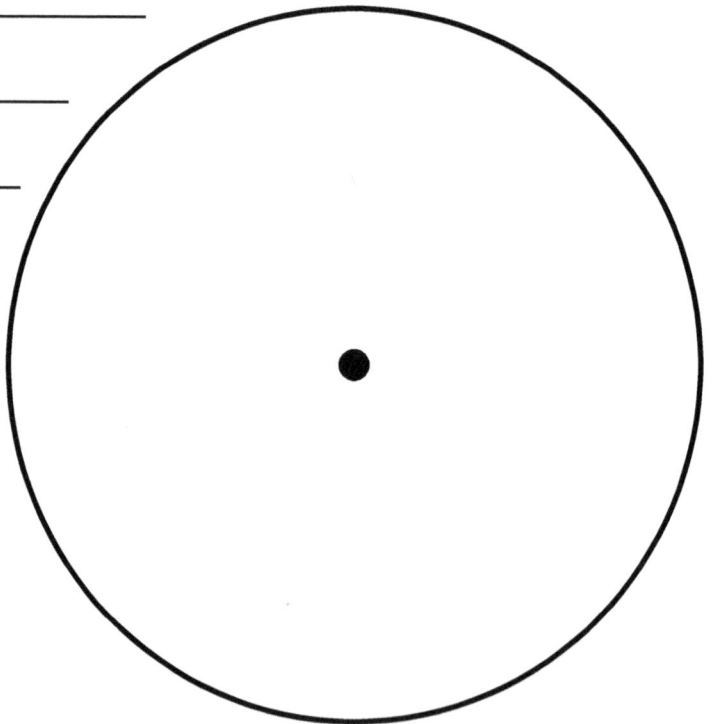

What did you learn from this exercise that you can use to help your child take responsibility for their actions?

_____

_____

_____

Topic 3: Self-Esteem and Confidence

People with ADHD may be highly susceptible to poor self-esteem, in part because they hear criticism all day from teachers, parents, and even themselves. If your child has ADHD, find opportunities to point out their successes.
Michele Novotni

ADHD can have quite a toll on a person's self-esteem. A child with ADHD has a hard time paying attention and difficulty structuring their time and prioritising tasks. They can be quite forgetful, and they tend to not pay attention or to interrupt frequently when others are talking. These behaviours can get quite frustrating for others, particularly teachers and parents. According to clinical psychologist Dr John C. Panepinto, these children can have huge cracks in their self-esteem even by the time they're seven or eight years old, and their identity is often centred on not being smart or good enough. They often feel they're letting others down, doing things wrong, or not being 'good'.

Furthermore, psychiatrist and author William W. Dodson adds that by the age of twelve, children who have ADHD receive 20,000 more negative messages from peers, parents, teachers and other adults, than their friends and siblings who do not have ADHD. Unfortunately, these messages are often internalised and affect the child's self-esteem and confidence.

You can help your child become more confident by helping them build and maintain self-esteem. Think of confidence as a muscle; when you work it, it gets stronger and more defined. Help your child define themselves by their strengths rather than their weaknesses. Make a point of highlighting your child's good qualities and praise them for handling situations well, rather than reminding them of what they messed up. This does not mean that you don't challenge them to grow and learn new ways of being in the world, like learning mindfulness, problem-solving and assertiveness; it means that they don't have to become someone else to be enough. No one is perfect. Those who claim to be are often the least confident and most insecure.

2

List three things that your child generally handles well and explain why you think so.

_____

_____

_____

Describe a personal struggle that has been bothering your child for some time.

_____

_____

_____

What critical self-talk do they engage in, in relation to this struggle?

_____

_____

_____

What have they done well in the face of this personal challenge?

_____

_____

_____

What could they do differently in similar situations in the future?

_____

_____

_____

Help Your Child Build Self Esteem and Confidence

It is easier to build strong children than to repair broken men
Frederick Douglass

As parents, we want our children to feel confident about who they are. We cross our fingers that as they enter their teen years, a developmental phase that encompasses much change, the encouragement and support we've given them up to that point has been enough to build strong self-esteem.

As our children search for their place in the world, many struggle through situations that challenge beliefs about themselves that they've held on for years. This can leave both parents and children feeling overwhelmed, exhausted, and confused. Be a family who does not give up. Follow the practical effective tips below to help your child grow into a strong, confident adult with a healthy self-worth.

Love unconditionally. Make sure your child can rest assured your love does *not* depend on their grades, performance, friend group, college, or any other factor – including their choices or behaviour.

When we tie love to performance, we miss the essence of unconditional love – that it is freely given because our child is enough just as they are.

This doesn't mean you and your child can't make mistakes or have bad days or arguments, and it certainly doesn't mean you ignore abuse. It's just a reminder the overall message your child should receive is: 'I love you no matter what. I'm committed to loving and supporting you through the ups and downs.'

Embrace a growth mindset in your home. Many children are stuck in a 'fixed mindset' about who they are or what they can or cannot accomplish and often feel unsure how to move forward.

Bring what you're learning about growth mindsets into your family conversations. Talk about the brain, use words like neuroplasticity, and make observations about areas in which you've seen your child grow.

Even if your child seems to reject it outright, sprinkle these messages into your interactions, reminding them their abilities are not fixed, inborn and inflexible. There is always room to grow and improve.

Make room for failure. Mistakes and setbacks can crush a delicate self-esteem and wreak havoc on a child's confidence. Your voice is essential in these situations. When you criticise, panic or gloss over a failure, you emphasise a fixed mindset, basically sending the message that this bump in the road is a sign there is no hope for improvement in the future.

Instead, take a deep breath and open up the conversation with your child. Ask questions like:

- Where did things get off track?
- What things influenced this decision?
- What did you learn from this situation?
- How are you planning to move forward in a positive direction?

Praise the effort and tie it to the outcome. It's easy to go overboard, pouring out praise on your child's awards, accolades and achievements. Unfortunately, these things can become tied to their self-esteem, causing them to feel they're only worthwhile if they achieve.

The negative side of this is that they believe they aren't worthwhile if they fall short or fail.

Instead, congratulate your child's accomplishments, milestones and growth by emphasising their hard work, effort and perseverance.

Focusing on the characteristics that got them to this point will help them make the connection between their effort and the result.

Help them gain new and lacking skills. Adolescence is a time of huge brain growth, but it can also highlight areas where your child struggles – physically, academically, socially or emotionally – more than they did when they were younger.

These new struggles can lead to feelings of negative self-worth. When you identify an area of concern or notice a challenge, encourage your child to see this as an opportunity to grow, learn and expand their interests and abilities.

Look for ways to build on things your child is already passionate about, and explore options for them to use these situations to practice or sharpen new skills.

Be a family that doesn't give up. Many people believe they need to feel confident before they tackle something difficult.

Carol Dweck states, 'A remarkable thing I've learned from my research is that in the growth mindset you don't always need confidence.'

Your child can still try something they're not good at or start something new, even if they don't feel super confident at the outset. If they stick to something wholeheartedly, and embrace a growth mindset, they can build confidence along the way.

Give reassurance. As teens navigate through the ups and downs of new situations and often overwhelming emotions, it helps to know these challenges are normal.

Building self-esteem and confidence often means taking bold stands and making decisions that impact peer groups or social standing.

Remind your child they are not a 'bad person' for moving on from a toxic friendship or choosing an activity over a boyfriend or girlfriend. Growth and maturity can be difficult, but it doesn't mean your child is doing something wrong.

Talk about assertiveness. Confident, clear and persuasive communication does not come easy to everyone. Many children don't have a grasp on the differences between assertive, passive and aggressive communication.

Discuss how nuances such as tone of voice can make or break a conversation. Point out how body language and nonverbal cues can send a message of their own.

Encourage your child to practice in front of a mirror so they can begin to identify the nuances of assertive communication. Standing up tall, rolling their shoulders back and speaking clearly can improve how your child feels, especially if they aren't feeling very confident going into a difficult situation.

Practice at home. Create a safe space for your child to process difficult situations. Give them the freedom to talk freely about challenges, peer conflict, and gripes about 'unfair' teachers and overwhelming homework assignments. Then, explore ways they can manage these situations with confidence, addressing others in a way that is respectful and keeps their self-worth intact.

For children who struggle to communicate clearly or are challenged in some social situations, use the safety of your home to explore their options. Roleplay potential conversations, using a variety of responses, tones of voice, volume and nonverbal cues.

Encourage self-compassion. Growth mindset requires kindness and patience with ourselves as we grow and learn. Contrary to popular messages in social media and influences from their peer group, your child doesn't need an outside opinion to prove personal worth.

If you notice your child is stuck in a negative or fixed mindset about their worth, encourage them to practice self-compassion.

Introduce mindfulness activities, create positive mantras, or list affirmations where they will be seen on a regular basis. When your child is struggling, encourage them to talk to themselves using the same words and tone of voice they would use if a close friend were struggling in the same way.

Encourage diversity in activities and interests. Children who are involved in a variety of activities, sports teams, volunteer opportunities and educational activities tend to have a higher sense of self-esteem. They aren't crushed by a setback in one area because they have other things feeding their self-worth.

2

Give less advice. It's not easy to sit back and watch as your child struggles to learn, or to manage the consequences of an impulsive decision. It's normal to want to share your wisdom or do what you can to smooth the path ahead for your child. However, learning to think through challenges, brainstorm options and problem-solve can all build your child's confidence.

Rather than solving all of your child's problems for them, engage them in the process. Practice collaborative problem solving. Listen as they explore where things went off track and then support your child's plan to move forward in a positive direction.

Ask for advice. Parents face challenges and failures in our everyday lives. We can use these moments to show our children that we are human and that we need help too! Be sure to discuss your challenges in front of your children. Let them see you make mistakes.

Discuss the situation with them. Perhaps ask them for advice or see how they would approach your problem. This not only creates connection but shows your child that you are *not* perfect and that you are learning and growing too.

Listen. Keep the relationship with your child strong and build their self-worth by resisting the urge to turn everything into a teachable moment or a long lecture.

Instead, focus on listening to what your child is saying. Don't make assumptions or judgments, or jump to the offense. Begin with empathy, putting yourself in your child's shoes.

Relate to them on an emotional level, realising that responding with logic or reasoning may push them away.

You don't have to agree with your child's perspective to be empathetic. Focus on improving your listening skills rather than needing to be right or have the last word.

Model confidence. Your child is watching you. They are observing how you manage challenging situations and how you feel about yourself.

Watch the conversations you have when your child is around – be careful you don't put others down, criticise yourself, or make your own happiness dependent on other people or circumstances.

Make an honest assessment of your own self-esteem and confidence. Then, embrace a growth mindset! Rather than beating yourself up, look for places or areas you want to improve and find things that will build your self-confidence – and then get started!

Your child's true confidence is reflected in their mindset, and their readiness to grow and learn from the challenges they encounter. Unfortunately, this may take time.

You can't force your child to embrace a growth mindset, practice positive affirmations or try challenging activities, but you can create a home environment that nourishes and encourages these behaviours.

There are many educational and inspirational games available that can help your child explore these issues in a fun, relaxed way. Start with the 'Family and Friends' boardgame on the next page. You may need to initially model appropriate answers to help your child explore these ideas.

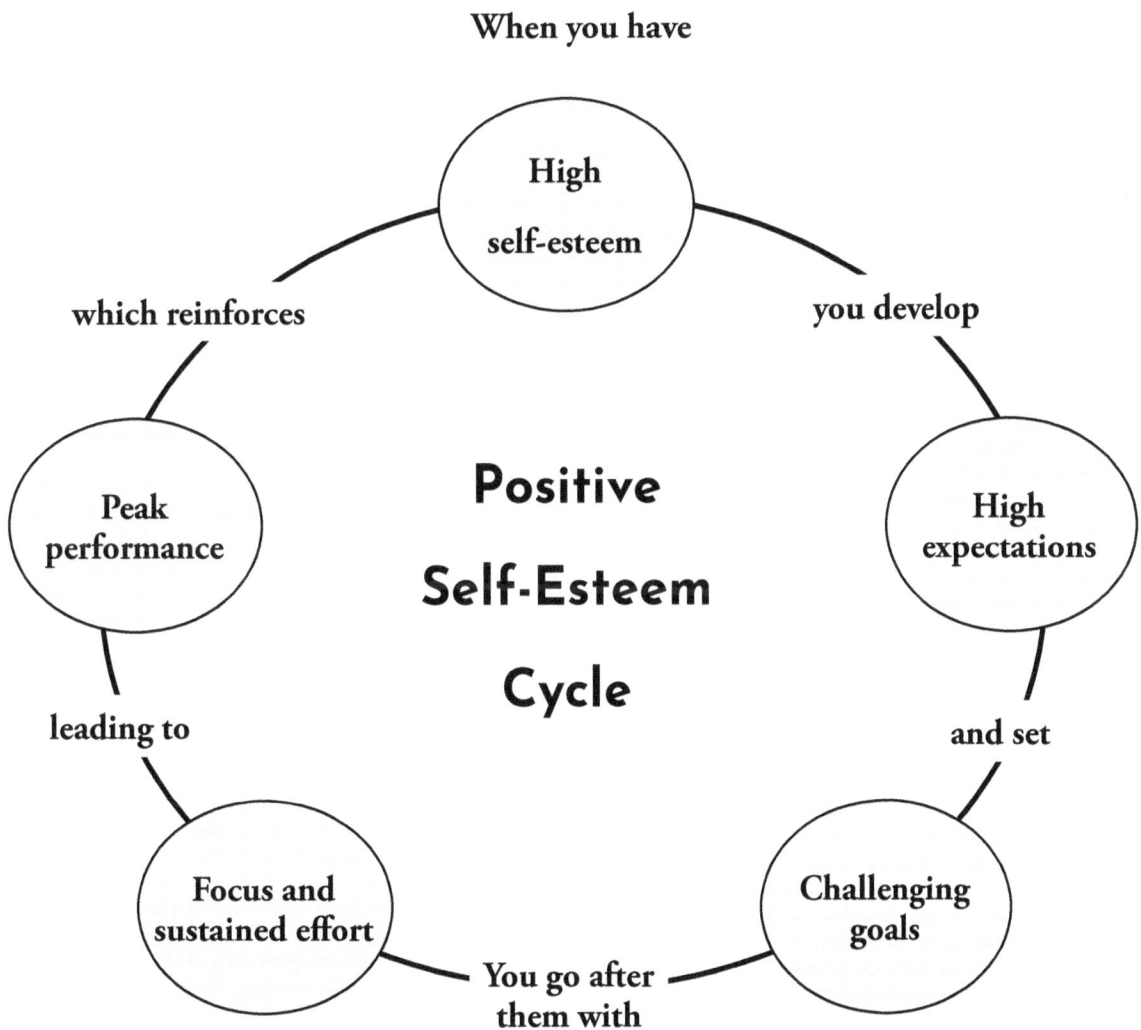

When you have

High self-esteem

which reinforces

you develop

Positive

Self-Esteem

Cycle

Peak performance

High expectations

leading to

and set

Focus and sustained effort

Challenging goals

You go after them with

Family and Friends Board Game

As you go around the board, answer each of the questions you land on.
If you land on a question mark (?), ask another player a question about family or friendship.

START 1	**Relax and enjoy!** 2	**Family is …** 3	**How would you define an ideal family?** 4	**A friend is someone …** 5
HOORAY!!! Go forward 4 spaces 6	**Are friendships important to you and why?** 7	**What do you think are the most difficult things that parents have to do?** 8	**?** 9	**Who is your best friend and why?** 10
Who do you look like the most in your family? 11	**What do you look for in a good friend?** 12	**Is it better to be male or female and why?** 13	**OOPS!!! Go back 4 spaces** 14	**Is it important for friends to have much in common? Give reasons.** 15
Is having siblings important? Give reasons for your answer. 16	**HOORAY!!! Go forward 4 spaces** 17	**Why is it important to say sorry?** 18	**How do you show your friends they are important to you?** 19	**Can boys and girls be good friends? Give reasons.** 20
Are you a good friend? Give reasons. 21	**OOPS!!! Go back 4 spaces** 22	**How important are family celebrations?** 23	**?** 24	**YOU WIN!** 25

Module 3:
Practical Coping Skills

Section 1:
Time and Task Management

Topic 1: Time Management

Individuals with ADHD experience time differently. Their inability to anticipate future rewards and consequences, remarkable ability to procrastinate, and inability to ignore the static around them, all contribute to trouble with deadlines, punctuality and planning. Looking at ADHD as being about the use of time will change how you understand and manage it.

Russell Barkley, PhD, has famously said that ADHD is not a disorder of knowing what to do, it's a disorder of doing what you know, at the right times and places. Executive function (EF) deficits explain many of the struggles experienced by people with ADHD.

Individuals with ADHD are stuck in the present and have a hard time doing what will benefit them later. The benefit to doing tomorrow's assignment or embracing healthy habits now might be avoiding problems and illness later.

When the school year picks up steam, it can sometimes feel nearly impossible to maintain time management and organisation. Important to note is that when your child's schedule gets crazy, keeping their space clean and organised and maintaining a good routine is what will keep you sane and them on track. Help them identify which of the tips below are helpful:

- **Get a planner, preferably a paper one:** First create a To Do list. List at random your commitments for the day. Then go back and allocate a time for each of your commitments, starting with the most important, for example, homework, studying, eating, sleeping, chores, relaxing or socialising. Stick to the plan as much as possible. Set alarms if you tend to forget to look at your planner.

- **Know when and where you're most productive:** Some people feel most productive in the morning; others later in the day. Some need to be in a quiet place to get things done. For others, some background noise, like music, helps. Note that some 'background noise' like TV or music with distracting lyrics can take away your focus.

- **Study with a buddy or sibling:** If the presence of someone keeps you more on track, study with a buddy. Or study alone if the presence of someone else is too distracting.

- **Prioritise your tasks:** If you tend to miss deadlines and have trouble finishing important things, start with the tasks that are most important and due soonest, then work on less-important stuff or things that have a longer deadline (apply the pebble-jar method described below). If, instead, you have trouble getting started, begin with easier tasks, then move on to harder ones once your brain is warmed up.

- **Set realistic day-to-day goals:** Work on one thing at a time and follow it through to completion. Break larger tasks (such as learning a few spelling words each day for the spelling test on Friday) into smaller chunks.

- **Be honest with yourself about how you spend your time:** Look at ways of cutting back on timewasters. Complete a time matrix. If you spend hours online before starting your homework, try to stick to a plan of starting your homework first, then using online time as a reward for finishing tasks.

- **Break up blocks of study time with short breaks to limit fatigue:** If you study solidly for a couple hours, make sure you give yourself 15–20 minutes before you start up again. Get away from the computer or books to stretch or take a short walk. Eat an energy-building, protein-rich snack like yogurt or almonds.

- **Use rewards rather than punishment for motivation:** Studies show that rewards are usually more motivating than punishment. Use this to your advantage by giving yourself a reward when you finish a task; for example, allow yourself to watch a favourite 30-minute TV show as a study break or give yourself some positive feedback. Self-criticism (a form of punishment) is usually not super effective for motivation, so work on recognising and limiting these sorts of thoughts. This is easier said than done, but is good to work on.

- **Watch your thoughts and work on thinking more positively:** Challenge the negative thoughts that creep into your mind and cause you unnecessary stress. Put more focus on what is going well. That doesn't mean denying or repressing unpleasant thoughts or feelings, but you also don't have to dwell on them. If you have a long-standing pattern of negative thoughts, learning a new way of thinking is a necessary process.

- **Consider asking a supportive friend or relative from your circle of support to be your mentor:** Agree to text or email the person a list of what you accomplished each day, or form a study group to keep each other on track. Studies show that being accountable to someone else can help keep you more focused.

- **Ask for help:** Don't wait until things are completely messed up!

- **Use apps:** There are many apps out there selected to be useful for students. One warning though – there is no perfect system. The best thing you can do is to get started and keep going. That is the only way the work gets done.

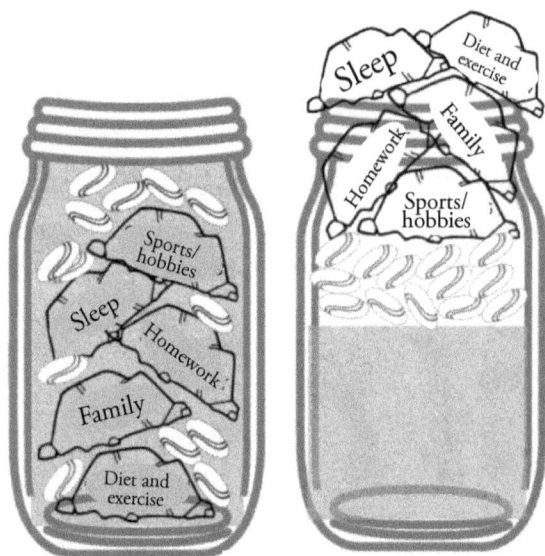

- **Use the pebble-jar metaphor:** The principle of this metaphor is that your day has a finite amount of time in it, just like a jar has finite capacity. Therefore it is important to start your day doing the things that matter the most (i.e. to put the bigger pebbles in the jar first). Generally, the smaller and easier it is to pour into the jar, the less it matters. The trouble is these are exactly the types of things we tend to end up filling our time with. The antidote, of course, is to set goals.

Tips for Creating a To Do List

Work through the following list with your child to help them learn how to get the most out of a To Do list.

- **Create a daily or weekly To Do list**. This may include things from many different categories. You might have several things you need to finish for school by the end of the day or week, as well as other personal and social commitments.

- **Set long-term goals**. This may include tasks that need to be broken down into multiple steps, and you'll need to prioritise. You might be working on an assignment to be handed in at the end of the school term, that involves many different smaller activities. The simple act of breaking it down will simplify it and reduce overwhelm.

- **Write down everything you need to do**. Select all the tasks, however big or small, that will need to be accomplished, and write them all down.

- **Categorise the things you need to do**. It may be helpful to break everything up into separate categories – for example, before school, after school, sports and social commitments, and weekend plans. Prioritise them in order of importance.

- **Allocate time slots in your planner in order of importance**. Identify the most important or urgent activities on the To Do list and allocate a time to do it. It's all relative to you and the topics on your list, so you might decide that school activities trump social commitments, or vice versa.

- **Tick things off the list**. Actively crossing out or checking off the items as you complete them can ease some of your stress about getting things done.

- **Keep the list visible.** Check your To Do list several times a day, to make sure that you are on track. Remember that you can have the best diary system in the world, but if you forget to check it, it will be of no use to you in the long run.

Tips for Prioritising Your Time

- **Rank the importance of each task.** What are the most important things on your list? In general, you might decide that school tasks will outweigh social and household chores, though certain outliers may exist. You've got to eat and bathe, for example, but gaming might be able to wait another day while you finish an important school assignment. You could rank the importance of things as high, medium, and low using colours. For example, you could use red to identify important or high priority items, orange for items of medium importance, and yellow for items that are not pressing at all. You can also ask the question, 'Is this a rock, pebble or sand task?'

- **Rank the urgency of each important task.** Consider upcoming deadlines and your ability to work within those deadlines. What needs to be done the soonest? What needs to be done by the end of the day? What might you be able to buy a bit more time on?

- **Consider the length of time.** It's important to estimate the length of time it will take to accomplish each of the tasks, maybe even assigning a set time to certain tasks. If you consider it a priority to exercise or play games every day, but you've got a crazy amount of work to do, give yourself an exercise or gaming cap of 30 minutes and find somewhere to fit it in.

- **Rank the effort required for each task.** Rank everything on your list in terms of its difficulty so you'll know how to situate it in relation to other tasks.

- **Compare all the tasks and allocate a time slot in the diary or planner.** Be realistic about how long tasks will take when allocating time slots.

To Do List

1.

2.

3.

4.

5.

How Much Time Do You Spend Doing What Matters?

This tool will help you recognise how much time you are spending doing what really matters and that moves you towards the life that you want to live.

Instructions:

1. Colour in the time blocks that you spend on **education or work-related activities** (e.g. your own studies or helping children with homework, projects and assignments) in **RED**.

2. Colour in the time blocks that you spend **outdoors** (e.g. exercising, gardening, cleaning, creating) in **GREEN**.

3. Colour in the time blocks that you spend doing **domestic chores** in your home (e.g. cleaning, doing laundry, organising, preparing and cooking meals) in **BLUE**.

4. Colour in the time blocks that you spend on **extra activities** (e.g. social sports, volunteering, socialising, going on dates, helping in school activities) in **ORANGE**.

5. Colour in the time blocks that you spend on **family enriching activities** (e.g. playing games, conversation, daily catch-ups, family walks, picnics) in **YELLOW**.

6. Colour in the time blocks that you spend on **screens or on social media** (e.g. texting, Instagram Twitter, Facebook, watching TV, gaming) in **BROWN**.

7. Colour in the time blocks that you spend on **alone time** (e.g. reading, exercising, mindfulness, personal care, hobbies etc.) in **PURPLE**.

8. Colour in the time block that you spend in **bed** in **BLACK**.

Time	Mon	Tue	Wed	Thur	Fri	Sat	Sun
5:00–6:00							
6:00–7:00							
7:00–8:00							
8:00–9:00							
9:00–10:00							
10:00–11:00							
11:00–12:00							
12:00–13:00							
13:00–14:00							
14:00–15:00							
15:00 –16:00							
16:00–17:00							
17:00 –18:00							
18:00–19:00							
19:00–20:00							
20:00–21:00							
21:00–22:00							
22:00–23:00							
23:00–0:00							
After midnight							
Rate your mood 1–10 (where 10 is great)							
Evaluate:							

Why Time Management Matters

Effective time management allows students to complete more in less time, because their attention is focused and they're not wasting time on distractions like social media. Efficient use of time reduces stress, as students tick off items from their To Do list. It can also provide a sense of achievement from fulfilling goals. For example, they might plan to complete an assignment by Friday so they can see friends on the weekend.

Furthermore, by using time efficiently, students can complete their work on time, stay engaged with their learning, and have more free time for pursuing activities that are important to them, such as sports, hobbies, and spending time with friends and family.

Other benefits reported included:

- increased independence
- increased self-control
- increased responsibility and discipline
- improved grades
- increased self-esteem and confidence
- decreased anxiety, stress and worry.

Complete the 'After-School Daily Routine', on the next page, for four consecutive weeks, recording your child's use of time. Get them to reflect on how their use of time is helping or hindering them to reach their goals.

Your Child's After-School Daily Routine

Use this tool to monitor how much time your child is spending doing what matters.

Instructions:

1. Colour in the time blocks that your child spends on **homework or doing school-related activities**, including organising and planning, in **RED**.

2. Colour in the time blocks that your child spends **outdoors** (e.g. playing, exercising, gardening, walking, creating), in **GREEN**.

3. Colour in the time blocks that your child spends on **chores** at home in **BLUE**.

4. Colour in the time blocks that your child spends on **extra activities** (e.g. sports, scouts, music lessons, church, community services etc.) in **ORANGE**.

5. Colour in the time blocks that your child spends on **family-enriching** activities (e.g. talking, sharing, helping, contributing, having meals) in **YELLOW**.

6. Colour in the time blocks that your child spends on **technology** (e.g. gaming, watching videos, texting, TikTok) in **BROWN**.

7. Colour in the time block that your child **goes to bed** in **BLACK**.

Time	Mon	Tue	Wed	Thur	Fri
4:00 – 4:30					
4:30 – 5:00					
5:00 – 5:30					
5:30 – 6:00					
6:00 – 6:30					
6:30 – 7:00					
7:00 – 7:30					
7:30 – 8:00					
8:00 – 8:30					
8:30 – 9:00					
9:00 – 9:30					
9:30 – 10:00					
Rate your child's mood 1–10 (where 10 is great)					
Evaluate:					

Reflection:

Are you happy about how much time your child spends doing what matters? Give reasons for your answers.

_____

_____

_____

How much time does your child spend on homework or school-related activities per day?

_____

Is your child achieving their academic goals? If not, how many more hours or blocks would they have to put in per day?

_____

_____

_____

Is your child using their diary and a To Do list? If so, how much and how well?

_____

_____

_____

In your opinion, does your child have to work harder or smarter?

_____

_____

_____

Vertical and Horizontal Time

When you have a task to complete, you can plan the completion time vertically or horizontally.

For example, suppose you are asked to complete a task that will take you 32 hours. There are two ways you can approach this, as illustrated below. Using vertical time, the task is completed quickly, in just two days. However, utilising vertical time leaves little time for other activities. If you focus on vertical time, then you are trying to get the task done in as short a time as possible. On the other hand, if you utilise horizontal time, you can go slowly and over time accomplish great things. Even ordinary effort over time can yield extraordinary results. The latter, however, requires planning, organising and prioritising – skills that you may be struggling with but that can be learned.

Vertical Time					
Horizontal Time					

	Monday	Tuesday	Wednesday	Thursday	Friday
Morning 6 hours					
Afternoon 6 hours					
Evening 6 hours					

Using a Diary

> *By failing to prepare, you are preparing to fail.*
> **Benjamin Franklin**

For some children, a diary or planner represents good self-management in relation to time and an opportunity for better planning and self-management, and less stress.

Unfortunately, for children with ADHD, maintaining a diary looks like a lot of painful work. But a well-organised planner is perhaps the most useful tool for middle- and high-school students with ADHD. It means the difference between success and failure both before and after graduation, so it's definitely worth the effort.

If your child cannot see how using a diary is going to help them, you may suggest that they give it a go for an agreed period, for example one month or one school term. If it does not improve their situation, they can always go back to doing what they were doing.

For example, if your child frequently forgets to do homework because they do not write it down anywhere, suggest that they make a point of having the diary open on their desk during every lesson. Having this tool ready increases the likelihood that when the teacher writes the homework on the board or gives them a date for when a project is due, they will write it down. They can use the diary to break a bigger task into smaller ones. With steady effort they can achieve their goals, reducing stress and last-minute panic.

Some Ideas on How to Set Up a Planner

We all have a unique brain and therefore unique time-management needs. This needs to be taken into account when sourcing a diary or planner. Those of us who are 'left-brain dominant' are typically more analytical, logical and objective. 'Right-brain dominant' people, on the other hand, are more creative, intuitive and subjective.

The following strategies have proven successful for many who are 'right-brain dominant' individuals:

- **Use colour.** Make the planner visually attractive, to help a creative brain stay interested, and easily recognise what needs to be done.
- **Personalised language.** Develop an easy-to-remember shorthand – like 'T' for 'test' or 'WS' for 'worksheet' – to keep track of assignments without getting stressed or overwhelmed. Your shorthand can include symbols or stickers – a useful tool for visual learners.
- **Routines.** If using a planner feels unnatural to your child, begin by establishing the structure of a daily routine. Set a time every day for reviewing and updating the

planner – right before homework time works for most. A daily review of assignments will help your child determine their most urgent priorities, and plan what they need to work on tonight, tomorrow, and further down the road, given their deadlines.

Other specifics to be considered include:

- Where will the diary be kept?
- How will you remember to use it every day?
- How will you remember to look at the task list every day?

One good idea that seems to work is to pick an activity that you do every day at the same time (e.g. eat breakfast or brush your teeth) and make that the time that you will look at your diary and your To Do list.

A planner should include more than just homework assignments. Help your child get into the habit of scheduling all activities, including personal and social events, and track other important information. The thinking is that once your child forms the habit of using their diary to track all commitments, it becomes easier to turn to it regularly and begin to see time more clearly – helping your child complete homework assignments, feel more in control of their time and improve their confidence.

Warning: It is important to remember that learning any new skill or forming new healthy habits takes practice and time. Your child may not be used to writing down what needs to be done daily or carrying a diary around. Be aware of what excuses your child uses that may sabotage their success down the road. For example:

- I don't have enough room in my bag for a diary.
- It's a hassle to have to bring a notebook everywhere with me.
- I've never been an organised person, so why start now?
- If I write down my appointments and assignments, I will then be responsible for them.

Help them stay focused on the reasons for wanting to bring about change, their values, the goals they hope to achieve and the accomplishment that they will feel for taking positive steps in their life.

Example of a Diary Page with a To Do List

Time	Task	To Do List
6:00	Wake up – take medication	Feed Buddy
6:30	Get out of bed, get dressed, make my bed	Work on shell project (A) 15 minutes
7:00	Have breakfast, feed Buddy, brush teeth, wash face and comb hair	Revise presentation (A) 15 minutes
7:30	Pack lunch in school bag Check that I've packed everything I need for school in my backpack	Other homework (A) 60 minutes Skype with Dad (A)
8:00	Walk to the bus stop	Walk Buddy (B)
8:30		Pack school bag (A)
9:00–3:00	School	Pack sports gear (A)
3:30	Catch bus home	In bed by 10:00 pm (A)
4:00	Arrive home, snack and play with Buddy	
5:00	HOMEWORK	
7:00	Dinner – do dishes when it's my turn Skype with Dad	
8:00	Screen time of choice, e.g. TV, gaming (as agreed with my parents)	
9:00	Bedtime routine – shower, brush teeth. Get school clothes ready for the morning Get sports gear ready, school bag packed Technology charging in designated area (no technology in bedroom)	
10:00	Lights off	

Topic 2: Organisation, Impulsivity and Distractibility

Being productive and effective when you have ADHD has less to do with your ability and a lot to do with your structure.
Unknown

Children with ADHD find organisation skills challenging, but organisation is a skill you can build over time. Just as a person who breaks a leg might use crutches as a tool you can develop organisation tools to help you succeed. Managing your time, planning, and prioritising are key skills to becoming a more organised individual.

Some advice you can give your child for school organisation: learning coping strategies and techniques for being organised can make school and home a lot less stressful, because it adds structure and order to your life. When you write down your assignments or homework, make certain that you write down all important information, including when they are due and any specific instructions from your teacher. Talk with your teacher and ask questions right away to prevent any misunderstandings. Keep a monthly calendar in an area where it is visible (in your locker or above your homework station at home). Mark important dates for school, home or social activities.

Below are some strategies you can help your child implement. Tick the ones that they already use, highlight any they would like to try.

- [ ] Day planner (paper diary)
- [ ] To Do list
- [ ] Wall calendar
- [ ] Consistent homework station
- [ ] Shelving and bookcases
- [ ] Storage bins (ideally see-through ones) for different items
- [ ] Stacking trays
- [ ] Launch pad
- [ ] Colour-coding different subjects
- [ ] Wastepaper bin
- [ ] Others

Help Your Child Become More Organised

Children with ADHD rarely keep their backpacks tidy, and that sometimes has serious consequences on overall academic performance. Organisation strategies can help children build the skills they need to stay neat – or at least neater! To be organised requires time, effort and sustained attention. Of these, your children may have only time – and they'd prefer to be doing something else with it. See if your child's teacher is open to implementing some of the strategies below.

Learning organisational skills at home (how parents can help)

- **Label where things should go.** Put pictures or text on clear plastic containers to show what goes in each container.

- **Schedule an after-dinner clean up.** Set aside five minutes after dinner to clean up the common areas in the house (e.g. living room, counter-tops, mudroom). Set a timer, put on some lively music, and have the family pitch in. Make it a daily routine.

- **Have your child stay put when cleaning up their work area.** Instead of taking away the stuff that belongs in other rooms, have them make piles: one for the bedroom, one for the kitchen, one for the playroom. If they walk off to another area, chances are, they will get side-tracked.

- **Buy your child a cork board and pins.** Hang up important papers that might get lost on a cluttered desk.

- **Assemble a homework supply kit.** Place in a see-through plastic container, with a lid, everything they will need to complete assignments – from crayons and a glue stick to a calculator and dictionary. With this system, it does not matter where your child chooses to study. The necessary supplies can accompany them anywhere.

- **Provide plastic sleeves for notebooks.** Insert them into your child's notebooks or binders for storing important papers that are not punched.

- **Colour-code entries on a calendar.** One colour for school-related activities, another for sports, a third for social activities.

- **Take a photograph of what tidy should look like.** When the backpack or workspace is tidy, take a photo to give the child something to work towards. Have your child compare their work to the photograph and critique themself. Did they do a five-star job (their work looks exactly like the photo), a three-star job (only a couple of things out of place), or a one-star job (they tried but seemed to run out of steam)?

- **Put up a large whiteboard with a calendar.** Give each family member a different-coloured marker to write tasks and events for the week, so each can easily spot their own.

- **Have your child design a system that works for them.** An organisational system that works for you is unlikely to work as well for your child.
- **Take out the academic component.** When helping your child organise their backpack or workspace, don't say anything about their terrible handwriting or a paper their teacher has marked up with comments; continue organising. You are working on organisation, not academics.
- **Ask permission before going into their backpack to organise it.** You wouldn't want them going into your purse or briefcase without asking first.
- **Make organisation a family affair.** Sometimes entire families are organisationally challenged. If so, admit your difficulties and ask the family to choose a problem to tackle. Design a system and get a commitment from family members to stick with the program for a few weeks to see if it helps. Hold a meeting after one week to evaluate and fine-tune the system; decide on a reward if everyone makes it through week two.
- **Tackle one mess at a time.** Parents' biggest downfall is having children organise their room, backpack and homework space all at once. Choose one task, get that system up and running, and after a month or two, move on to another task.

Learning organisation skills at school (how your teacher can help)

- **Make desk-cleaning a part of the daily routine.** A half hour before dismissal, a teacher might say, 'Okay, let's do a speed cleaning!' to her first-grade class, prompting children to tidy up their desks and other common spaces. When the classroom is tidy, they can play a short group game before getting ready to go home for the day.
- **Talk about it.** Have a class discussion about what it means to be organised. Ask children to design a system for cleaning up their cubbies or a common play area. Talk about how to organise classroom routines to make them go more smoothly. Set up a suggestion box children can use if they think of other ideas.
- **Instruct the class in how to set up and organise a notebook and binder.** Each time you tell students something that should go in the notebook or binder, tell them exactly where it goes and supervise them to make sure it gets there. Work in pairs to ensure each follows the plan.
- **Use brightly coloured paper for project assignments, providing details and due dates.** Give each student two copies – one for the notebook and one to be posted at home.
- **Stay organised yourself.** Have classroom systems in place for daily routines – turning in homework assignments, collecting lunch money and permission slips, and so on. Teach students the systems and appoint student monitors to make sure the routines are followed as much as possible.

- **Make organisation a team effort.** Divide the class into two teams, appoint team leaders, and award points for keeping desks clean, cubbies or lockers organised, or notebooks neat. With the class, create a checklist that can be used for inspections. Hold daily or random spot-checks and award points based on the checklist. The team with the most points at the end of the week gets to choose the class reward from a rewards menu.

- **Keep classroom systems simple.** Use two colour-coded folders – red for incomplete homework assignments, green for completed assignments. Use this for class work as well, and teach the class to move their work from red to green as the morning progresses. Make sure they pack the folders before they go home. First thing in the morning, ask them to get out their green folders with completed homework and place them on top of their desk for review.

- **Give bonus points,** or some other reward, for improved organisational skills. Reward disorganised students when they can quickly locate a certain book or paper in their desk or notebooks.

- **Take photos and display them.** Take photos of what an organised desk, locker and classroom looks, like and display them in the classroom so that students know what neat looks like.

What reasons does your child give for not wanting to try new skills or strategies? Check the familiar ones from the list below.

- ☐ I have tried this before, and it did not work.
- ☐ It takes too long to learn how to use a calendar, and it won't work anyway.
- ☐ Once I get it started, I'll forget all about it.
- ☐ I can't throw things out because I might need them someday.
- ☐ I can't throw things out because I need to hold on to the memories in them.
- ☐ Getting organised is going to take time away from doing my homework.

Other reasons:

- ☐ _____
- ☐ _____
- ☐ _____

Help your child challenge each statement that is limiting their progress in organisation.

Impulsivity

Before you make a decision, ask yourself this question:
will you regret the results, or rejoice in them?
Rob Liano

One of the core symptoms of ADHD is impulsivity – not being able to stop an action before it starts, or to stop or change a behaviour once it's started. The urge to act seems to be independent of reason. Even if the person is aware of the consequences of the behaviour, they still have great difficulty controlling it. Impulsivity can create severe consequences, from school failure to life -hreatening situations. The cycle of frustration, acting impulsively, and then feeling more frustration about not controlling your own behaviour, gets replayed over and over.

Reflect:

- Does your child engage in risky behaviours (e.g. shoplifting, taking things from their friends, cheating in a test, spreading rumours?)
- Of all the risky behaviour/s that your child has engaged in, which had the most negative consequence?
- Are you worried about your child's impulsive behaviours?
- What can you do to help your child stop these behaviours?
- What role does peer pressure play in your child's involvement in risky behaviour?

Distractibility

I may look like I'm doing nothing... But in my head I'm quite busy.
Unknown

Distractions are everywhere and are part of life. Generally, when someone is interrupted in the middle of a task, they will temporarily shift their attention and then move back to the original task. This is not as easy for those with ADHD. It is harder to transition between activities and get back on track. Often, the original task is forgotten, and they move on to whatever distracted them. Distractions come in different forms and include inner urges to take breaks, raid the refrigerator, or just sharpen your pencil when the task gets boring. Removing distractions from your child's environment is key to helping them be productive and exercise good time management.

What tasks distract your child the most?

_____

_____

_____

What environments distract your child the most?

_____

_____

_____

What three activities does your child find most boring, and what distractions draw them away when they are bored?

_____

_____

_____

Name three things that your child loves doing that never makes them bored.

_____

_____

_____

3

Distractibility delay

Distractibility delay can help your child delay attending to distractions while working on boring or difficult tasks. Children with ADHD often say that they are unable to complete tasks because less important tasks or distractions pull them away.

Help your child understand that having a short attention span is part of ADHD. It is not because of a lack of intelligence or ability. If your child expresses frustration in trying to implement distractibility delay and not seeing results right away, encourage them to see this as a process that may take some time to get right. Remind them that they have been doing things in a certain way for many years and that it is unrealistic to expect that new habits can be learnt overnight. Our brains don't have a delete button, and so we have to learn the new with the old program running. This can be challenging for some of us.

The first step in distractibility delay is to gauge the length of time that your child can work on a boring or difficult task. Record this length of time and repeat this exercise several times. Get an average.

The second step is to break down the task into smaller chunks that take the amount of time that your child can concentrate for, as identified in step one.

During that time, ask your child to write down distractions but to not act on them. After the agreed-upon period, they can decide if the distractions that they wrote down are tasks that need to be done immediately, tasks that can go into their To Do list, or tasks that are pure distractions and can be discarded.

Reflect:

- Do you at times feel that your child's grades do not reflect the amount of time that they invest in their schoolwork? If so, is it possible that your child needs to work smarter and not harder?

Modifying the environment

One of the most important things that parents and teachers can do to assist their children with ADHD – apart from following the recommendations regarding medication – is to put in place a range of environmental modifications. Simply put, environmental modifications are about structuring a child's environment, and having supports in place that enable a child to be more successful in various areas of their life. Many of these strategies can be used in multiple settings. Discuss the environmental modifications below with your child to get them to reflect on what might work for them.

Structure and routine

Structure and routine are important for all children, but particularly so for children with ADHD. Because they struggle with organisation, if their day is organised for them, it is much easier for them to do the things they need to do. Routines around transitions are particularly important. Morning routines for getting up and getting ready for the day, for the transition from home to school, routines around homework and bedtime routines can help a child's day to flow better, with more success and less negative feedback from adults. Structure and routine are important at school too. If there are options available at your child's school (i.e. if there is more than one teacher teaching a particular grade), request a teacher who is both kind, and uses a structured approach in their classroom. There should be routines for transitioning into the classroom and starting the day, routines around transitions (to sport, music, recess, etc.), a daily schedule posted at the front of the class, and structure within each subject period (e.g. instruction time followed by question or demonstration time, followed by work time).

Regardless of the setting, warnings of upcoming transitions are often helpful (e.g. a 5 minute and a 1 minute warning). These can be given verbally, but visual timers often work best.

Use checklists

Checklists can be used to break large tasks or assignments down into smaller parts. This helps children to remember what they have to do, and also helps them monitor their completion of the task. Checklists can be used to support routines (e.g. a task list posted in the bathroom or child's bedroom with the steps involved in getting up and ready for the day), chores, and homework. You can also ask your child's teacher to use checklists at school. Younger children might need cueing from adults to refer to the list to know what they are supposed to be doing. Older children can learn to check the list themselves and self-monitor. For older children, as assignments at school get more involved, their teacher should be able to provide guidelines for detailed or project-based assignments.

Provide reminders as needed

Children with ADHD typically require frequent reminders to remain on task. Parents often need to sit with young children, or check in with older children to remind them to attend to the task at hand. Some parents make the mistake of thinking that their child is lazy because they have difficulty getting work done independently. This is not true. Difficulty with work completion is one of the symptoms of ADHD. Use both verbal cues (e.g. 'Ok, Let's get back to your math now', or 'What are you supposed to be doing?') and visual cues (task lists, visual schedules, and assignment rubrics, as described above).

In a classroom setting, there are usually many more distractions than there are at home. However, if the teacher is cueing your child verbally all day, other children may find this annoying or develop the impression that your child is the 'bad' child. Speak with your child's teacher about nonverbal cues that can work. This may be as simple as the teacher touching your child lightly on the shoulder and pointing to the work on their desk as they walk by. It may involve catching your child's eye and giving them a hand signal (agreed upon in advance) to listen or to get back to work. There will be times when verbal cues will be necessary. However, using a mix of visual and verbal cues can help to protect your child's self-esteem and social standing with their peers.

Minimise visual and auditory distractions

Many people mistakenly think that when a child has ADHD, they are not capable of attending. It is more accurate to say that ADHD makes it extremely difficult to attend to the correct thing. For most people, when they are focusing on something, other things in the environment fade into the background. For individuals with ADHD, everything in the environment remains foreground. So, the sound of the TV on in the next room is just as 'front and centre' as the voice of the parent who is telling them to do (or not do) something. The sound of a conversation at the back of a classroom is just as 'front and centre' as the teacher explaining a lesson. When this is the case, it is very difficult to focus on the correct thing, and the child is frequently distracted by other things in the environment.

This is why it is helpful to reduce the number of extra things a child might see or hear when they are trying to focus on a particular task. At home, when a child is doing homework (or a chore), the TV should be off, or in a different room with the person watching using headphones so that there is no sound. The house should be as quiet as possible. The child should be seated away from windows, or the curtains should be drawn so that they are not distracted by movement on the street. It would be best if the wall in front of the desk or table where your child is doing their homework is not covered with brightly coloured posters or artwork. Homework should be done in low-traffic areas of the house. Avoid the kitchen unless it will be out of bounds for walk-through traffic during homework time.

These same principles apply to school. Your child should be seated in a low-traffic area of the classroom, facing away from windows and the wall where artwork is displayed, and ideally would be seated amongst quiet peers. Because it is not possible to eliminate all extraneous noise, some children find it very helpful to use ear defenders. These may be purchased from school supply companies, and are also often available at an inexpensive price from automotive parts stores. Many teachers will have a basket of these available for use by anyone in the class, thus normalising their use among the peer group. Beyond about Grade Four, children tend not to want to use ear defenders at school. In that case, some children may require a period of time each day when they can work in a quiet setting outside of the classroom (provided supervision is available to ensure they are on-task).

Provide various workstation options

Increasing proprioceptive or tactile sensory information often helps children with ADHD to focus. Movement and touch help to provide sensory information that compensates for that which is lost due to neurotransmitter deficiencies, yet often do not distract from the task at hand. So, while your child is doing school work or homework, it is helpful to use one or more of the following items: a chair that rocks, a wiggle stool, a standing desk, a yoga ball for a chair (provided it is in a base and won't roll away), any other desk modification that provides sensory feedback (e.g. a 'sit cushion' – a rubber cushion with bumps; a Theraband™ around the front chair legs), or a light table.

Many classrooms use several of these strategies. For example, there may be a standing desk (or two) at the back of the class; three or four chairs that rock (one of which would be strategically allocated to a student with ADHD); and two or three wiggle stools – perhaps at a table were group work happens. There may also be a light table at the side of the class that can be used by any student, and a basket of focus tools at each table grouping. Setting up classrooms to meet the sensory needs of students is not only helpful to students who have ADHD, but to many other students as well. As a parent, you can speak to your child's teacher and school administrator to advocate for sensory-friendly classrooms.

Provide focus tools

Focus tools are things that a child can quietly manipulate with the hands (such as a stress ball, a small ball with hard bumps on the outside, a Tangle™, a pen with threads and a nut that can be rotated up and down, etc.). Many focus tools are available in school supply stores, or less expensive alternatives can often be found in dollar stores.

It is important to teach children how to use focus tools appropriately. Focus tools often help a child to attend to instruction while their teacher is speaking; however, they do not work for all children. Some children will impulsively throw the focus tools across the room or at their peers, in which case other strategies will have to be used. For example, when hand-held focus tools don't work, another option is to glue a small strip of Velcro inside the child's desk, which they can rub while listening to the teacher. When focus tools work, however, children are often able to take in far more information, thereby increasing their academic success. As noted above, it is not unusual for teachers to have a basket of focus tools at each table grouping in their classroom, thus normalising their use. Focus tools can naturally also be used at home, while your child reads or does homework.

Provide movement breaks

Because movement helps children with ADHD to focus, taking movement breaks is also often helpful. These need only be 5–10 minutes in length, but should include some type of physical activity. At home, this can be any easily-accessible physical activity such as walking, running, bike riding, playing basketball or skateboarding. At school, this can be as simple as going for a walk down the hallway to get a drink of water. Some schools may have other options available such as the use of a trampoline, treadmill, or other weight-room equipment (depending on the age of your child, and the school's budget). Some teachers will simply address an empty envelope to the principal or school secretary, and ask a child who needs a movement break to take the 'message' to the office. Another school-based strategy is to have a child hand out textbooks or other school supplies as opportunities arise, thus providing them with a movement break without leaving the classroom. The frequency with which these breaks are necessary will be determined by the severity of your child's ADHD, and the number of other strategies being used to assist your child.

Choose appropriate chores

Active, hands-on chores will be easier for a child than more sedentary tasks (for example, it will be easier for a child to maintain their attention to task when shoveling the walk than when sewing on buttons). This principle applies at school too. Permitting students to demonstrate mastery of a concept in alternate ways – for example, by doing a presentation or building a model rather than writing a paper – will increase your child's experience of success in the classroom. As a parent, you can request that these sorts of accommodations are made for your child.

It is important for individuals with ADHD to work in environments that have few distractions. Think about the environment in which your child does homework or study. What are the things that typically distract them in that environment?

Some typical distractions include:

- ☐ Hearing the telephone ring
- ☐ Surfing the internet, chatting online, playing online games
- ☐ Replying to messages
- ☐ Noticing other things on the desk or table that need attention
- ☐ Listening to the radio
- ☐ Watching television
- ☐ Speaking to a friend or relative who is in the room
- ☐ Looking at something going on outside the window
- ☐ Worrying, negative self-talk and other internal distractions
- ☐ Other distractions

For each item that is distracting your child, help them come up with a strategy that reduces their susceptibility to this distraction.

For example, they can:

- Turn off the phone
- Shut off notifications
- Clear off their desk or homework space
- Turn off the radio and television
- Ask others not to disturb them because they are working
- Place a 'Do Not Disturb' sign on their door
- Turn their desk away from the window

Topic 3: Procrastination

Knowing is not enough, we must apply. Willing is not enough, we must do.
Bruce Lee

'You found out about this assignment weeks ago. Why did you wait until tonight to start working on it?' Does this sound familiar?

Procrastination is one of the most common concerns I hear about from parents.

Whether it is waiting to start an assignment until the night before the due date, or beginning tomorrow's homework at 7 pm, procrastination is a regular way of life for many children.

For parents, this can be incredibly frustrating, because it seems so easy to avoid ('If you had just started your homework when you got home, you'd be finished already… now you're going to be up half the night!').

It is extremely tempting to call child out for being lazy, lecture them on the costs of procrastination, or point out the bad decisions that got them into this mess. Unfortunately, these responses rarely help.

I have found that when children don't feel judged or criticised and can let go of their need to justify their behaviour, they admit that they wish they could procrastinate less. They know the damage procrastination does, and that their lives would be easier if they did not do it. They just don't know how to change. So, what works?

The first step is to develop an understanding of *why* your child procrastinates. An effective solution depends on understanding the root of the problem. Awareness and self-knowledge are the keys to defeating procrastination.

Common Reasons for Procrastination

Forgetfulness: Some children leave their work until the last minute because they forget or are unaware. Maybe they were distracted when it was announced, didn't write it down or forgot to check the class website. Until a friend mentions it the day before it's due, or they walk into class on the day, they genuinely have no idea there was homework to be done. Technically speaking, this common cause of leaving things until the last minute would not be classified as 'procrastination' because the student is not resisting their work – they simply do not realise they have any work!

Lack of understanding: When a child doesn't understand what an assignment is about, what is expected of them, or where to start, they can become overwhelmed by the apparent enormity of the task. They often put off the assignment in hope that they will understand it better later. Unfortunately, when they look at it the night before the deadline, they usually have no more information than they did before, and no time left to ask their teacher for clarification or advice on where to start. The inherent difficulty of the project is compounded by the fact that they have run out of time to complete it.

Optimistic time estimates: Optimism is a wonderful quality – in most situations. But when it comes to estimating how much time it will take to complete an assignment, unrealistic optimism can create big problems. Students commonly overestimate how much time they have left to complete assignments and underestimate how long it will take to complete them. Consequently, they fail to leave themselves enough time to complete the work.

Overly lenient deadlines: When teachers don't enforce deadlines and allow students to turn in late work without a penalty, students learn that deadlines are not meaningful and stop taking them seriously. Without meaningful consequences, external deadlines can start to feel as arbitrary as internal deadlines, which – while helpful – are not as effective at discouraging procrastination.

Poor study routines: Habitual behaviour can cause children to procrastinate automatically, without even thinking about it. Watching TV after school can lead to procrastination because it is hard to turn off. A pattern of leaving the hardest work until last, when they have the least energy and the smallest amount of willpower, will reduce the chances of the work being done well.

Distractions: Sometimes students set aside time to complete their work but end up distracted with other things. These distractions can be external (social media, text messages, etc.) or internal (their own thoughts and impulses). Either way, this results in them spending time that had been budgeted for their work in other ways.

Perfectionism and fear of failure: When children are overly concerned about doing perfectly and not making mistakes, it creates anxiety that makes it difficult for them to even get started. They avoid the project even more as the deadline approaches because they become less and less likely to be able to do a good job on it. Eventually they are so close to the deadline that producing an ideal assignment is no longer possible, and their only options are to do an imperfect job or turn in nothing at all.

Too many commitments: If a child has so many scheduled activities and so little free time that their life feels like an endless string of obligations and chores, they may use procrastination to artificially create 'free time' for themselves. Unfortunately, this type of free time is usually not very satisfying because it's also accompanied by a sense of guilt for avoiding the things they should be working on.

Resistance: Procrastination can be a form of rebellion. When children view work as something that is being forced on them by an unreasonable teacher or authoritarian parents, procrastination becomes their way of resisting authority, showing teachers and parents, 'You can't make me do it.'

Difficulty regulating emotions: Recent studies have suggested that procrastination is less of problem with time management than we had once believed, and more of a difficulty with emotional regulation. Students who feel bored, tired, frustrated or nervous when they work on assignments will often pursue a strategy of trying to make themselves feel better in the short-term by downplaying the assignment ('It's no big deal; it won't affect my grade much anyway') and distracting themselves with fun, rewarding activities in order to improve their mood.

Unrealistic expectations: Research shows that parents who have unrealistic expectations of their children risk their child's mental, emotional and physical well-being. Academically bright children stop trying at school to the point of failing, because of their parents' unrealistic expectations. This often leads to putting tasks off and procrastination.

The solutions are different for each of these scenarios, which is why it is so important to identify the root cause of your child's procrastination before choosing strategies to try. For example, reminders about the consequences of an impending deadline may help a child who hasn't been taking deadlines seriously but, for a child with a fear of failure or difficulty regulating emotions, it could actually make things worse by increasing their anxiety about the assignment and their desire to do something else in order to avoid these negative emotions.

Which of the above reasons for procrastination are true to your child?

_____

_____

_____

What type of support or encouragement would help your child get started rather than leaving it until the last minute?

_____

_____

_____

If you can't provide your child the support that they need, who in your child's Circle of Support could provide that support and encouragement?

_____

_____

_____

Procrastination Excuses

Below are some of the excuses that people use to justify, or make themselves feel better about, their procrastination. Check the ones that your child often uses. Then add your own!

- [ ] I will do it once this other thing is finished.
- [ ] I don't have everything I need, so I can't start it now.
- [ ] I don't have enough time to do it all, so I will wait until I do.
- [ ] It is too late to start it now.
- [ ] I won't get much done, so I'll just leave it for now.
- [ ] It is better to do it when I am in the mood or feeling inspired.
- [ ] I will miss out on the fun happening now – I can do it another time.
- [ ] It is too nice a day to spend on this.
- [ ] I've got to organise my desk/drawers/backpack first.
- [ ] I've got to exercise first.
- [ ] I am too busy to do it now.
- [ ] I have plenty of time, so I can do it later.
- [ ] I work better when I am stressed, so I will leave it to the last minute.
- [ ] It might not be good enough, so why bother doing it?
- [ ] _____
- [ ] _____
- [ ] _____

Help Your Child Challenge Their Procrastination Excuses

The Truth	Unhelpful Conclusion	Helpful Conclusion
I am really tired.	I am better off doing it after I have rested.	Yes, I am tired, but I can still make a small start now.
I will miss out on the fun going on now.	I can always wait until nothing fun is happening.	If I get some work done, I can reward myself with other fun later.
I don't have everything that I need.	I will wait until I have everything before I start.	I can still make a start with what I have.
I have other things to do.	I will do it once those things are completed.	But they are not more important and can be done after this.
I have plenty of time.	I don't have to start it now.	But it is better to get on top of it now than leave it to the last minute.
I work better under pressure.	I will leave it to the last minute.	But it is still worth making a start now.
I don't like maths.	I am not even going to try.	I can try on my own and ask Dad for help if I need to.

Reflect:
- Consider the pros and cons of your child's existing behaviour.
- Weigh up the pros and cons of the new behaviour.
- Identify possible obstacles to change.

Module 3:
Practical Coping Skills

Section 2:
Communication and Social Skills

Topic 1: Communication and ADHD

When we look at something from only our own perspective, we see just one part of the situation. We must see things from different perspectives to understand a situation fully.
Unknown

Symptoms of ADHD can be barriers to communication. Core symptoms of ADHD like hyperactivity can lead to dominating the conversation and impulsivity can lead to interrupting while others are talking. Communication is much more than simply speaking words and includes:

- conveying emotion to another person
- listening to what someone is saying with words and with their body language
- being a good listener
- give and take – listening to another person and waiting your turn to speak.

The best thing a parent can do is brush up on their own communication skills, so they can model better communication for their children.

Are You a Passive, Aggressive or Assertive Communicator?

Every person has a unique communication style or way in which they interact and exchange information with others. There are several communication styles, but for the purpose of this workbook we will concentrate on the following three basic styles: passive, assertive and aggressive. It's important to understand each communication style and why individuals use them. In some situations a combination of these styles might be most effective.

Read the list of traits for each style, and tick the ones that relate to you.

Passive communication

	Speaks softly if at all		Keeps the peace
	Allows others to take advantage		Does not inspire respect from others
	Does not express their own needs		Lacks confidence
	Makes poor eye contact		Gives in to others

Aggressive communication

	Speaks loudly, over others		Can lead to shouting or violence
	Will not compromise		Damages others' self-esteem
	Forcefully expresses own needs		Bullies others
	Will not listen to the needs of others		Easily frustrated

Assertive communication

	Cares for needs of both people		Makes good eye contact
	Stands up for own needs		Listens without interruption
	Respects needs of others		Builds self-esteem
	Is willing to compromise		Enhances relationships

It is important to note that learning to communicate assertively doesn't guarantee you will have your needs met, but it makes it more likely, and it can improve your relationships with other people and improve your self-esteem.

What is your preferred communication style?

_____

_____

_____

Based on how well you know your child, which communication style do they use the most and what behaviours are indicative of this?

_____

_____

_____

In your opinion, which is your partner's preferred communication style and what behaviours are indicative of this?

_____

_____

_____

Common Communication Obstacles

To help improve communication within your family, identify the communication methods that you use and that your child uses. Circle how often each one is used.

(1 = little; 2 = a lot).

Communication Method		Parent/Caregiver		Child	
1	Use the words 'always' and 'never'	1	2	1	2
2	Yell, shout, raise your voice	1	2	1	2
3	Tease or make fun of the other person	1	2	1	2
4	Use big words	1	2	1	2
5	Threaten to do something unpleasant	1	2	1	2
6	Call the other person names	1	2	1	2
7	Repeat your opinion over and over	1	2	1	2
8	Interrupt	1	2	1	2
9	Give unhelpful responses, like 'Uh huh' or 'I don't know'	1	2	1	2
10	Make suggestions that are not helpful	1	2	1	2
11	Make demands of the other person	1	2	1	2
12	Argue about small and big things	1	2	1	2
13	Say very little, remain silent or refuse to talk	1	2	1	2
14	Talk a lot	1	2	1	2
15	Talk as though the other person hasn't said anything	1	2	1	2
16	Make jokes about the other person	1	2	1	2
17	Reject any compliments or praise the person offers	1	2	1	2
18	Ignore the person when told what they want or like	1	2	1	2
19	Make accusations or blame the other person	1	2	1	2
20	Use put downs or criticism	1	2	1	2
21	Exaggerate how bad things are	1	2	1	2
22	Lecture, preach or give long sermons	1	2	1	2
23	Talk in sarcastic tone of voice	1	2	1	2
24	Think that you can read the person's mind or know their opinion	1	2	1	2

3

25	Get off topic	1	2	1	2
26	Monopolise the conversation	1	2	1	2
27	Swear	1	2	1	2
28	Dwell on the past	1	2	1	2
29	Look away when speaking or avoid using eye contact	1	2	1	2
30	Use inappropriate hand gestures, threats	1	2	1	2

Communication Alternatives

Write down the communication obstacles that you use most often.

1. _____

2. _____

3. _____

4. _____

5. _____

6. _____

7. _____

8. _____

9. _____

10. _____

Consider using the alternative communication skills below. Tick the ones that you want to try.

- ☐ Talk directly to another person
- ☐ Speak calmly and monitor your voice tone
- ☐ Use few and simple words
- ☐ Listen to the other person
- ☐ Acknowledge a strength of the other person
- ☐ State our feelings by using an 'I' statement
- ☐ Keep to the facts rather than emotions
- ☐ Use humour appropriately

☐ Wait your turn to speak
☐ Keep dialogue focused on the here and now
☐ Keep emotions in check
☐ Pick your battles
☐ Tell the person what you want and need
☐ Make eye contact
☐ Accept responsibility for your actions
☐ Summarise and reflect what the other person is saying
☐ Use appropriate words to express criticism
☐ Other: _____

What alternative skills will replace your communications obstacles?

1. _____

2. _____

3. _____

4. _____

5. _____

6. _____

7. _____

8. _____

9. _____

10. _____

How can you develop the habit to utilise these alternatives?

_____

_____

'I' Statements

Taking responsibility for your feelings will help you improve your communication when you feel upset or angry. One way to achieve this is by using 'I' statements. This technique will allow you to communicate what is upsetting you without blaming. If you sound too accusatory, your child may become increasingly defensive.

'I' Statement format: I feel ____ when you ____ because ____ .

Examples

Regular	'You're so rude, you're always talking back.'
'I' Statement	'I feel disrespected when you talk back to me because I feel that it's rude.'

Practice

Scenario	Your friend keeps cancelling plans at the last minute. Last weekend you were waiting for her at a restaurant when she called to tell you that she could not make it. You left feeling hurt.
'I' Statement	

Scenario	You are working on a project with a group and one member is not completing his tasks on time. In the past you have lost marks for not meeting the deadline. You don't want the same thing to happen and you feel frustrated.
'I' Statement	

Help Your Child Use 'I' Statements

Use the steps below to help your child develop their use of 'I' statements.

I felt/feel sad/upset (say how you feel using the feeling words below)

When you called me names (describe what was said or done)

I would like to be treated with respect (describe what you would like to happen instead using the ideas below)

Feeling Words				
worried	angry	sad	shy	lonely
afraid	mad	grouchy	jealous	rejected
scared	upset	blue	bored	uncomfortable
fearful	aggressive	down	helpless	sick
disappointed	out of control	insecure	frustrated	overwhelmed
annoyed	enraged	anxious	hyper	weak
irritated	furious	grief	attacked	distressed
silly	bothered	pain	judged	cranky
tired	offended	hurt	antsy	empty
discouraged	shamed	alienated	desperate	devalued
disrespected	agitated	exasperated	defensive	embarrassed

Examples of **what I would like ...**

- to share and take turns
- to be treated with kindness
- for everyone to follow the rules
- to play together
- to find a solution we agree on
- to have a second chance
- to be able to focus and work
- to have more say over my life

- to feel included
- to spend time together
- to be in a quiet and calm space
- to feel safe
- to work out the conflict
- to have some space and privacy
- to make my own decision
- to be heard and listened to

3

Topic 2: Levels of Domination in Conversation

Communication must be HOT. That's Honest, Open, and Two-Way.
Dan Oswald

Children with ADHD and other EF conditions can find reciprocal conversation skills particularly difficult. They may say little or nothing in the playground or in class discussions. Or, they may dominate in monologue fashion, not noticing the signs that others are becoming impatient. This can have a negative impact on peer relationships. The following exercise will help you become more aware of your child's level of domination in a group conversation.

Exercise: Monitor how much time your child spends listening and how much time they spend talking in relation to others in the group (e.g. family or peers). Colour in the portion of the pie that they spend talking in red and the portion that they spend listening in green. Have your child do the same, and see if you and your child agree by comparing yours to theirs.

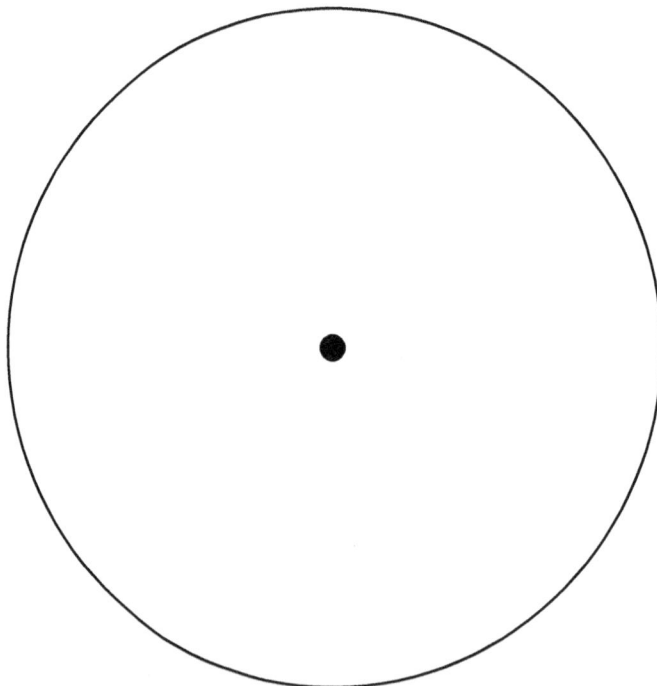

Is your child happy with the proportions/distribution? If not, what can they change?

_____

_____

Finding Common Interests

For children who struggle to start and maintain a conversation, it can be helpful to think about where your interests overlap with the other person's. Conversation is easier and more satisfying when both participants are interested in the topic being discussed.

Person 1: Write down some things that you like to talk about

Person 2: Write down some things that you like to talk about

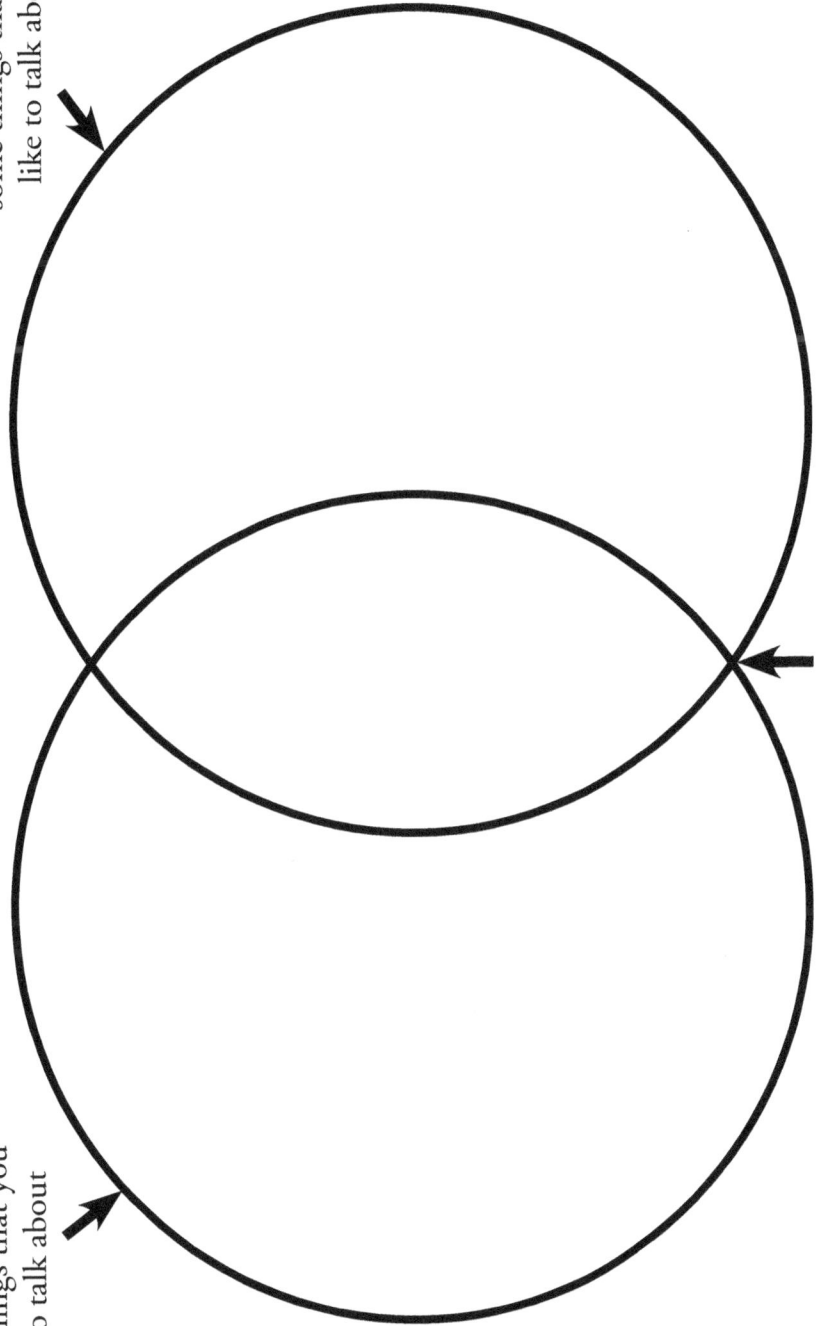

Here, write what you have in common

Topic 3: Social Relationships

I just want people to take a step back, take a deep breath, and actually look at something with a different perspective. But most people will never do that.
Brian McKnight

Many children with ADHD struggle with appropriate behaviour for social settings and situations in which they must interact with others. This can be because they did not receive this guidance in the home or because another system of values and behaviours was being taught.

Perhaps they did have good role models in the home and neighbourhood who promoted and modelled appropriate behaviour, but didn't pick it up as well as most children – just like some children learn to read without formal instruction prior to school, and some need the structured process of reading instruction. Some of these struggles can lead to rejection from their peer group and feeling isolated, different, unlikeable and alone. These are perhaps the most painful aspect of ADHD related impairments, which can have long-lasting effects. For friendships to grow and be maintained, children need to be able to control impulses, take turns, share, listen, be empathetic, attentive and focused, communicate effectively with others, be aware of and respond to social cues, and have an ability to problem-solve situations and resolve conflicts as they arise – skills that can be challenging for a child with ADHD. Unfortunately, once a child is labelled negatively by their peers because of social-skills deficits, it can be very hard to dispel this reputation.

In fact, having a negative reputation is perhaps one of the main obstacles children may have to overcome socially. Studies have found that the negative peer status of children with ADHD is often already established by early-to-middle primary school years, and this reputation can stick with the child even as they begin to make positive changes in social skills.

Does your child find understanding social cues challenging? _____

Does your child tell you they feel misunderstood? _____

Does your child struggle with forming and maintaining relationships? If so, what has this struggle cost your child?

_____

_____

Identify Your Child's Social Skills Needs

The following skills are useful when dealing with other people. Read each skill and check the box that shows how good your child is at using that skill. This checklist will help you determine where improvement is needed. The lower the score the more improvement you need.

1 = never good	2 = hardly ever good	3 = sometimes good	4 = usually good	5 = always good				
					1	2	3	4	5

	1	2	3	4	5
Listening: Can your child pay attention to someone who is talking?					
Starting a conversation: Can your child talk to others about simple and then more complicated stuff?					
Asking a question: Can your child decide what questions to ask someone and then ask?					
Saying thank you: Can your child let people know that they are thankful for something?					
Introducing themself: Can your child go up to people on their own and introduce themself?					
Introducing other people: Can your child help other people get to know each other?					
Giving a compliment: Can your child tell people that they like something about them or things they do?					
Asking for help: Can your child request assistance when they need it?					
Apologising: Can your child say sorry when they have done something wrong?					
Knowing their feelings: Can your child name the emotions they are feeling?					
Expressing their feelings: Can your child tell others the emotions they are feeling?					
Understanding the feelings of others: Can your child figure out what other people are feeling?					

Which of the above social skills are most difficult for your child?

_____

_____

_____

What strategies have you tried to manage the identified needs?

_____

_____

_____

Are there any social skills your child is exceptionally good at?

_____

_____

_____

Is Your Child an Introvert or an Extrovert?

> *Your vision will become clear only when you look into your own heart. Who looks outside dreams, who looks inside awakes.*
> **Carl Jung**

You probably know people who are outgoing, and people who are shy. Those who are outgoing are named extroverts and those who are quiet and prefer small groups are named introverts. In your view, which is it better to be, an extrovert or an introvert?

The answer is: neither! The world needs both styles of people, and people who fall everywhere in-between. If you would like to know a bit more about your child's preferred style, read the pairs of statements in the questionnaire on the next page and circle the one that sounds most like them.

Score as follows:

10 or more A's suggest that your child is an introvert. This means that they are more comfortable when in small groups or one-on-one social settings. They often feel that people drain their energy.

10 or more B's suggest that your child may be an extrovert. They are the happiest when they are with others and feel energised from being around others.

If the scores were similar for A's and B's, your child probably feels comfortable wherever they are, with people or alone.

Introvert or Extrovert Questionnaire

Circle A or B for each one. Do not overthink.

1	A	My child is seldom bored	B	My child is easily bored
2	A	My child does not like fast, scary rides	B	My child loves fast scary rides
3	A	My child would rather spend the evening at home with a few friends	B	My child would rather spend the evening at a loud party with lots of people
4	A	My child enjoys being alone	B	My child hates to be alone
5	A	My child likes to have a few close friends	B	My child likes to have many casual friends
6	A	My child would rather write a book than sell things to people	B	My child would rather sell things to people than write a book
7	A	My child is not likely to take a dare	B	My child will take almost any dare
8	A	My child thinks that April Fool's Day is stupid	B	My child thinks that April Fool's Day is fun
9	A	You won't find my child watching Mr Bean	B	My child thinks that Mr Bean is funny
10	A	My child likes talking about ideas	B	My child would rather do things than discuss them
11	A	In hide-and-seek, you'll find my child behind the tree	B	In hide-and-seek, you'll find my child in the tree
12	A	My child avoids crowds	B	My child likes crowds
13	A	My child does not like to dance	B	My child likes to dance
14	A	My child believes that convertibles aren't safe and that you shouldn't ride in one	B	My child believes that convertibles are fun and that you should ride in one
15	A	My child enjoys working behind the scenes	B	My child wants to be on stage

What is your child's style? Total their A's and B's: A ___ B ___

Give this questionnaire to other members of your family and see how they score. Are they extroverts or introverts?

Should you child change their style?

Some introverts think they're too shy and wish they could be different. But there is nothing wrong with being quiet, enjoying solitude, or being a thinker. However, if being introverted worries your child, encourage them to speak to an adult they trust.

Some extroverts are funny. But after a while, they can get tired of being the life of the party. If this is your child, help them take a break. Encourage them to let their family and friends know that they'd like to engage in some solitary activities for a while.

Remind your child that they do not have to be the same all the time. What's most important is for them to talk about these things and to be themself.

Topic 4: The Impact of Bullying

Right is right even if no one is doing it; wrong is wrong even if everyone is doing it.
Saint Augustine

Bullying can exist in many forms: it can be physical (pushing, punching, or hitting); verbal (name-calling or threats); or psychological and emotional (spreading rumours or excluding someone from a conversation or activity).

The first step to dealing with bullies is knowing when your child is a victim.

'Typical bullying symptoms include physical complaints such as tummy aches, as well as worries and fears, and a child not wanting to go to school', says Steven Pastyrnak, PhD, the Division Chief of Psychology at Helen DeVos Children's Hospital in Michigan, USA. 'A normal defense is to avoid or withdraw from things that are causing the stress.'

Ask questions and get your child talking about their social situation. Know which friends they're getting along with and which ones they're not. 'Establishing good communication should start well before the children are having bullying problems', says Dr Pastyrnak. 'Keep it very general for the younger children, but if you suspect a problem or if your child has vocalised a problem, press for more details.'

As children get older, they have an increased awareness of peer relationships, so you can be more direct with your questions. When your children talk, really listen to what they share and keep your own emotions in check.

If your child is being bullied, remind them that it's not their fault, and that you have their back. It's important for children to identify their feelings so they can communicate what's going on; therefore, parents should talk about their own feelings.

'Often parents will get angry or frustrated, but children don't need you to overreact. They need you to listen, reassure, and support them. They need to see you as stable and strong and able to help them in any situation.' Below are some ways to help them deal with bullies.

Create a list of responses. Practise phrases your child can use to tell someone to stop bullying behaviour. These should be simple and direct, but not antagonistic: 'Leave me alone.' 'Back off.' 'That wasn't nice.' They could also try, 'Yeah, whatever', and then walk away. 'The key is that a comeback shouldn't be a put-down, because that aggravates a bully.' Also, it is important to be mindful of when your child is the one doing the bullying!

194

Role-play 'What If' scenarios. Role-playing is a terrific way to build confidence and empower your child to deal with challenges. You can role-play the bully while your child practices different responses until they feel confident handling troublesome situations. In your role play, teach them to speak in a strong, firm voice – protesting or crying will only encourage a bully.

Keep an open line of communication. Check in with your children every day about how things are going at school. Use a calm, friendly tone and create a nurturing climate so they aren't afraid to tell you if something's wrong. Emphasise that their safety and well-being are important, and that they should always talk to an adult about any problems.

Build your child's confidence. The better your child feels about themself, the less likely the bullying will affect their self-esteem. Encourage hobbies, extracurricular activities and social situations that bring out the best in your child. Tell your child the unique qualities you love about them and reinforce positive behaviours that you'd like to see more. 'As parents, we have a tendency to focus on negative situations, but children actually listen better when their good behaviours are reinforced', Dr Pastyrnak says. Honouring children's strengths and encouraging healthy connections with others can affect self-esteem, increase your children's long-term confidence, and prevent any potential bullying situations.

Praise progress. When your child tells you how they defused a harasser, let them know you're proud. If you witness another child standing up to a bully in the park, point it out to your child so they can copy that approach. Above all, emphasise what your own mum may have told you when you were a child: if your child shows that they can't be bothered, a bully will usually move on.

Teach the right way to react

Children must understand that bullies have a need for power and control over others and a desire to hurt people. They often lack self-control, empathy and sensitivity. With that said, it's helpful for children to use these strategies when dealing with bullies:

Don't let a bully make you feel bad. When someone says something bad about you, say something positive to yourself. Remind yourself of your positive attributes.

Tell the bully how you feel, why you feel the way you do, and what you want the bully to do. Learn to do this with a calm and determined voice. Say, for example, 'I feel angry when you call me names because I have a real name. I want you to start calling me by my real name.'

Don't reward the bully with tears. The bully wants to hurt your feelings, so act like their name-calling and taunts don't hurt. You can do this by admitting the bully is right.

For example, when the bully calls you 'fatty', look them in the eye and say calmly, 'You know, I do need to start getting more exercise.' Then walk off with confidence.

Disarm the bully with humour. Laugh at their threats and walk away from them. Use your best judgment and follow your instincts. If the bully wants your homework, and you think they are about to hurt you, give them your work and walk off with confidence. Then tell an adult what happened.

Don't expect to be mistreated. When walking toward a group of children, think of them as being nice to you, and do your best to be friendly. Most important, treat others the way you want to be treated. Stand up for other students who are bullied and ask them to stand up for you.

Take action to stop bullying

Ultimately, it's up to parents to help young children deal with a bully. Help them learn how to make smart choices and take action when they feel hurt or see another child being bullied and be ready to intervene if necessary. Report repeated severe bullying.

Contact the offender's parents

This is the right approach only for persistent acts of intimidation, and when you feel these parents will be receptive to working in a cooperative manner with you. Call or email them in a non-confrontational way, making it clear that your goal is to resolve the matter together. You might say something like:

'I'm phoning because my son has come home from school feeling upset every day this week. He tells me that Peter has called him names and excluded him from games at the playground. I don't know whether Peter has mentioned any of this, but I'd like us to help them get along better. Do you have any suggestions?'

Partner with your school

Communicate with your child's school and report bullying incidents. 'You can't expect the school staff to know everything that's going on. Make them aware of any situations', Kaplan says. Though more schools are implementing bullying-prevention programs, many still do not have enough support or resources. 'Parents and teachers need to be aware and get involved so that they can monitor it appropriately', says Dr Pastyrna. Learn how to start anti-bullying and anti-violence programs within the school curriculum.

Dealing with Bullying

Standing up to a bully can be difficult. Bullies will pick on their target over and over, and it can be hard to make them stop. But learning ways to respond to a bully without escalating the situation can help.

One way of doing this is fogging – when a person who is being bullied responds with neutral statements or agrees with what the bully says. For example, 'Thanks for noticing', or 'maybe I will'. The idea is to show the bully that what they are saying is not bothering you.

Another strategy to deal with bullying is Bold Talk – using strong, assertive statements to resist the bully's pressure.

Role-play these strategies with your child so they are prepared to deal with any bullying situation that arises.

Fogging

When the bully says:

Everyone hates you

You're such a loser!

You have stupid hair

How does it feel to have no friends?

You're such a nerd

You're so dumb

You have ugly teeth

You can't even catch a ball, dummy!

Your fogging response could be:

Oh, okay

Whatever

That's interesting

Thanks for noticing

You're probably right

Just fine, thanks

That's your opinion

You're right, I do well at school

Why do you care?

Use Bold Talk when you are:	To get result when using Bold Talk	Bold Talk statements that work
▪ Telling someone to stop doing something ▪ Politely saying no to someone ▪ Disagreeing with bullying or gossip	▪ Look the person in the eye ▪ Use an assertive tone of voice (not too harsh but not too soft) ▪ Your face needs to reflect your message. Look serious but not mean ▪ Own what you say by using 'I' statements (e.g. 'I feel … when…') ▪ Role play with someone in your Circle of Support. Have the other person be rude, mean or make you do something you know is wrong. You will feel strange at first, but with practice it gets easier ▪ Report ongoing behaviour before it goes too far Using Bold Talk does not mean that the other person will stop the first, second or third time, but keep at it. Using Bold Talk will help you feel better and more confident.	▪ 'Stop.' ▪ 'I told you to stop.' ▪ 'Don't talk to me like that.' ▪ 'I think that is mean.' ▪ 'No thanks.' ▪ 'I don't want to do that.' ▪ 'I don't like how you are playing.' ▪ 'I don't like talking about people who aren't here.' ▪ 'That is harsh. How would you like it if they did that to you?' ▪ 'How about if I think my way and you think your way?' Agree to disagree.

Bold talk for peer pressure	Bold talk for gossip	Bold talk for hurt feelings
Things you can say when you don't want to do what a friend wants you to do:	Things that you can say when a friend is gossiping, and you don't like it:	Things you can say when a friend hurts your feelings:
▪ 'I don't really want to do this.' ▪ 'This is mean. I don't want to do this.' ▪ 'I changed my mind – I don't want to do this.' ▪ 'This is making me feel bad. I don't want to say that.' ▪ 'I am feeling worried about this – I want to be left out of this.' ▪ 'This does not sound like a good idea. I want out.' ▪ 'This is not cool. I don't want to do this.' ▪ 'I can just tell that this is going to go wrong, and I am going to get busted. I am out!' ▪ 'I think this is going to hurt someone else's feelings. Let's not do it.'	▪ 'Are you sure you should be saying this? I don't think this is right.' ▪ 'This sounds like gossip. Let's change the subject.' ▪ 'Hey – I don't want to talk like this. It's not who I am!' ▪ 'Come on guys. This is how rumours get started.' ▪ 'Oh, come on, let's stop the drama and change the subject.'	▪ 'I feel upset. You seem mad at me and I don't understand why.' ▪ 'I was really sad when you didn't invite me. It was embarrassing.' ▪ 'I am angry because you broke your promise and told my secret.' ▪ 'I am confused. We were together all weekend and now you aren't acting like my friend.'

Bold Talk - Role Play

Example:

Friend: Hey can I use your phone to text Sarah and pretend that its Sam?

You: Why?

Friend: She's totally obsessed with him. It'll be funny. You'll see.

You: No thanks. My mum reads all of my texts. Besides, I don't like drama.

Friend: You know you can delete all of your texts. Come on!

You: Look, I don't want any part of this. It sounds mean and stupid. Use your own phone and keep me out of this.

Friend: You're so lame.

You: Whatever. If I was with her, I wouldn't text you and pretend to be someone else. What you want to do is mean and dumb.

Module 3:
Practical Coping Skills

Section 3:
Making Change

Topic 1: Bringing About Change

Change involves the courage to do things differently. The secret of change is to focus your energy not on the old, but on building the new.
Socrates

There is an old saying that 'if you always do what you've always done, you will always get what you've always got'. Change involves doing things differently and involves taking action, and that can be hard to do. Before your child embarks on the journey of real change, it is helpful to reflect on the following questions:

Does my child talk about needing to make changes? If so, what are they saying?

_____

_____

_____

Do they talk about change but refuse to take action?

_____

_____

_____

Change can be scary, but you know what's scarier?
Allowing fear to stop you from growing, evolving, and progressing.
Mandy Hale

Stage of Change

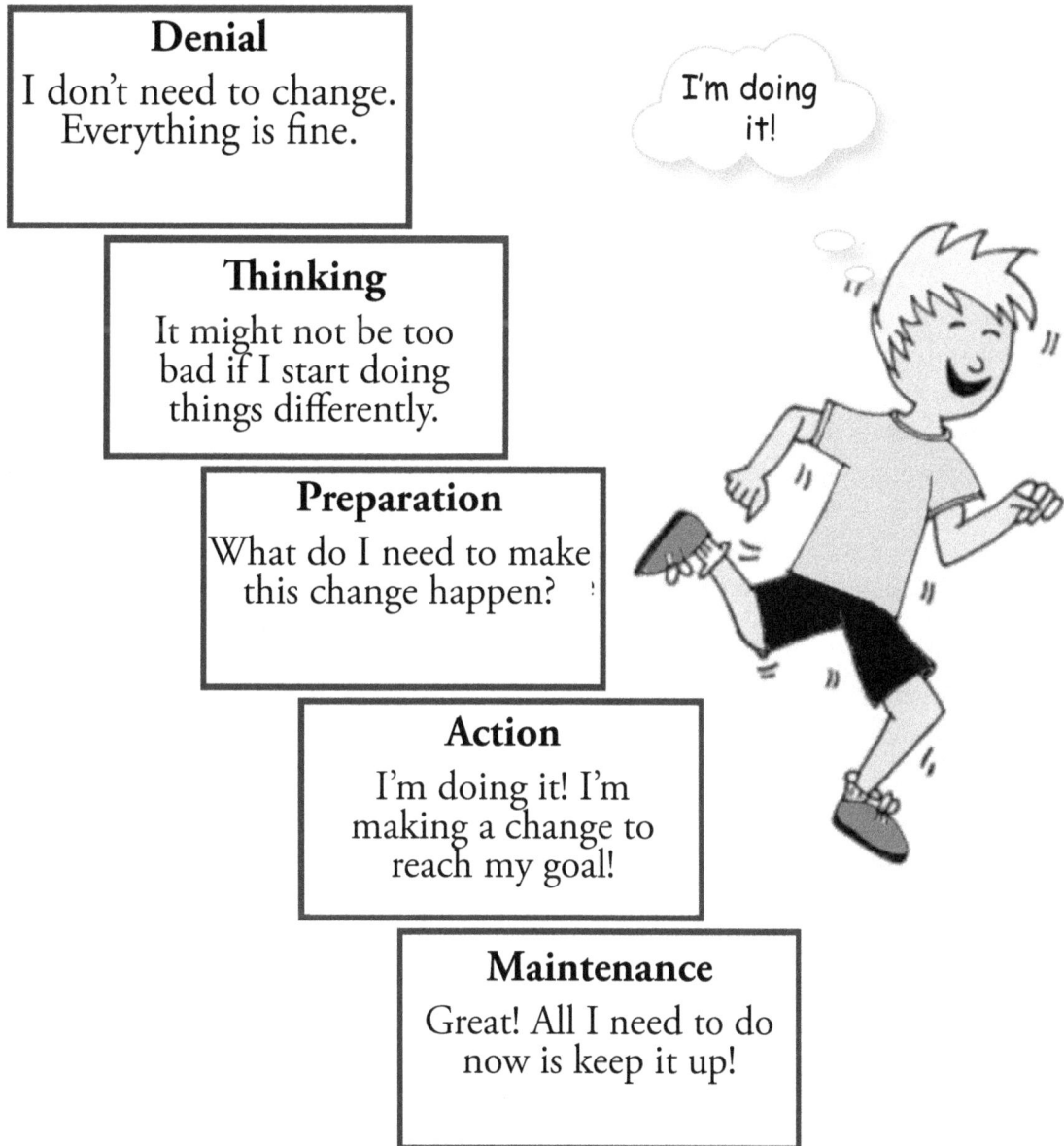

> **Denial**
> I don't need to change.
> Everything is fine.

> **Thinking**
> It might not be too
> bad if I start doing
> things differently.

> **Preparation**
> What do I need to make
> this change happen?

> **Action**
> I'm doing it! I'm
> making a change to
> reach my goal!

> **Maintenance**
> Great! All I need to do
> now is keep it up!

Success is not final. Failure is not fatal. It's the courage to continue that counts.
Winston Churchill

Types of Change

When we look at positive changes we have made in our lives, we can divide them into two categories:

Category 1: Someone tells us we must change and if we don't, something bad is going to happen. A parent tells their child that if they fail the weekly spelling test, they will be grounded for the whole weekend. A teacher tells a student that they need to complete their writing assignment by the next day or face failing the class. A judge mandates someone to counselling or they will go to juvenile detention. In these cases, we change in order to avoid the bad thing that could happen if we don't change.

Category 2: At other times, we change because we want to change. We make the decision to change. We decide to change on our own. No one tells us something bad is going to happen if we don't change. We weigh the pros and cons of changing or not changing in our minds and decide for ourselves that we will do. It is possible for one kind of change to cross over into the other. For instance, someone tells you that you should consider changing your technology habits. Your first reaction might be to resist and even tell them off; however, after a few late nights spent scrolling social media, you revisit the idea of change and decide to make adjustment to your technology use. The change you made started when someone told you to change and later you decided it was a good idea.

Exercise: Think of a change you made in your life.

When did you first decide there was a problem that had to be fixed? Did you realise it gradually or did it happen all at once?

_____

_____

_____

Do you remember when you didn't think you had a problem? And how other people tried to tell you that you had a problem, and you didn't believe them, or you thought they were exaggerating the problem?

_____

_____

_____

What feelings or obstacles did you have to overcome to recognise the problem?

_____

_____

_____

Bringing About Change

Whether it is actions or behaviours, what could you stop doing, do less, start doing and keep doing in order to bring about constructive change in your parenting and family life in general?

Date	Stop Doing	Do Less	Start Doing	Keep Doing

Expectations vs Reality

There are two ways to be happy: improve your reality or lower your expectations

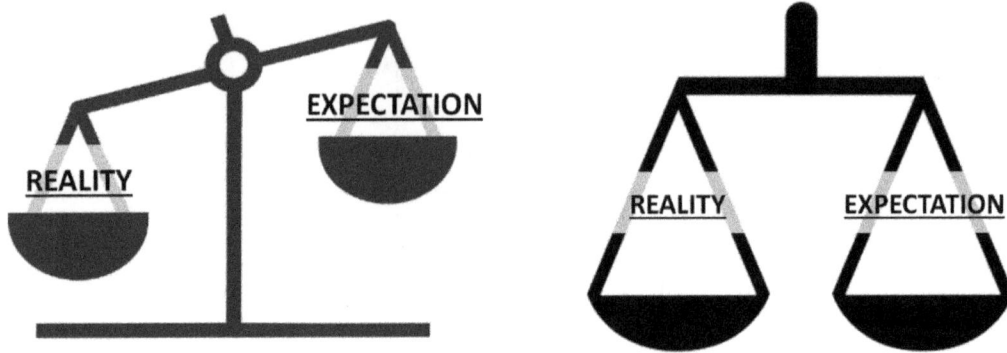

Research shows that parents who have unrealistic expectations of their children risk their child's mental, emotional and physical well-being. These expectations can be academic, or in any other sphere of their lives. Children who perceive this kind of pressure can often refuse to attempt anything unless they are convinced that they will be the best at it. I have worked with academically bright children who have stopped trying at school to the point of failing, because of their parents' unrealistic expectations. They reason that regardless of how hard they try, it is never good enough for their parents. Parents who put this kind of unhealthy pressure on their children would benefit from stepping back and realistically evaluating their own issues underpinning these expectations. Often a discussion with the child's teachers can be helpful.

Reflect:

What do I expect my child's life to be like in the following five domains?

- Family domain: _____
  _____

- School domain: _____
  _____

- Academic domain: _____
  _____

- Social domain: _____

- _____

- Health domain:_____
  _____

If you drop your expectations, how will your relationship with your child change?

_____

_____

_____

How might your life change if your expectations were more realistic?

_____

_____

_____

> *Maybe that was the problem – Expectations!*
> **Unknown**

It has been said that happiness equals reality divided by expectations. If our reality is lower than how we expect life to be, then we're likely to feel unhappy or discontent. This formula therefore suggests that our reality needs to be balanced with our expectations. The more we can get them in balance, then the happier, more content, accepting or peaceful, we are likely to be.

Therefore, to make positive change, we can choose to improve our reality, and/or lower our expectations.

Step 1: improve my reality	Step 2: lower my expectations

Topic 2: Underachievement and ADHD

In many cases underachievement is not because a lack of knowing butbecause of the lack of structure and planning.
Unknown

Many children with ADHD struggle with underachievement; they know they could do better but somehow don't. Research has shown that medication can help children with ADHD improve their performance at home and at school. Medications used to treat ADHD help the neurotransmitters dopamine and norepinephrine work more efficiently. When this happens, attention and concentration improve; more chores and schoolwork are completed; compliance increases, hyperactivity and impulsivity decrease; and other negative behaviours decrease. Examining current behaviours, in relation to what is needed to achieve goals, can help put a plan in place that targets your child's needs and increases their motivation to achieve more.

There can be many reasons for underachievement. Check the ones that are true for your child:

- ☐ Stress
- ☐ Self-doubt
- ☐ Having unrealistic expectations
- ☐ Lack of family support
- ☐ Too much family pressure
- ☐ Distraction by video games, TV and other technology
- ☐ Lack of interest in school
- ☐ Preferring to spend time with friends
- ☐ Being too disorganised to create a schedule for schoolwork
- ☐ Anger at parents
- ☐ A belief that school is not important, that it does not relate to the real world
- ☐ Giving priority to other interests, such as sports and fun

Succeeding with ADHD

> *I had to learn to work with my ADHD and not against it.*
> **Student**

Despite the serious challenges that individuals with ADHD face daily, they can still be successful in their life.

'Despite all the challenges I encounter daily, I would not trade ADHD for anything – but this only happened once I accepted my condition. At this time, I stopped wishing ADHD away and sought help. One thing that my parents and I realised soon after I was diagnosed and medicated, was that pills didn't teach skills. The medication was needed but I also had to learn additional skills to help me manage the challenges that the new environment that I had transitioned into, high school, presented. Although I was never late for classes I had to realise that I no longer had all the support that I had in primary school and that high school demands so much more; academically and socially. I also had to realise that there is more to time management than being punctual for appointments. I had to accept that I was not good at using time, at prioritising or planning. Once I identified my challenges, I became more open to accept help and learn compensatory skills.'

Children with ADHD can become successful adults.

What is your view of this statement?

_____

_____

_____

_____

_____

_____

_____

_____

_____

_____

_____

What do you think is missing from your child's life at present that would increase their chances of success? Please check the list below:

- ☐ One good friend
- ☐ A few close friends
- ☐ Ways to describe how they feel to us
- ☐ Ways to ask for help and support
- ☐ Finding something that they really like and look forward to
- ☐ Ways to express their thoughts and feelings
- ☐ Fun activities
- ☐ Adventure
- ☐ Acceptance of their condition
- ☐ Other _____

_____

_____

What can you start doing today to help your child reach their full potential?

_____

_____

_____

Topic 3: Screen Time and ADHD

Technology can be a weapon of mass distraction.
Credit needed

Controlling Screen Time for Children with ADHD

Parents are often concerned about their child's screen time and report difficulty enforcing limits. Screen time includes all screens including social media, online gaming and watching TV or streaming. Enforcing limits on screen time can be particularly challenging for children who have ADHD due to their difficulties with self-monitoring and inattention. As a child therapist, I am often told by parents that their child grabs their phone out of their purse, asks to use their tablet constantly, and cries when denied. This leads to parents often giving in to such requests, which only encourages this behaviour in the future. Screen time is a frequent topic of discussion in child therapy, and many parents can benefit from learning skills to manage their child's screen time.

Screen Time Today

Screen time is nearly impossible to avoid. The majority of children between of five and sixteen years old play video games regularly (at least one hour per day), and a recent Norwegian study found that over 75% of children play for over two hours per day. The American Academy of Pediatrics currently recommends a maximum of one hour per day of screen time.

Screen time in moderation is a part of everyday life. It is important for children to learn skills related to electronic devices in order to function in the modern world. Your child's friends at school are using devices regularly, and if your child doesn't play similar games, it can be difficult for them to participate in related conversations. However, too much screen time can deprive children of face-to-face social interactions, exploring other interests, working on homework and reading. Regulating your child's screen time can help them to regulate their own use in the future and develop other skills and interests.

ADHD and Screen Time

Children with ADHD are particularly vulnerable to the exciting colours, sounds and images appearing in quick succession on a screen. Video games, internet videos, and social networking sites provide immediate rewards that strongly encourage continued use.

Children with ADHD also have difficulty with self-monitoring. This means that children with ADHD, and children in general, have a hard time recognising when they have spent too much time on a game and when it is in their best interest to put the game down or go to sleep. Children with ADHD have difficulty with impulse control and may be more likely to view inappropriate videos, sext or make poor decisions regarding internet use.

Sleep and Media Use

Individuals with ADHD are also known to have sleep difficulties, including not sleeping for enough hours, frequently waking, and moving a great amount during sleep. Children may turn to a tablet or mobile phone to 'help' them go to sleep, which results in the opposite effect. A recent study published by the *Journal of Physical Activity and Health* concluded that children with ADHD, compared to children without ADHD, obtained less than optimal hours of sleep and exceeded recommendations for screen time. Parents reported that they set limits for their children's screen time, but many children had TVs in their bedrooms and were not complying with their parents' request.

There are many benefits to be enjoyed from technology. Like most things in life, it is not the technology that is the problem but rather our inability to use it responsibly. Some children with ADHD are at increased risk for problematic overuse of technology. Although most cases do not reach the point which is considered an addiction, a small percentage of children struggle to resist the temptation of technology. Valuable time is wasted on texting, social media, and in particular, gaming; time that could be used doing priority tasks such as homework, studying and building face-to-face relationships. This not only impacts on performance but also leads to much family conflict.

Scenario

Kate picked up the remote and flipped on the TV. Her favourite program was about to start. She flopped comfortably on the couch as the theme song started, her mobile phone close at hand so she could chat with her best friend Sally throughout the show. They often watched shows 'together' like this, enjoying it more because they shared the experience.

'Have you finished your homework?' Dad called from the kitchen.

'Yes, Dad' Kate replied, not entirely truthfully. But she had plenty of time, she'd get those Science questions done later.

Right in the middle of the show, Mum came home with a ton of shopping. 'Come and help carry', she told Kate.

Kate knew better than to argue, so she raced out to the car and grabbed as many bags as she could, hurrying back inside so she didn't miss anything. She dumped the bags on the kitchen floor and jumped back onto the couch, grabbing the phone to message Sally at the same time.

What happened? What did I miss?

Mum was shouting from the kitchen about the shopping being dumped on the floor. Kate ignored her and turned up the TV to hear it better.

The show was nearly over, with all the most exciting things happening, when Toby came into the lounge room, dragging his noisy xylophone toy. He plopped onto the floor and started singing and banging the xylophone.

Kate was mad. Her stomach felt as if it was filled with boiling hot lava. 'Get out!' she shouted. She snatched the xylophone off Toby and threw it towards the lounge room door. She missed the doorway. The xylophone hit the wall and broke, falling to the floor in several pieces. Toby burst into tears, Dad came shouting into the lounge room, and suddenly Kate was in her bedroom, grounded and in tears over her phone being confiscated, and she'd missed the end of the show.

Can you relate to the scenario above? Explain.

_____

_____

_____

Is your child's technology use having a negative impact on their school performance? Please give a reason for your answer.

_____

_____

_____

Is your child's technology use causing conflict in your relationship? Please give a reason for your answer.

_____

_____

_____

If you've answered yes to the above questions, what do you think is preventing your child from using technology more responsibly?

_____

_____

> *Technology is a useful servant but dangerous master.*
> **Christian Lous Lange**

The following strategies you can try at home to help control your child's screen time:

- Set a time limit for screen time and consistently enforce limits.
- Choose a consistent time of day. This helps your child predict when they will be able to use electronics and not beg for the device 24/7. You may want to choose 30 minutes or 1 hour after your child has completed their homework. Choosing a time in the morning may distract your child from getting ready for school.
- Help your child tell time and encourage them to monitor when the time to use the device is up. You can provide your child with a digital clock and/or a timer that makes a sound when it is time to put the device away. Avoid having to be personally responsible for keeping track of their screen time and instead help your child develop the skill of monitoring their time.
- Have your child use electronic devices in the common living area so they can be monitored for safe and appropriate use.
- Do not allow your child to use devices during meal times or in situations where they can be conversing with friends, such as at a party.
- Do not allow your child to reach into your purse, backpack or other personal space in order to retrieve a device. This encourages inappropriate boundary crossing that can cause issues for your child with friends or others. Instead, hand your child the device when it is time to play. If possible, provide your child with their own tablet or device to play games instead of using your mobile phone that may have texts, emails and other information you do not want your child viewing.
- Have your child store electronics in your bedroom overnight so that they are not temped to use games when they should be sleeping. Additionally, remove TVs from your child's bedroom.
- Praise your child when they respect limits for device use and provide appropriate and reasonable consequences if they purposefully disobey limits. This may include losing device time the following day.

- Be prepared – when you enforce new rules in the home, your child may become upset and defiant at first until they learn the new routine. Be prepared for this and don't let it discourage you. If you have ongoing difficulties with this topic and/or notice a decrease in your child's sleep, grades, or that your child is choosing screen time over spending time with other children face to face, it may be time to seek out therapy to address individual concerns.

One thing to remember is that although your child is fighting your rule, it does not mean that you should not implement it. Be consistent but fair.

Screen Time Checklist

Morning	Afternoon	Weekend
Check that you have:	**Check that you have:**	**Check that you have:**
☐ Made your bed	☐ Unpacked your bag	☐ Dressed for the day
☐ Had breakfast	☐ Put your bag and shoes in your launch pad	☐ Put your pyjamas away
☐ Dressed for the day	☐ Had 30 minutes of outside time	☐ Made your bed
☐ Put shoes and socks on	☐ Completed your homework	☐ Brushed your teeth
☐ Put your pyjamas away	☐ Completed your chores	☐ Combed your hair
☐ Brushed your teeth		☐ Had breakfast
☐ Combed your hair		☐ Had 20 minutes of reading
☐ Packed your bag		☐ Had 30 minutes of outside time
☐ Placed your lunch in your bag		☐ Completed a chore
Completed the list?	**Completed the list?**	**Completed the list?**
You can now have _____ minutes of screen time!	**You can now have _____ minutes of screen time!**	**You can now have _____ minutes of screen time!**

Play Ideas	
Indoor	**Outdoor**
Lego	Run/walk/skip
Board games	Ride a bike/scooter
Exercise	Play with your pets
Listen to music and dance	Take your dog for a walk

Earn Screen Dollars

Tasks	Dollar value
Clean your room	3 SD
Vacuum carpets	2 SD
Fill dishwasher	1 SD
Empty dishwasher	1 SD
Sweep floors	1 SD
Pack away groceries	1 SD
Mop floors	2 SD
30 min walk with the dog	1 SD
Fold a load of laundry	1 SD

Add your own tasks and dollar value.

Example: of using screen dollars:

- 1 SD = 30 minutes of screen time
- Trade 20 SD for $10 in real money

Comments:

_____

_____

Parent signature: _____ Date: _____

Child signature: _____ Date: _____

Topic 4: Learning Styles

Every child has a different learning style and pace. Each child is unique, not only capable of learning but also capable of succeeding.
Credit needed

We all learn differently. Which of the following styles do you relate to the most? Explain why.

_____

_____

_____

Visual Learner	Auditory Learner	Kinaesthetic Learner
Visual learners may: - express themselves through facial expressions - be interested in videos and images - use their eyes to find solutions to a particular problem	Auditory learners may: - express themselves through their words - enjoy sound and music - want to discuss the possible solutions	Kinaesthetic learners may: - express themselves through their body language - be generally interested in physical activities - look for solutions using their hands

Do you know your child's learning style?

Knowing your child's learning style makes it easier to understand what accommodations they may benefit from. This might include classroom accommodations. Speak to your child's teacher about their preferred learning style and what can be implemented in the classroom to enhance learning. Further information about strategies for different learning styles can be found in the supplementary information.

Describe your child's natural talents that you feel are not given credit at school.

_____

_____

_____

Accepting Accommodations

Children with ADHD can get classroom accommodations designed to increase their success. Some children are embarrassed about these accommodations or afraid that others will find out that they have ADHD or other challenges.

Help your child realise that accepting accommodations is not a sign of weakness but rather a sign of wisdom. These environmental supports are available to help them meet their individual learning needs and allow their true ability and gifts to be acknowledged and developed.

Reflect:

- Has your child been given accommodations at school?
- How do they feel about using accommodations in the classroom?

Find out if any of the support that your child needs are available as accommodations.

Typical accommodations include:

- [ ] Special use of computers
- [ ] Note takers
- [ ] Untimed tests
- [ ] Extra time for timed tests and exams
- [ ] Permission to make up missed work
- [ ] Alternative assignments
- [ ] Alternative grading, such as minimising deductions for minor errors
- [ ] Homework help
- [ ] Special setting assignments
- [ ] Verbal (instead of written) tests
- [ ] Student Aid

Further information about classroom accommodations can be found in the supplementary information.

Troubleshooting Struggles

Identify the struggles that are most challenging for your child and help them to apply the solutions in the right-hand column. Check the ones that you have implemented.

Struggles	Solutions for your child to consider
Fails to give adequate attention to details and makes careless mistakes in schoolwork or other activities	☐ Recheck your attention span and ability to break activities into smaller units. ☐ What is your learning style? ☐ Is your worry, anxiety or anger interfering with your ability to listen? ☐ Practise mindfulness. ☐ Use your problem-solving skills to come up with options.
Has difficulty sustaining attention in tasks	☐ Check management of space (is your work environment too distracting?). ☐ What is your mind telling you? ☐ Ask yourself, 'Am I doing what I am supposed to be doing?' If not, get to the task without delay. ☐ Use your problem-solving skills to come up with solutions. ●
Fails to listen when spoken to directly	☐ Talk to someone in your Circle of Support or your mentor about ways to improve your listening. ☐ Talk to others about finding optimal times for a conversation. ☐ Keep your eyes on the person that is speaking. ☐ Is your worry, anxiety or anger interfering with your ability to listen? ☐ Practise mindfulness. ☐ Use problem-solving skills to brainstorm solutions.
Has difficulty in organising, planning and prioritising tasks	☐ Have your To Do list in your diary (avoid sticky notes). ☐ Prioritise from your To Do list. Use the pebble-jar concept. ☐ Carry over, to the next day, what you don't get done on a specific day. ☐ Use your problem-solving skills to come up with an action plan.

Procrastinates	▪ Identify why you procrastinate. ▪ What has procrastination cost you? ▪ What excuses do you use for your procrastination? ▪ What is your mind telling you? ▪ Use your problem-solving skills to manage your procrastination.
Loses things necessary for tasks or activities	▪ Use a single work area. ▪ Get into the habit of placing things back in their place. ▪ Declutter frequently. ▪ Use your problem-solving skills to minimise this problem.
Is forgetful in daily activities	▪ Use a diary and a To Do list. ▪ Set alarms to remind you to check your diary. ▪ Link checking your diary to activities that you do habitually (e.g., brushing your teeth, before going to bed). ▪ Use your problem-solving skills to minimise this problem.
Is demotivated, has low self-esteem and lacks confidence	▪ Are you motivated from the outside or from within? ▪ Are you eating, sleeping and exercising well? ▪ Are you communicating assertively? ▪ Are you living consistent with your values? ▪ Use your problem-solving skills to explore solutions to this problem.
Has difficulty with emotional control	▪ Name what you are feeling. ▪ Practice mindfulness. ▪ Use 'I' statements to communicate your feelings and your needs. ▪ Are you living consistent with your values? ▪ Use your problem-solving skills to explore solutions to this problem.

Your job as a parent is not to sculpt your child to fulfil your own expectations, but to be a guide, supervisor, provider, nurturer, and protector of their unique gifts and strengths.
Russell Barkley, PhD

References

American Psychiatric Association (2013). *Diagnostic and Statistical Manual of Mental Health Disorders* (5th ed.). American Psychiatric Association.

Bellak-Adams, K. (2010). *AD/HD Success! Solutions for Boosting Self-Esteem: The Diary Method for Ages 7–17*. Loving Healing Press.

da Camara, G. (2018). *Fridays with Tristan: Understanding ADHD from a mentoring perspective*. Blackjack Books.

da Camara, G. (2021). *What Lies Beneath Matters: A Workbook for Tweens and Teens with ADHD*. Achievers World Publishing.

Ramsay, J. R., & Rostain, A. L. (2015). *The Adult ADHD Tool Kit: Using CBT to Facilitate Coping Inside Out*. Routledge.

Ramsay, J. R., PhD. *How Cognitive Behavioural Therapy Unlocks Positivity and Productivity for Adults with ADHD*. ADDitude webinar.

Ratey, J., & Hagerman, E. (2008). *Spark: The Revolutionary New Science of Exercise and the Brain*. Little, Brown.

Shapiro, L. E. (2010). *The ADHD Workbook for Children: Helping Children Gain Self-Confidence, Social Skills & Self-Control*. Raincoast books.

Recommended Books for Parents

Barkley, R. A., & Robin, A. L. (2008). *Your Defiant Teen: 10 Steps to Resolve Conflict and Rebuild Your Relationships*. Guilford Press.

Cox, A. J. (2006). *Boys of Few Words: Raising Our Sons to Communicate and Connect*. Guildford Press.

da Camara, G. (2023). *What Lies Beneath Matters: A Workbook for Tweens and Teens with ADHD*. UWA Publishing.

Dendy, C. Z. (1995). *Childagers With ADD: A Parent's Guide*. Woodbine House.

Goldstein, S., Brook, R., & Weiss, S. (2004). *Angry Children, Worried Parents: Seven Steps to Help Family Mange Anger*. Specialty Press.

Greene, R. (2005). *The Explosive Child* (3rd ed.). Harper Collins.

Hallowell, E., & Ratey, J. (1996). *Driven to Distraction: Recognising and Coping With Attention Deficit Disorder From Childhood Through Adult*. Simon & Schuster.

Lougy, R. A., DeRuvo, S. L. & Rosenthal, R. (2009). *The School Counsellor's Guide to ADHD: What to Know and Do to Help Your Students.* Corwin.

Murphy, T., & Oberlin, L. H. (2002). *The Angry Child: Regaining Control When Your Child is Out of Control.* Three Rivers Press.

Useful Websites:

Australian Guidelines for ADHD – https://www.racp.edu.au/docs/default-source/advocacy-library/pa-australian-guidelines-on-adhd-draft.pdf

Attention Deficit Disorder Association (ADDA) – www.add.org

ADHD Aware – www.adhdaware.org

National Resource Center for ADHD – www.help4add.org

ADDISS – www.addiss.co.uk

ADD Resources – www.addresourcs.org

ADDitude – www.additudemag.com

Canadian ADHD Resources Alliance (CADDRA) – www.caddra.ca

Children and Adults with Attention Deficit Disorder (CHADD) – www.chadd.org

Conduct Disorders – www.conductdisorders.com

Understood – www.understood.org

Supplementary Information

Does My Teen Need Help?

Items	Check
Does your teen struggle with basic family rules and expectations?	
Has your teen ever been suspended, expelled or truant, or had a significant drop in school grades?	
In your opinion, does your teen associate with a bad peer group?	
Has your teen lost interest in former productive activities, such as hobbies and sports?	
Do you have difficulty getting your teen to do simple household chores or homework without a major fight?	
Has your child ever been verbally abusive?	
Has your teen had problems with the law?	
Do you find yourself picking your words carefully when speaking to your teen so as not to elicit a verbal attack or rage from them?	
Are you worried that your teen may not finish high school?	
Does your teen at times seem depressed and/or withdrawn?	
Is your teen's appearance or personal hygiene outside your family standards?	
Has your teen ever displayed violent behaviour?	
Is your teen manipulative or deceitful?	
Does your teen seem to lack motivation?	
Do you suspect that your teen is telling lies or has been dishonest with you?	
Are your concerned that your teen may be sexually promiscuous?	
Have you seen any evidence of suicidal thoughts, such as statements that your teen wanted to be dead?	
Do you suspect that you've had money or other valuables taken from your home?	
Are you concerned that your teen's behaviour is a threat to their safety and wellbeing?	
Does your teen seem to lack self-esteem and self-worth?	
Do you have a lack of trust with your teen?	
Is your teen angry or displaying temper outbursts?	
Does your teen have problems with authority figures?	
Does your teen engage in activities you don't approve of?	

Do you think your teen is experimenting with drugs and/or alcohol?	
Does your teen seem to be in constant opposition to your family values?	
No matter what rules and consequences are established, does your teen defy them?	
Are you exhausted and worn out from your teen's defiant or destructive behaviours and choices?	
When dealing with your teen, do you often feel that you are powerless?	
Are you concerned about your teen's wellbeing and future?	
Total Score	

Based on the number of your checked responses, my recommendations are as follows:

18+ checks = High risk – get help!

Speak to your GP and consider a psychiatric assessment, residential centre treatment may be needed.

9–17 checks = Borderline risk

The problems may be resolved by evaluating your parenting style. Establish the function of your teen's behaviour and try the principles of collaborative parenting (see Dr Greene).

If things do not improve, residential treatment may need to be considered.

Up to 8 checks = Moderate risk

Be consistent with your parenting and monitoring – most importantly, follow through. When you say that something will happen, your teen must see it happen.

The above merely serves as a point of reference in understanding the severity of the challenges your teen is facing. Sometimes these problems are so severe that they can only be addressed by getting professional help in a controlled environment, such as residential centre treatment or alternative educational paths. Other times, problems can be resolved in the home setting by creating more consistency and structure.

Progression of ADHD from Preschool to Adulthood

Although it was previously thought that children eventually outgrow ADHD, studies suggest that a substantial proportion of affected individuals continue to show significant symptoms of the disorder into adulthood. An important consideration in the effective treatment of ADHD is how the disorder affects the daily lives of children, young adults and their families. No longer is it enough to only consider ADHD symptoms during school hours. A thorough assessment of the condition should consider the functioning and wellbeing of the entire family.

As children get older, the way the disorder impacts upon them and their families changes. The core difficulties in executive functioning seen in ADHD result in a different outcome in later life, depending on the demands made on the individual by their environment and the type of coping strategies available. This varies with family and school resources, age, cognitive ability and the level of insight of the individual.

Preschool and early primary (self-esteem)

Poor concentration, high levels of activity, poorly developed self-control and emotional impulsiveness are frequent characteristics of normal preschool children. Consequently, a high level of supervision is the norm. Even so, children with ADHD may still stand out as needing more help. This difference can impact the child's self-esteem negatively. Other associated difficulties, such as delayed development, oppositional/emotional behaviour and poor social skills may also be present. If ADHD is a possibility, it is important to offer parental advice and support in order to improve parent–child interactions and reduce parental stress.

Primary school years (self-esteem, disruptive behaviour, learning delays, poor social skills).

The primary school child with ADHD often begins to show differences from non- ADHD children as they start to develop the skills and maturity that enable them to learn successfully in school, often in the second half of primary school. Although a teacher who is sensitive and understands ADHD may be able to adapt the classroom to help a child with ADHD succeed, frequently the child experiences academic failure, rejection by peers and low self-esteem. Co-morbid problems, such as specific learning difficulties, may also start to impact on the child, further complicating diagnosis and management.

At this age, difficulties at home, on outings to shops and parks, and on visits to family members become more apparent. Other children may not invite them to birthday parties or play dates. Many of these children also have poor sleeping patterns, and although they may appear not to need much sleep, daytime behaviour is often worse when sleep is poorly affected. As a result, parents have little time to themselves; whenever the child is awake, they must be watching them. This contributes to strained family relationships and in some cases even relationship breakdown, bringing additional social and financial difficulties. This may cause children to feel sad or even show oppositional or aggressive behaviour. Although limited attention has been given to siblings' relationships in families of children with ADHD, it has been reported that siblings of children with ADHD are at increased risk for conduct and emotional disorder. In a recent study, siblings reported feeling victimised by aggressive acts from their ADHD brothers through overt acts of physical violence, verbal aggression, manipulation, and control. Furthermore, siblings reported that parents expected them to care for and protect their ADHD siblings because of the social and emotional immaturity associated with the disorder. These siblings also reported feeling anxious, worried and sad.

High school years (oppositional defiant disorder, school exclusion, challenging behaviours, criminal activities, lack of motivation, conduct disorder, complex learning difficulties)

Adolescence may bring about a reduction in the hyperactivity that is often observed in younger children, but impulsivity and inattention, executive function problems and inner restlessness remain major difficulties. A distorted sense of self and a disruption of the normal development of self has been reported by adolescents with ADHD.

A young person who previously tried hard in the face of difficulties may start to give up and may no longer feel that everyday tasks and successes are achievable for them. They may start to be more reliant on 'feel-good' escape behaviours such as gaming and internet use, at the expense of engagement with school or hobbies. Excessively aggressive and antisocial behaviour may develop, along with potentially associations with other young people who have given up on mainstream attainment.

Oppositional defiant disorder, is defined by the presence of defiance, disobedience and provocative behaviour (but without the aggressive and demeaning behaviours that are the hallmark of conduct disorder) and by absence of more aggressive acts that violate the law or rights of others. Studies examining teens with ADHD and oppositional defiant disorder showed increased parent–teen conflict, as well as a severe lack of friendships. This age group is also at risk of academic failure, dropping out of school or college, teenage pregnancy and criminal behaviour. Individuals with ADHD are easily distracted from concentrating on driving, and this poses an additional risk. Studies have shown that when compared with age-matched controls, drivers with ADHD are at increased risk of traffic violations, especially speeding, and are at fault in more traffic accidents, including fatal ones.

Adult life

As many as 50–80% individuals with ADHD symptoms in childhood continue to have difficulties in adult life. Adults with ADHD are more likely to be dismissed from employment and have often tried several jobs before being able to find one in which they can succeed. In the workplace, they experience more interpersonal difficulties with employers and colleagues. Further problems caused by lateness, absenteeism, excessive mistakes, and an inability to prioritise and meet expected workloads and deadlines. At home, relationship difficulties and breakups are more common. The risk of drug and alcohol abuse is significantly increased in adults with ADHD, especially if it is not treated. Also, the genetic aspects of ADHD mean that adults with ADHD are more likely to have children with ADHD. This in turn causes further problems for parents with ADHD who are already tired and overwhelmed. The success of parenting programs for parents with ADHD is highly influenced by parental ADHD. Thus, ADHD in parents and children can lead to a cycle of difficulties.

ADHD Symptoms in Children Vs Adults

Symptoms of inattention in childhood	Symptoms of inattention in adulthood
Has difficulty sustaining attention	Has difficulty sustaining attention to reading or paperwork
Is easily distracted and forgetful	Is easily distracted and forgetful
Does not follow through	Has poor concentration
Cannot organise	Manages time poorly
Loses things	Misplaces things
Does not listen	Has difficulty finishing tasks
Symptoms of hyperactivity in childhood	**Symptoms of hyperactivity in adulthood**
Squirms and fidgets	Shows inner restlessness
Runs or climbs excessively	Fidgets when seated
Cannot play or work quietly	Self-selects active jobs
Talks excessively	Talks excessively
Is always on the go	Feels overwhelmed
Symptoms of impulsivity in childhood	**Symptoms of impulsivity in adulthood**
Blurts out answers	Drives too fast, has traffic accidents
Cannot wait their turn	Impulsively changes jobs
Intrudes on or interrupts others	Is irritable or quick to anger

What Can I Do to Help My Child Cope Better?

While ADHD is believed to be hereditary, effectively managing your child's symptoms can reduce both the severity of the disorder and development of more serious problems over time. Early intervention holds the key to positive outcomes for your child. The earlier you address your child's problems, the more likely you will be able to prevent school and social failure and associated problems such as underachievement and poor self-esteem that may lead to delinquency or drug and alcohol abuse. Having said that, it is never too late to improve the behaviour of your young person and your experience as a family! Although life with your child may at times seem challenging, as a parent you can help create home and school environments that improve your child's chances for success. Let's see how!

- Learn all you can about ADHD. While a great deal of information on the diagnosis and treatment of ADHD is available, not all of it is accurate or based on scientific evidence. It is up to you to be a good consumer and learn to distinguish the accurate information from the inaccurate. How can you sort out what will be useful and what will not? In general, it is good to be wary about ads claiming to 'cure' ADHD. Currently, there is no cure for ADHD, but you can take positive steps to decrease its impact. In addition, pay attention to the source of the information. If you are using the internet, stick with reputable websites. Those that end with (.edu) often have most evidence.

- Don't waste your limited emotional energy on self-blame. ADHD is a neurodevelopmental disorder and is inherited in the majority of cases. It is not caused by poor parenting or a chaotic home environment, despite parents often receiving negative comments, which can be hurtful. However, the home environment can make the symptoms of ADHD better or worse.

- Make sure your child has a comprehensive assessment. The diagnostic process must include medical, educational and psychological evaluations (involving input from your child's teacher). Other disorders that either mimic or co-exist with ADHD such as autism, behavioural/emotional problems, and intellectual or learning disorders must also be considered.

How to Make Life at Home Easier

- Join a support group. Parents will find additional information, as well as support, by attending a support group.

- Seek professional help. Ask for help from mental health professionals, particularly if you are feeling depressed, frustrated or exhausted. Reducing your stress will benefit your child as well.

- Work together. It is important that all the adults that care for your child (parents, grandparents and relatives or carers) agree on how to handle your child's problem behaviours as much as possible. Working with a professional, if needed, can help you better understand how to work together to support your child.

- Learn the tools of successful behaviour management. Behavioural techniques have been widely established as a key component of treatment for children with ADHD. Parent training will teach you strategies to change behaviours and improve your relationship with your child. You can find parent training programs in your community through ADHD Australia, ADHD WA or your family doctor or child's paediatrician.

- Find out if you have ADHD. Since the condition is often inherited, many parents discover that they also have ADHD when their child is diagnosed. Parents with ADHD may need the same types of evaluation and treatment that they seek for their children in order to function at their best. ADHD in the parent may make the home more chaotic and affect a parent's ability to be proactive rather than reactive. Even parents with ADHD traits but no diagnosis may find that they can improve their self-management and the way they structure life for their young person.

How to Help Your Child Succeed at School

- Become an effective case manager. Keep a record of all information about your child. This includes copies of all report cards, teacher notes, disciplinary reports, evaluations and documents from any meetings concerning your child. You might also include information about ADHD, a record of your child's prior treatments and placements, and contact information for the professionals who have worked with your child.

- Form a team that understands ADHD and be the team captain. Meetings at your child's school should be attended by the principal, as well as a special educator and a classroom teacher who knows your child. You have the right to request input at these meetings from others that understand ADHD or your child's special needs. If you have consulted other professionals, such as a psychiatrist, psychologist, educational advocate or behaviour management specialist, the useful information they have provided should also be made available at these meetings. A thorough understanding of your child's strengths and weaknesses and how ADHD affects them will help you and members of the team go on to develop an appropriate and effective program that takes into account their ADHD.

- Become your child's best advocate. You need to represent and protect your child's best interest in school situations, both academic and behavioural. Become an active part of the team that determines what services and placements your child receives in an Individualised Education Plan (IEP).

- Communicate regularly. Adopt a collaborative attitude when working with your child's team. After all, everyone has the same goal – to see your child succeed! Let your child's teachers know if there are some major changes going on in your family, since your child's behaviour can be affected. Invite the teachers to contact you with any issues or concerns before they become a problem. Having open lines of communication between you and the school will help your child.

- Be prepared for it to be an ongoing process, with some ups and downs. You may not get the perfect education plan every year, but working alongside the school and maintaining a good relationship will give your child the best possible chance.

How to Boost Your Child's Confidence

- Set aside a daily special time for you and your child. Constant negative feedback can erode a child's self-esteem. A special time, whether it's an outing, playing games or just positive interactions, free from criticism or placing demands, can help fortify your child against assaults to their self-worth.

- Notice your child's successes, no matter how small. Make an effort to notice when your child is paying attention well or doing what they are supposed to be doing. Tell your child exactly what they did well. This can improve your child's self-esteem and teach them to notice gradual improvements, rather than be too hard on themselves. Celebrating partial successes will provide the motivation to keep trying.

- Tell your child that you love and support them unconditionally. There will be days when you may not believe this yourself. Those will be the days when it is even more important that you acknowledge the difficulties your child constantly faces and express your love. Let your child know that you will get through both the smooth and rough times together.

- Assist your child with social skills. Children with ADHD may be rejected by peers because of hyperactive, impulsive or aggressive behaviours, or not paying attention to social cues the way other children do. Parent training can help you assist your child in making friends and learning to work cooperatively with others.

- Identify your child's strengths and good qualities. Many children with ADHD have strengths in certain areas such as art, athletics, computers or mechanical ability, and lovely qualities such as kindness, creativity or a sense of fun. Build upon these strengths and good qualities, so that your child will have a sense of pride and accomplishment. Make sure that your child has the opportunity to be successful while pursuing these activities, and that their strengths are not undermined by untreated ADHD. Avoid targeting these activities as contingencies for good behaviour, or withholding them as a form of punishment when your child misbehaves.

Helping Your Child Understand Emotions

There are three primary ways we use to refer to our states of mind. These are:

Emotional mind – occurs when our thoughts are being controlled by our emotions. If the emotions are fear or anger, they may keep our thoughts so volatile that we have trouble being reasonable.

Reasonable mind – is when we can think logically and be rational about what is occurring.

Wise mind – is the interception between emotion and reasonable mind. Wise mind is part reason and part emotion. What makes us know we're in this mind is often a sense of intuition.

When one experiences wise mind, we have a sense of stepping back from the situation. For example, we might look at a person and be able to see how they're struggling, but we do not take their struggles personally. Rather, we experience a sense of compassion that makes us want to be validating toward them. Below is a personal experience that helps you understand how these three mind states interplay.

Example:

I have a relative who is extremely self-centered. When I talk to him, he goes on and on talking about himself. Occasionally, he might ask me a question, but never remembers my reply. The only time he remembers what I've said is when it's about him. For many years, I took this personally. I thought he didn't really respect or care about me and only wanted an audience.

Then one day it dawned on me. He was talking, but I had put up a bit of an emotional shield because I was tired of being disappointed. I suddenly saw how sad it was that he couldn't listen to me or anyone else, that his self-esteem was so damaged that in all his social encounters he tried repeatedly to prove that he was okay. I tried to understand what that must feel like, and I saw him with more compassion and didn't get caught up in caring about whether he ever listened to me.

I saw his desperation, and without thought or effort, I began to be more validating. Instead of walking away wounded, I congratulated him for his achievements. When he spoke about problems, I didn't give him suggestions or advice, I just said, 'That must have been very difficult for you.' He stopped trying to pull a response out of me and said, 'That's right. It was. I'm glad you understand.'

This realisation and acceptance without taking it personally is an example of wise mind. Some people experience wise mind when making a decision that they know is absolutely the right thing to do. They know they are in wise mind because they don't have any sense of dread or anxiety. They just 'know' they are doing the right thing. There is absolutely no doubt.

Sometimes, wise mind can be like the calmness that comes after the storm recedes; something experienced immediately following a crisis or enormous chaos. It's about suddenly getting to the heart of the matter, seeing or knowing something directly or clearly. It is grasping the whole picture when only parts were previously understood. It is 'experiencing' the right choice in a dilemma, when the feeling comes from deep within rather than from a current emotional state.

Reflect:

- Which mind state does your child tend to engage with the most – emotional mind, reasonable mind or wise mind? What clues are indicative of this?

Help your child stop taking things personally and respond with their wise mind by:

- not accepting responsibility for someone else's rudeness. When someone is rude it's likely to be a reflection of their own issues.
- taking comments or criticism in a constructive way. Ask whether there's any truth to it, and what can be learned from it.
- taking a different perspective. Ask how someone they trust would see the situation.
- realising that they cannot please everyone.
- understanding that they are not defined by their mistakes or criticism.
- realising that their self-worth depends on them. It does not depend on what others say about them.

Help Your Child Manage Change

Life is filled with new challenges and adventures for young children with ADHD. Change is always happening, and our children have a tough time handling transitions, big or small. They find it hard to process experiences quickly or to shift to new tasks and situations. Getting used to a procedure or routine takes a long time for a child with ADHD, and it can be overwhelming and scary. Their growing brains thrive on structure and consistency, yet they may fight it.

During times of change, children can experience a range of emotions that they may not be able to name or deal with. As parents, we can help them to manage their own feelings of sadness, anger or anxiety when life changes in unexpected ways. When children understand that these feelings are as normal as being happy, they are better able to deal with stressful events, such as when they lose a loved one, a relationship or a job. Your child needs to know that challenging situations might make you feel upset too, but that you can handle these strong emotions. Acknowledging and talking about these feelings shows your child it's okay to feel this way.

Negative emotions may not disappear overnight, but talking about things will help your child to process and accept what's happened, as well as form a 'mental model' of the new routine that their minds can get used to. Children need to be reminded that change is a normal part of life, and that it can help us to develop strengths such as courage, flexibility and resilience. You can also help your child feel like they're not alone and reassure them that this, too, will pass.

Conversation starters:
- You've had a rough time recently. How are you feeling?
- It's hard to fight with friends/lose someone/etc. How are you feeling about it?
- This new classroom seems kinda different, hey. What are the things that are different this year? Is there anything we can practice at home?

Validate Your Child's Feelings

Adults can sometimes be dismissive of young people's reactions to problems, because their problems don't seem like such a big deal to us. Try not to ignore or brush off your child's moods, as it's important that they learn how to process these negative emotions. Mood changes when things aren't going right in their lives are actually a sign of healthy brain activity. They need to feel that you 'get' them, and that what's happening and how they feel about it is valid. There'll be time to reflect on their reaction together later down the track. Encourage them to talk about what's going on, rather than simply encouraging them to 'get over it'.

Help Your Child Figure Out What They Can and Can't Control

When something unexpected or unwanted happens, it's easy to get stuck feeling sad, angry or out of control. A helpful way for your child to cope is to learn how to figure out what they can and can't control. This will help reassure them that they're not powerless and give them something positive to focus on. Work with your child to break down what's happened. For example:

- What we can control: how we treat other people; what activities we do the next day; how we spend our time, what goals we have; who we spend time with; how hard we try to do the best we can, etc.
- What we can't control: losing a loved one; natural disasters; pandemics; how someone has treated us; what others say, what others do, etc.

Accept challenging events

Sometimes, it takes a while to accept events that we have no control over, but acceptance will help us to move on. The feelings of hurt, anger and frustration may return every now and then. Remind your child not to be too hard on themselves, because this reaction is normal and to be expected. Teach them to accept those feelings and to acknowledge that today is a bad day. But also remind them that they've had good days and they'll have them again. You can help your child to accept the changes in their lives by guiding them to identify the positive things that are happening for them.

Try asking your child:

- School has been hard for you this week/month. What are some things that have gone well?
- Let's talk about another time in your life when things felt really hard. What are some of the things that also happened at that time that made you feel good?

Support your child to cope with change

Your child might need help to respond appropriately to changes that have occurred. It might mean a new daily routine or finding time in their existing schedule for an activity that's enjoyable or will give them opportunities for personal development. When it comes to developing a new routine, do you think that they have the skills to manage this independently, or will they need a guiding hand? When learning a brand-new skill, it is common for a child to require reminders, a checklist of their new routine and the steps involved, as well as some rewards and encouragement for times when they have managed the routine or made a good attempt.

Parents can help the child feel supported by providing scaffolding – facilitating learning and making adjustments for executive function weaknesses. It involves demonstrating, teaching and slowly stepping back. The aim is to reach goals that may overwhelm your child at first, and to do so in a gradual and meaningful way.

Look After Yourself, Too!

By staying calm when your child is anxious or upset, you are helping to reduce their stress levels. Remind yourself not to take their stress responses personally, and don't forget that your mental and physical health is important, too. The stronger you are, the better able you will be to help your child. Often, the situations that cause anxiety in our children are also difficult for us. Try to:

- take some time out to maintain your adult friendships
- commit to your own exercise routine
- eat well and model healthy eating (and drinking) habits
- spend time on hobbies, such as reading, arts, sports or volunteering.

By looking after yourself, you'll also be role modelling to your child how you deal with change and tough times. With the right support and time, you can both cope with what's going on.

If You ... Then I

From my clinical experience, children with ADHD have a strong sense of fairness. If this is challenged – be it in a classroom or at home – it can break down trust and build resentment.

> *Be patient with me. Understand why I do the things I do.*
> *Don't yell at me. Believe me, I don't want to have ADHD.*
> **Joane E Richardson**

If you (parent) will...	Then I (child) will...
Give me a chance to explain my thinking	Think through my choices more carefully
Help me take risks by trying exciting new things	Stay away from risks that would get me in trouble
Hear me out respectfully when I have trouble with your rules	Accept your right to set limits on my behaviour
Respect my choices when they only involve my personal taste	Respect your rules when they involve my health or safety
Give me a second chance when I mess up	Try again to live up to your trust
Look for common ground when I disagree	Look for a compromise we can both live with
Focus on the positive, not what I do wrong	Appreciate how much you care about me

Reflect:
- Do any of the statements above resonate with you?

Giving Children the Language to Explain Their ADHD

Helping a child understand ADHD and how it impacts their life is an important aspect of psychoeducation, as it:

- gives children the language/terminology they need to explain their ADHD diagnosis to peers
- helps parents explain their children's condition to family members and friends who may see ADHD as a character flaw
- helps understand the downside of sugarcoating ADHD by calling it a 'superpower' or 'gift'
- helps fathers who may not believe in the diagnosis or think that their child's ADHD-related behaviours are intentional.

Many of the children that I've worked with have never had ADHD explained in a way that gives them a holistic understanding of what ADHD means for them. Often this is because parents take ownership of their condition to the point that they just tag along to doctor appointments and therapy because parents say so. This is quite normal up to a certain age, but there comes a time when the child needs to take responsibility for their condition. This process needs to be gradual, through collaborative problem-solving and management of symptoms and struggles.

My general explanation of ADHD for children (which I modify based on the age and cognitive ability of the child that I am working with) is as follows:

The prefrontal cortex is the operating system of your brain. It's developing a few years slower than the rest of your brain. Everyone's brain has certain things that are easier or harder to learn. The things that your brain finds difficult to learn are not things really taught in school. Let's use the video game analogy.

If you try playing Minecraft on a computer from 2016, it may be glitchy because you're playing on an older operating system. ADHD is kind of the same thing. Your brain's operating system is developing a little behind the rest of your brain so that makes it harder to learn and do certain things. This has nothing to do with what you're good at, your intelligence and what kind of job you'll have one day, etc.

Things that ADHD can make harder for your brain to do:

- Picture things that you have to do in the future (future planning)
- 'Feel' time

- Remember information or emotions from the past and apply it to the present (high insight/episodic memory)
- Consider other people's thoughts about what you're saying or doing (perspective thinking)
- Switch from doing something you like to something you think is boring, like getting off the computer to do a chore

ADHD is a description of how your brain works; it is not your identity or a mental problem.

The role of self-directed talk

Self-directed talk or 'brain coach' is the voice in your brain that helps you:

- Get through tasks that are boring or difficult
- Figure out what you should be doing (without an adult having to tell you what to do)
- Figure out what is a little, medium or big problem
- Think about someone else's thoughts before you say or do things

ADHD turns the volume of your 'brain coach' to very low, making it difficult to understand the issues mentioned above.

The problem with sugar-coating ADHD as a gift

This can be misleading and eventually most children will come to realise that ADHD is no gift, given the challenges it presents, or question the need to take medication to deal with a gift or a superpower.

The message here is to help children understand that we all have strengths and weaknesses, regardless of any medical or mental health condition we may be struggling with. Gifts are talents we naturally have, so when we engage in activities where our natural strengths are, we feel happier and life becomes easier. For this reason, it is especially important for someone with ADHD to explore fields they love, and talents that come naturally to them, when considering a career path.

Language for young children to explain ADHD to their peers

- My brain makes it hard for me to picture what I'm supposed to be doing and to pay attention to things that I'm not interested in.
- ADHD makes it hard for me to think about the future before I do something, that's why I call out a lot in class.
- Sometimes my brain makes it hard for me to figure out the difference between a little problem, a medium problem or a big problem. That's why I get really mad sometimes.

- When you have ADHD, your brain makes it hard for you to pay attention or sit still for anything that you think is boring.

Language for older children:

ADHD means that the operating system part of your brain called the frontal lobe is developing about three years slower than the rest of your brain, so it makes it hard to remind yourself of things you need to do, to get through boring things and think about what you say before you say it.

Explaining ADHD to family members

ADHD is a neurodevelopmental disability. It means that the frontal lobe, the self-control part of the brain, is developing about three years behind the rest of the brain. This means that children with ADHD may have lagging skills in the areas of:

- Emotional regulation
- Their ability to think in a social context
- Resiliency to persevere through non-preferred tasks
- Using self-directed talk (internal dialogue). This all falls under the umbrella term of executive functioning. ADHD should really be called Executive Function Developmental Delay.

You can't speed up development of the frontal lobe by being stricter or punishing a child. It's hard for people to 'see' ADHD-related challenges because people with ADHD look like everyone else.

Fathers who don't believe in ADHD or think it's an excuse

- The existence of ADHD is scientific fact; it is not debatable.
- When we were growing up, ADHD was rarely diagnosed. If it was diagnosed it was rarely talked about or explained to children beyond 'trouble paying attention or sitting still'.
- Not learning about ADHD or denying it exists will most likely impair your relationship with your child.
- I encourage you to watch the videos on the 'ADHD Dude' YouTube channel explaining ADHD. Some of these videos are specifically for fathers.

Discipline Without Raising Your Voice

Whether it's scheduling pit stops or reaffirming your love, here are some strategies that will help you feel less like a tyrant and more like a mum or dad the next time your child needs a wake-up a call.

What Does Your Struggle With ADHD Behaviour Look Like?

You've told your child with ADHD to place their dirty clothes in the laundry. Not a single sock has been placed in the laundry basket. Did they not hear you or did they ignore your discipline?

Annoyed, you shout and feel yourself getting angry and nearing a power struggle. Then the threats start: no mobile for a week, no going out with friends for a month, and whatever else you can think of in your rage. The incident costs everyone dearly. Your child feels angry and demoralised, and you feel like anything but a loving parent. All because of a pile of dirty washing – a pile of clothes in need of a washing machine.

Later that evening, during a quiet moment at the kitchen table, you think back to what happened and what has been happening for months now. You wish you had used more effective communication and question whether you love your child anymore or whether you're a fit parent.

If the above scenario resonates with you, don't feel alone or ashamed. This seems to be the plate of the day in many homes with children with ADHD. You're feeling the emotional turmoil and stinging regret every parent experiences when trying to love and discipline your child. Below are some strategies that will help.

Discuss why it's wrong. Make sure your child understands how their action or inaction has hurt someone or goes against the grain of your expectations. Then ask if they think it would be a good idea to apologise, suggesting that they would probably want the same courtesy extended to them if their feelings had been hurt.

Be reasonable when grounding. If your child or teen abuses a privilege, remove the privilege briefly. Depriving a teen access to their mobile for a month because they exceeded the plan's calling minutes is overkill. They are your child, after all, not a criminal. Withdrawing the privilege for a short time – and allowing your teen to earn it back by developing a credible game plan for not abusing the privilege next time – teaches the necessary lesson.

Say it a couple of ways. Different children respond to direction in different ways. When giving your child a task, such as putting their games away, state it two ways. Say, 'I'd like you to stop leaving your games all over your room. You paid good money for them, and you want to take care of them, right?' Then state the same request in a positive way: 'Please put your games away.' Chances are, they will get the message. Do your own experiment and see what yields the best outcome.

Schedule pit stops. Race car drivers periodically pull their cars into the pit – to change tyres, add fuel, and talk over race strategy with the pit crew. Do the same with your child when things get tense and you feel the urge to yell. Tell them you want to have a pit stop, a private conversation in a quiet area of the home where nobody will interrupt, or better yet, at their favourite coffee place. Scheduling pit stops cuts off an ugly exchange that you will regret later.

Figure out a better way. Turn discipline moments into learning opportunities. Remind your teen that we all make mistakes, then invite them to brainstorm better ways to deal with a similar temptation or stress in the future. Listen to their ideas and value their input. It shouldn't just be your way or the highway. Practice collaborative problem-solving (see liveinbalance.com).

Encourage a redo. When your child messes up, patiently re-enact the situation – doing it the right way. If your child spills a glass of drink while clowning around at the table, have them wipe up the mess and pour another glass. Then ask them to place the glass in a better location on the table and be on their best behaviour.

Take a moment. Breathe and count to ten before opening your mouth; it will short-circuit a great deal of verbal nastiness.

Strengthen the bond. The best discipline combines a firm expectation of how to behave or act, along with basic respect for the worth and dignity of your child. Bedtime tuck-ins, listening to their concerns, empathising with their feelings, and defending your child when necessary all show that you are more than a drill sergeant. You're a loving parent.

Reaffirm your love. Always remind your child, no matter what they've done, how much you love them. Love and leadership are the twin functions of effective parenting. Make it clear that disciplining them doesn't diminish your affection for them. It's the behaviour that you disapprove of, not the child.

How to Stop Doing Everything for Your Children and Teach Responsibility

It is possible to teach responsibility and stop doing everything for your children. Here are three ways to lead your children towards greater independence.

'It's time to get up!' you exclaim for the fourth time, as you stick your head into your thirteen-year-old son's bedroom. Every morning it's a struggle to get him out of bed.

Sometimes he's so resistant you literally have to sit next to him and prod until he puts his feet on the ground. After a number of moans and groans, your son finally complies. But with only twenty minutes before his school bus arrives, he's going to have to move quickly to get out the door in time. As he gets dressed and brushes his teeth, you help him pull his backpack and lunch together. You're tired of this agonising daily routine. It means less time for you to get ready and results in a grumpy start to everyone's day. But, you tell yourself, if you weren't persistent every morning, and he was left to his own devices, your son would sleep the entire morning through.

How to stop doing everything for your children

Many parents assume their children are incapable of being responsible on their own. After all, time and again, it's proven to be true: your daughter frequently forgets her homework at home, your son constantly leaves dirty dishes on the dining room table, and neither seems able to get ready for school on time. So you keep bringing homework to school, putting dishes away, and reminding your children to wake up every morning. You've become so accustomed to doing all these things (and more) that they've simply become part of the routine. Besides, you reason, it's often easier to do these things for your children than struggle to get them to do it themselves. In the past when you've tried to teach responsibility, an argument ensues, the situation doesn't improve, and you're back to managing your children's lives once more. What most parents don't realise is that the way they've tried to teach their children responsibility is hindering progress.

Why nagging and lecturing doesn't teach responsibility

It feels like a primal instinct for parents to nag and lecture their children when they aren't demonstrating the responsibility we expect from them. We assume that if we tell our children what they're doing wrong or constantly remind them of what they need to do, our children will begin to do it for themselves. But this is rarely the case.

Instead, nagging and lecturing are interpreted by children as negative signals that their parents feel they're incapable and incompetent. And this poor assessment of their abilities diminishes any intrinsic desire to do or act better. Even worse, too much nagging can wear down positive communication between parents and children. And if our children are continuously hearing negative messages from us, they'll eventually tune out everything we're saying.

Children act better when they feel better

Jane Nelson, the author of *Positive Discipline*, summed up how parents can promote better behaviour in children – without nagging or lecturing – in this simple statement. No one has the desire to act or be better if they feel poorly about themselves. If we want our children to demonstrate greater responsibility, we'll first need to help them feel capable and competent. It may seem like a tall hill to climb, especially if your child shows zero desire to act responsibly on their own.

But parents can do a number of things to help children get there. These acts may take practice and require some up-front work. But eventually – gradually – children will rise to the challenge. And the benefit for us is that in the long run we can take a few steps back from managing their lives. Here are a few ways you can begin to lead your children toward greater independence and teach responsibility.

Get children involved in solutions

One way to demonstrate to your children that you feel they're capable is to ask them to help solve the issue at hand. Asking our children for help, instead of telling them what to do, sends the message that we believe they're capable of doing better and coming up with a solution. And this sense of empowerment makes children want to do better. Often, younger children will jump at the chance to problem-solve. This age group loves to demonstrate maturity when given the opportunity. Teens and sometimes tweens, on the other hand, may be more reticent. After years of having a parent do things for them, they won't view their lack of responsibility as a problem or even as something they want to fix, so persistence is key.

When to approach children about problem-solving

The best time to get children involved in problem-solving is far from the time when the problem occurs. For example, your son won't be open to finding a solution to waking up on his own if you ask him shortly after he gets out of bed. Instead, talk to him about the issue in the afternoon or evening – during a moment when he's eating a snack or isn't focused on anything else. Better yet, especially if more than one child has trouble waking up in the morning, use your family meeting time (or call a special family meeting) to discuss the issue and come up with solutions together.

How to guide children toward a solution

When you help your child come up with a solution, let them take the lead. Giving children this agency to make decisions will make them more invested in the outcome and motivated to follow through. And children can be excellent problem-solvers when given the chance. Problem-solving will feel more natural to children as it becomes more commonplace and built into your family culture. And as children get more accustomed to problem-solving, they'll grow to appreciate it as a responsibility they're proud to take part in. An important part of this activity is to maintain a respectful, non-accusing tone when talking to your children. Although it's aggravating (to say the least!) that your son doesn't recognise how frustrating it is that you have to remind him to wake up multiple times every morning, blaming him won't teach him how to be more responsible. And it will shut down any desire for him to do better.

Take time to train and then step back

While problem-solving can be a solution in many situations, in some cases it's possible that your child simply needs to be taught how to be more responsible.

Young children, for example, would have no idea what's meant by the phrase 'clean up the playroom' unless a parent showed them how to pick up toys and put them away. And while we can ask children what they think is required to clean up a room to encourage participation, they'll also likely need guidance from us about exactly what to do. Teens, even though they appear to be young adults who should know better, still often need coaching and guidance in skills too – such as time management and organisation. Coaching and teaching children is different than lecturing, since it's an act of working together to help your child learn. And, as always, keeping a respectful tone keeps the discussion from feeling like an accusation.

Here are a few suggested steps to take when training your children in a specific task:

1. As you perform the given task, have your child look on. Explain what you're doing step by step.

2. The next time the task needs to be done, or in the moment, if possible, do it with your child. Or you could do part of the task (such as washing dishes) while they do the other part.

3. When the opportunity arises again, have your child do the task by themselves while you supervise. Be careful at this stage not to point out every mistake being made – that could cause discouragement. Instead, praise when possible and make suggestions that will set them up for success.

4. When your child feels ready, let them perform the task on their own.

Use routines to encourage independence

One other way to teach responsibility and independence in children is through the use of routines. Think of routines as guardrails that help keep children in their lane.

When children have a routine, the need for parents to remind them to do daily tasks diminishes and simply becomes more…routine.

While young children usually can't be expected to follow a routine independently, a routine can lessen power struggles such as when it's time to brush teeth, take a nap or get ready for bed. The comfort of knowing what comes next in a day's rhythm is often all a child needs to cooperate.

Another way to encourage children's participation in a routine is to get them involved in creating it. Being given that responsibility, children feel more in control, which inspires greater willingness to follow through.

Our patience and respectful guidance will help ensure children's success as they get used to following a routine. You may even eventually find that your children will begin to develop routines of their own.

Lessons learnt from mistakes and setbacks, long term

Even after we help children problem-solve, take time for training, and get children started on routines, our children will still likely make mistakes and occasionally be irresponsible.

And that's OK.

Our children are learning responsibility and, as with any endeavour, there will be setbacks along the way.

It's helpful to reflect on our own lives and the time we were late picking up our daughter from ballet or accidentally slept past our alarm.

Mistakes happen.

Remember that everyone, including our children, learns from mistakes. While our children will make mistakes – as painful as it is for us to see – it's the long-term progress that's important.

Sometimes big leaps in responsibility happen when a mistake occurs, the painful consequences are felt, and our child determines they never want to repeat that experience again.

Keep this in mind too when it's tempting to save your child from failure. Because, believe me, we've all had moments when deep in our hearts we want to save our children from experiencing the discomfort of failure.

But if we don't let our children work through their mistakes now, in childhood, we'll likely find that they need to endure them as adults when the stakes are often higher.

Make sure your identity isn't wrapped up in your child's life

One other trap to be mindful of when letting go and handing over more responsibility to your child is to make sure your identity isn't wrapped up in your child's life.

It feels good to feel loved and needed and necessary. Each time our child takes on more responsibility and becomes more independent, it means they need us less, and that realisation can be painful.

But the truth is that the most loving thing we can do for our children is to prepare them for the world they'll face without us. And the more we coach and train them and show our confidence in their ability, the more they'll willingly take on more responsibility.

Teaching Children to Problem-Solve Makes Parenting Easier

Strong problem-solving skills are essential for our children to navigate the world independently. And as our children grow in their ability to problem-solve, they'll demonstrate greater autonomy and responsibility, making parenting easier.

'Mum, I forgot my maths homework today', your son says shortly after coming home from school.

Your stomach sinks because, unfortunately, this isn't the first time he's left homework at home – and his grades are starting to reflect this habit.

Given your son's lack of organisation and lack of cleanliness in his room, it's not surprising that his homework was misplaced in the shuffle. You've talked to him a number of times about the benefits of a tidy room, to no avail.

So, it's frustrating to once again see the natural consequence of his disorganisation – and more than tempting to point out that if he was better organised this wouldn't happen.

But you also recognise there's also an opportunity in this challenge – a chance to help your son practice his problem-solving skills and grow independently to find solutions.

Daily challenges are opportunities for teaching children problem-solving skills

Nearly every day our children present challenges to us that need a solution.

Whether it's living in a messy and disorganised room, forgetting to pack sports clothes the night before practice, or eating chocolate on your white couch and leaving stains, you're almost always facing a challenge.

For most parents, the natural reaction to these issues is (naturally) frustration, irritation and general disappointment. Especially if we've repeatedly reminded our children to clean their rooms, pack their sports clothes the night before, and never eat chocolate in the living room.

But if we take a step back and consider what's really happening when our children face these challenges (or create them), we can not only take advantage of an opportunity to help them learn, but also gradually make it easier to parent them.

Here's why: the more we teach our children problem-solving skills to find solutions to their challenges, the more we're setting them up for greater self-sufficiency. With practice, our children can begin to solve their own problems independently. And at the same time, as we eschew traditional consequences or punishment and instead focus on teaching and solutions in our discipline, we avoid arguments and power struggles with our children.

Parenting mindsets that get in the way of teaching children to problem-solve

But before diving into how to encourage our children to problem-solve, it's important to point out that our culture and society is ripe with mindsets that would have us do otherwise.

One of the most common parenting mindsets is that children must 'pay,' or rather, be punished, for their mistakes or wrongdoing. The thinking is that parents shouldn't let children 'get away' with bad behaviour and children will only learn if they're made to suffer.

It can be especially tempting to take on this mindset when children have done something that we've told them endless times not to do, like eat chocolate on our white couch. Or their behaviour has triggered a heightened sense of annoyance or frustration in us such as creating a mess or arguing with a sibling.

Making children 'pay' for their wrongdoing – or, in other words, suffer – is punishment. And research shows that punishment not only doesn't teach children better behaviour, it can also exacerbate the behaviour by making children feel bad or revengeful.

One other mindset that keeps modern-day parents from encouraging children to problem-solve is the belief that children are incapable of coming up with solutions on their own.

But history and even other cultures prove that children are very capable of coming up with their own solutions. And the more we encourage children to think for themselves, the better they'll be at problem-solving independently.

Is Fibbing Just a Self-Preservation Strategy?

Fibbing – Character Flaw or Self-Preservation?

Many parents are appalled at the idea of their child lying to them. It smacks of deception and manipulation and leads you to worry that you can't trust anything your child says. Most parents aim to raise good, upstanding citizens, and take it as a personal failure when they catch their child consistently lying to them.

As with many behaviours, it is important to take a breath and a step back and investigate untruthfulness, to find out what triggers the behaviour and what the payoff is for the child.

Many are familiar with the concept of fight or flight as a response to danger. Adrenaline pumps around the body and prepares us to either run away or fight back. A third response is to freeze, also known as reactive immobility, which causes stillness in the face of a perceived threat.

The key component of the fight–flight–freeze response is that it is an automatic response and is outside voluntary control. Perceiving danger, the body sends the signals to prepare for the actions required to ensure safety. What happens as a response to the threat is instinctive and is carried out without thought.

As psychologists continue to study this phenomenon, they have identified other responses to this acute stress response, namely fawn and fib. The fawn response involves displaying appeasing behaviours designed to please, thereby averting the threat. Fibbing similarly averts the danger by turning aside threatening attention and allowing a temporary reprieve. In evolutionary terms, it is a new line of self-defence achieved through language.

Rather than demonstrating a flawed character or a pattern of deception, fibbing in an individual with ADHD may be an impulsive action rooted in poor EF skills, a lack of inhibition and emotional regulation, and deficits in working memory and attention.

Understanding the reasons behind your ADHD child's fibbing is essential in finding the best way to deal with this issue. As the fib is not a conscious action, counteracting the impulse involves investigating what happened before the lie, and how the child could have steered the situation to make the lie unnecessary. The fib is a fear response when confronted with real or perceived danger. Harsh disciplinary tactics will merely underline the child's feeling of danger, making it more likely that lying will continue.

Remember that the child has usually not chosen to lie. It is an impulsive attempt to escape from fear, embarrassment, judgment, guilt, or shame. The fib is designed to preserve self-worth and avoid a reduction in self-esteem resulting from a failure.

Overcoming the tendency to lie requires a gentle touch, acknowledging the child's awareness of danger and helping them examine their own response to it. Providing a safe space and time for them to process what has happened and how it led them into the fibbing behaviour can help lead them towards a better response in similar situations in the future. See the fibbing as a symptom rather than a behaviour, so you can help the child manage the symptom instead of punishing a bad behaviour.

Mindfulness practice can increase the child's ability to remain calm in stressful situations and look for a truthful way to respond rather than react. Talking through what you see and hear from your child, giving them time and space to evaluate what is happening and how they can respond to it, will also help your child learn appropriate ways to deal with the perceived threat without resorting to fibbing.

When Consequences Don't Work – and What Will

Consequences have become something of a buzzword in parenting circles. Rather than punishing a child by sending them to their room or using physical punishment, parents now feel they are teaching their child a lesson by using consequences, setting up situations so the child will feel the ramifications of their behaviour.

What often trips parents up is not understanding that the 'consequences' they impose on their children are actually disguised punishments instead of logical consequences. Rather than teaching children, they make them feel bad about themselves and unhappy with the parent. This damages the parent–child relationship, making it harder for the parent to really teach the child anything, and makes it more likely that the child will misbehave or be defiant in the long run. This is why these sorts of 'consequences' ultimately don't work.

Fortunately, there are other ways to parent, using positive discipline techniques, which teach and empower children, and inspire them to want to do better. Here are some tools you can use instead of imposing consequences. The more you use these tools while remaining positive and respectful, the more your children will want to behave better and be more willing to cooperate.

Set a routine. Creating a routine for when it's time to get dressed, eat a meal, brush teeth, or start and stop an activity, can mean less resistance because everyone knows what's expected of them. Many people, adults and children alike, dislike being taken by surprise. In addition, those with ADHD can struggle with transitions and change.

Develop understanding and problem-solving. Sometimes you can feel that your child is being defiant or disobedient, when in fact they just don't know how to behave properly. Children, especially those with ADHD, may have more problems with compliance when there are multiple steps involved. Instructing a child to clean their room when they don't know the steps to follow or being angry with a child who can't get ready on time in the morning is unlikely to be effective, and needs a change in both attitude and approach.

Work with the child to come up with a solution. Ask for their thoughts on how to solve the problem and keep it from being an issue in the future. Help them create a procedure or routine that works for them, and they are more likely to follow it and improve their behaviour.

Family meeting. Many problems can be solved through effective communication, and family meetings offer an excellent forum for communication, problem-solving, and allowing all members of the family to have their voices heard.

Limiting choices. Overwhelming situations can be defused or de-escalated by reducing the available choices. Rather than telling the child what to do, offer them a limited choice between two or three options that are acceptable to you. If your child struggles with getting dressed and can't decide what to wear, or objects to what you tell them to wear, offering a choice of two outfits can make the decision easier. Reducing the number of toys available to play with can make cleaning up easier.

Get them involved and feeling useful. Many a parent has found shopping trips to be less stressful when the children are helping. Give them a list of items to collect, even let them have their own basket or child's trolley if available. Give them some agency over how things are done, such as choosing whether to go to the post office or the park first.

Model self-control. Telling your child what to do invites a power struggle. Instead, tell them what you will do and how it will affect them. For example, if you are doing laundry you could say: 'I'm going to wash the clothing that you bring to the laundry. If you don't bring it to the laundry, you will not have any clean clothes.' Or when your child is yelling at you, you could calmly state, 'I want to hear what you have to say but I don't talk to people who yell at me.' Just be sure that the message isn't delivered to try to shame the child. It should simply be a calm explanation of your own values.

Earning privileges with responsibility. Children should be taught to treat their belongings with respect, use them appropriately and know that they will be taken away if they do not follow through on this. It is very important not to confuse this lesson in responsibility with taking away privileges as a punishment. Taking away a mobile phone because curfew wasn't obeyed is a punishment, not a logical outcome of the behaviour.

When Logical Consequences Do Work!

Logical consequences, when used correctly, are an effective way to teach a child a lesson and lead them toward better behaviour. For the consequence to truly be positive, effective and non-punitive, it must have the following characteristics:

It's related to the situation. For example, after a child draws on a wall with a crayon, a related consequence would be cleaning the crayon marks off the wall.

It's respectful. Consequences that are condescending, humiliating, cause pain or come across as bossy are not respectful.

It's reasonable. Having a child clean the crayon off the wall and also wash the floor and windows is not a reasonable consequence.

It's revealed in advance. Sometimes if a consequence isn't revealed in advance, it can easily be misconstrued as a punishment. Whenever possible, a parent should set expectations in advance, so the child is aware of the consequence of their actions.

Natural consequences in parenting

Outside of logical consequences that are externally imposed, children also sometimes face natural consequences, i.e. situations that follow naturally from a choice the child makes.

An example of a natural consequence is when a child leaves their lunch money at home and has no lunch to eat. Another example is a teen who procrastinates studying for a test and receives a bad grade.

If the child or teen facing the natural consequence isn't saved by an adult's interference, they'll likely learn a deep lesson that will stay with them as they grow and mature.

When thinking about the parenting tools you employ, always keep in mind your ultimate goal – to help your children develop independence and self-reliance.

How to Disengage From a Power Struggle With Your Child

It is a power struggle when:

- you are feeling controlled or the need to control
- either of you is arguing, blaming, demanding or being disrespectful
- you feel the need to win.

Don't argue when your child starts to argue about the facts – when, why, where etc. – don't get pulled in. Refuse to argue.

Give effective commands

- Make sure you mean it.
- Do not present the command as a question or favour.
- Do not give to many commands at once.
- Tell the child what **to do** rather than what **not to do**.
- Be realistic about commands that involve the concept of time.
- Say exactly what needs to happen in a short and clear way; for example, 'You need to complete all of your homework before you get you 20 minutes of screen time'.

Don't take your child's resistance or anger personally

Remember, your child is just trying to change your mind so they can have or do what they want. The child is using tactics that have probably worked in the past (or that they have seen work for others).

Ignore attempts to rope you in

Let your child know, 'I am not going to talk about it anymore. I am going to ignore you if you continue to argue about it.' Engage yourself in another activity.

Talk about the problem later, when you are both calm

Bring up the discussion again later when you have some relaxed time together. Use skills you have learned to talk about the problem, such as problem solving, listening, and acknowledging feelings.

Ask yourself: Is this something I am willing to negotiate about?

If the situation is something you are willing to negotiate about, let your child know. 'Let's talk about how we can meet halfway on this'. Calming thoughts for you, the parent, include:

- I cannot control their behaviour, but I can control my behaviour.
- I don't have to deal with this right now; it will only make it worse.
- They are responsible for their feelings.
- They are responsible for their behaviour.
- Let it go for now. I can talk about it later when we are both calm.
- I am calm and in control.
- I will go into another room and take some deep breaths.
- I don't have to engage in this battle. I can take a time-out, calm down and think about how I want to communicate.
- I don't have to 'win'.
- The strongest influence I can have with my child is to model the behaviour I want them to learn.

Time-out for You, the Parent

A time-out is a constructive way to try to solve problems in your family. It is a way each family member can take responsibility for their actions. When your teen is starting to use abusive behaviours (name calling, yelling, put-downs or anything physical), taking

259

your own time-out lets your teen know that you refuse to engage in abusive behaviour and that abuse will not be tolerated. If done right, a time-out can:

- help you stay calm
- help you make good decisions
- help you find better ways to set limits with your children
- help to reduce conflict in your family
- increase the understanding in your family.

Identifying your own red flags

Paying attention to your own red flags will help you know when you need to take a time out. Red flags include:

- body signs such as feeling tense, stomach-ache, headache or shoulder tension
- emotions such as anger, frustration or revenge
- thoughts like 'he's not going to get away with this', 'she's a selfish brat'.
- verbal signs such as saying hurtful things, put-downs or criticism
- actions like pointing your finger, getting too close to the person or slamming your fist.

When a Child is Abusive: Effects on Parenting

Many parents believe they are at fault for their child's behaviour. It is important for you to remember:

- Your child is responsible for their behaviour.
- Your thoughts and feelings can affect your parenting.
- Changing the way you think about a situation can help you respond in more effective ways.

Change your thinking

Irrational beliefs are common for parents. A professional can help you identify and modify unrealistic expectations and distorted attributions by following these four steps:

- Identify the extreme thought.
- Provide a logical challenge to the extreme thought.
- Help the family member identify an alternative, more realistic thought.
- Help the family member explore evidence to disconfirm the extreme thought and confirm the more reasonable thought.

For example:

Irrational thought: 'I should be able to control them.'

Rational thought: 'I can help them make good choices through incentives and consequences, but they are in charge of their behaviour.'

Keep your child's developmental level in mind. Remember that your 13-year-old with ADHD may developmentally be a 9-year-old. Your expectations need to be appropriate to your child's developmental age, not his or her chronological age.

Finally, parenting a child with ADHD requires patience and endurance. Be sure you have support from those around you. Find time to take a break for yourself. Take a step back, look for positive changes and remind yourself that this task is always going to be 'a work in progress'.

Strategies for the Different Learning Styles

Strategies for Visual Learners

Visual learners learn best by seeing, or watching others do something before they try it themselves.

- Organising work and living space to avoid distractions.
- Sitting in the front of the room to avoid distraction, and away from doors or windows where action takes place. Sitting away from wall maps or bulletin boards.
- Using neatly organised or typed material.
- Using visual association, visual imagery, written repetition, flash cards, and clustering strategies for improved memory.
- Reconstructing images in different ways, trying different spatial arrangements and taking advantage of blank spaces on the page.
- Using note pads, To Do lists, and other forms of reminders.
- Using organisational format outlining for recording notes. Use underlining, highlighting in different colours, symbols, flow charts, graphs or pictures in notes.
- Practising turning visual cues back into words as you prepare for exams.
- Allowing enough time for planning and recording thoughts when doing problem-solving tasks.
- Using test preparation strategies that emphasise organisation of information and visual encoding and recall.
- Participating actively in class or group activities.
- Developing written or pictorial outlines of responses before answering essay questions.

Strategies for Auditory Learners

Auditory learners learn best by listening to instructions before they try it themselves.

- Working in quiet areas to reduce distractions, avoiding areas with conversation, music, and television.
- Sitting away from doors or windows where noises distract you.
- Rehearsing information orally.

- Attending lectures and tutorials regularly.
- Discussing topics with other students, siblings and parents. Ask others to hear your understanding of the material.
- Using mnemonics, rhymes, jingles, and auditory repetition through audio recording to improve memory.
- Practising verbal interaction to improve motivation and self-monitoring.
- Using audio recorders to document lectures and for reading materials
- Remembering to examine illustrations in textbooks and convert them into verbal descriptions.
- Reading the directions for tests or assignments aloud, or have someone read them to you, especially if the directions are long and complicated.
- Reminding yourself to review details.
- Leaving spaces in your lecture notes for later recall and 'filing'. Expand your notes by talking with others and collecting notes from the textbook.
- Reading your notes aloud.

Strategies for Kinaesthetic Learners

Kinaesthetic learners learn best if they are involved directly in whatever is being taught/done.

- Keeping verbal discourse short and to the point.
- Participate in discussions.
- Using all your senses: sight, touch, taste, smell, hearing.
- Using direct involvement, physical manipulation, imagery, and 'hands-on' activities to improve motivation, interest, and memory.
- Organising information into the steps that were used to physically complete a task.
- Seeking out courses that have laboratories, field trips, etc. and lecturers who give real life examples.
- Using case studies and applications (example) to help with principles and abstract concepts.
- Allowing for physical action in solving problems.
- Reading or summarising directions, especially if they are lengthy and complicated, to discourage starting a task without instructions.
- Using taped reading materials.
- Using practice, play acting, and modelling to prepare for tests.

- Allowing for physical movement and periodic breaks during tests, while reading, or while composing written assignments.
- Role playing the exam situation.
- Teaching the material to someone else.
- Writing practice answers, paragraphs or essays.

Classroom Accommodations For Common ADHD Challenges

Adapted from: Bob Seay & Sharon Saline, Psy.D

Students with ADHD often benefit from special accommodations. When teachers and parents spend thoughtful time pinpointing problematic ADHD symptoms and work together to devise classroom accommodations, they create effective solutions to those problems. The best IEP is the one with accommodations designed for your child's very specific symptoms.

Following is a list of common challenges faced by students with ADHD, and the accommodations that can help bring success at school.

1. **Classroom setup accommodations for ADHD**

   If your child: Is easily distracted by classroom activity or by activity visible through door or windows

   Try: Seating the student front and centre, away from distractions

   If your child: Acts out in class to gain negative attention

   Try: Seating the student near a good role model

   If your child: Is unaware of personal space; reaches across desks to talk to or touch other students

   Try: Increasing distance between desks

2. **Assignment accommodations for ADHD**

   If your child: Is unable to complete work within given time

   Try: Allowing extra time to complete assigned work

   If your child: Does well at the beginning of an assignment but quality of work decreases toward the end

   Try: Breaking long assignments into smaller parts; shorten assignments or work periods

   If your child: Has difficulty following instructions

   Try: Pairing written instructions with oral instructions

3. **Distractibility Accommodations for ADHD**

   If your child: Is unable to keep up during classroom discussions and/or take notes effectively

Try: Providing peer assistance in note taking and ask student questions to encourage participation in discussions

If your child: Complains that lessons are boring

Try: Seeking to involve student in lesson presentation

If your child: Is easily distracted

Try: Cuing your student to stay on task with a private signal

If your child: Turns in work with careless mistakes

Try: Scheduling a five-minute period to check over work before turning in homework or tests

4. Behaviour accommodations for ADHD

If your child: Is constantly engaging in attention-getting behaviour

Try: Ignoring minor inappropriate behaviour

If your child: Fails to 'see the point' of a lesson or activity

Try: Increasing immediacy of rewards and consequences

If your child: Blurts out answers or interrupts others

Try: Acknowledging correct answers only when hand is raised and student is called upon

If your child: Needs positive reinforcement

Try: Sending daily/weekly progress reports home

If your child: Needs long-term help with improving behaviour

Try: Setting up a behaviour contract

5. Organisation/Planning Accommodations for ADHD

If your child: Can't keep track of papers

Try: Recommending binders with dividers and folders

If your child: Has trouble remembering homework assignments

Try: Providing student with assignment book; supervise writing down of assignments

If your child: Loses books

Try: Allowing the student to keep a set of books at home

If your child: Is restless and needs to move around

Try: Allowing the student to run errands or to stand at times while working

If your child: Has difficulty focusing for long periods of time

Try: Providing short breaks between assignments

6. **Social Accommodations for ADHD**

If your child: Is unclear about appropriate social behaviours

Try: Setting up social-behaviour goals with student and implement a reward program

If your child: Does not work well with others

Try: Encouraging co-operative learning tasks

If your child: Is not respected by peers

Try: Assigning special responsibilities to the student in presence of peer group

If your child: Has low self-confidence

Try: Complimenting positive behaviour and work; give student opportunity to act in leadership role

If your child: Appears lonely or withdrawn

Try: Encouraging social interactions with classmates; plan teacher-directed group activities

If your child: Is easily frustrated

Try: Acknowledging appropriate behaviour and good work frequently

If your child: Is easily angered

Try: Encouraging the student to walk away from angering situations; spend time talking to student

How to Guide and Not Carry Your Child Toward Fulfilment

———○———

Your job as a parent is not to sculpt your child to fulfil your own expectations, but to be a guide, supervisor, provider, nurturer, and protector of their unique gifts and strengths. Use the 'shepherd' parenting style and these eight strategies for raising happy children and well-adjusted adults.
Russell Barkley, Ph.D.

Your child is a unique being with a distinct mix of strengths and weaknesses. As a parent, you get the chance to shepherd – not carry – your child into adulthood by understanding their patchwork of developed and still-developing executive functions. This steering takes place indirectly, primarily through the environment in which you raise your child with ADHD and the resources you provide.

The 'Good Shepherd' Parenting Style

1. Provide protection

Job one of parents is obviously to protect their child from disreputable forces at play in their homes, neighbourhoods, schools, and communities.

Children with ADHD are three to five times more likely than other children to endure accidental injuries and poisonings; to experience bullying, victimisation, and physical and emotional abuse at the hands of other children and adults; and to generally get into more trouble because of their affinity for risk-taking and sensation-seeking. They are also nearly twice as likely to die from an accidental injury before age 10. Most parents are psychologically wired to engage in this protective behaviour instinctively. These protective efforts are especially important for parents of children with ADHD.

2. Find the right environment

Do whatever you can to find the best neighbourhood in which to raise your child. Not all of us have a lot of choices, but we usually have some discretion.

- Does your neighbourhood provide good-quality schools, pro-social peers, and adults who can be good role models?
- Are there resources that can foster your child's physical and social development, like sports, clubs, scouts, and church groups?

Judith Harris wrote in *The Nurture Assumption* that where you choose to buy or rent a home has more to do with your child's development than what you are likely to do inside of it. Find the best neighbourhood that you can reasonably afford. Then, monitor your child's relationships, and steer them toward friendships with well-adjusted and inspiring peers.

3. **Engineer quality time**

    The younger your child, the more your interactions with them matter. Predictable, supportive, rewarding, and stimulating interactions with your child help them become better adjusted and more confident and competent.

    Make your home's rules, routines, family rituals, and other activities reasonably predictable, and as pleasant and respectful as you can. Keep your interactions with your child stable, not chaotic, emotional, capricious, or disparaging. And lastly, never be psychologically absent or uninvolved. Stay engaged.

4. **Find accommodations**

    Make adjustments as needed to accommodate your child's needs and executive dysfunctions. You can reduce the hurdles that come with ADHD by changing the environment. For instance, you might have your child do their English homework at the kitchen table while you are preparing dinner. That way, you can set a timer for completing a small quota of problems, allow short breaks from work, and dispense encouragement and approval throughout. Touch them affectionately on the shoulder occasionally as a sign of approval. Reward them with their choice of dessert after dinner.

    Doing so in no way changes your child's degree of ADHD impairment, but it does make it more likely that they will complete the assignment than if they had been sitting in her bedroom, with no break, working unsupervised.

5. **Adopt a child's eye**

    Look for ways to change your child's settings to make them more educational, stimulating, or fun to be in and interact with. Adding a swing set to the backyard, more books in the bedroom, more educational toys, DVDs, video games, and more sports gear to the home environment will have a positive impact on a child's development.

6. **Prioritise nutrition and nourishment**

    Take a close look at what your child eats to make sure the foods are contributing to health and wellness. Is it slanted toward junk, starchy, sugar-laden foods and beverages? On average, children with ADHD eat less nutritiously than typical children. We think that is because junk foods are what a child with ADHD will make less of a fuss about eating. This has led to the risk of health problems among children with ADHD that increases with age.

Try to provide access to balanced and nutritious foods; reduce and remove the less nutritious ones from the house. Some children with ADHD have vitamin (usually D), omega 3 or 6, or iron deficiencies that could be addressed through foods. A small percentage have allergies to food colourings that can worsen their ADHD symptoms. Ask your paediatrician if this might be the case and take steps to improve these deficiencies and allergies.

7. Provide consistent and predictable routines

- Are the family's morning routines consistent and effective at getting your child prepared and out the door for school?
- Are your dinnertime and evening routines fairly consistent as to when you eat, do homework, prepare your children's things for the next day, bathe or shower, brush their teeth, and get them off to bed?

The routines of ADHD families are often inconsistent and chaotic, which can lead to poor health, increased stress, and impaired coping abilities. Worse, it can sow the seeds for oppositional and defiant behaviour in children.

8. Take good care of yourself

You can't be your best at raising your child if you have health problems, emotional distress, or general life stress.

Assess your habits:

- Do you use alcohol or other substances excessively? Do you eat nutritious meals?
- Are you exercising enough to remain in good physical and mental shape?
- Are you getting enough sleep to avoid being a fog-brained, irritable, emotionally brittle, or spaced-out shepherd?
- What are you doing to recharge your emotional batteries, so you can cope with and shepherd your child with ADHD? Don't skimp on emotional self-maintenance while trying to be the best shepherd you can be.

If you have concentrated on improving in the areas above, you have done as much as you can to be a good shepherd. The rest is largely out of your power to control. You can raise a unique individual and build a close and supportive relationship that will last a lifetime. Having done your best, enjoy the show!

ADHD In College/University

The Case for Gap Years

Not every teen is ready to fly the nest. Many could benefit from a few more years of transition into adulthood. Here's how to nurture and instil independence in your teen – without helicoptering or overwhelming them.
Wes Crenshaw, Ph.D.

Research tells us that children with ADHD are between 2–4 years behind their peers in maturity and self-regulation. At no time is this more apparent and challenging than graduation from high school, college, or trade school. According to Stanford University Dean Julie Lythcott-Haims, every 18-year-old should have the following skills in order to manoeuver these transitions:

- Talking to strangers (not fearing them)
- Finding their way around (including maintaining a car)
- Managing assignments, workload, and deadlines
- Contributing to the running of a household
- Resolving interpersonal problems
- Coping with the many ups and downs inherent to adulthood
- Earning and managing money
- Taking appropriate risks

After 24 years of practice, and helping several thousand young adult clients set out into the real world – and with one of her own about to finish community college – Lythcott-Haims says that most children with ADHD struggle with all eight skills mentioned above. She adds that although medication and therapy can help, it cannot make up for the three- or four-year maturity gap, but that families can improve their child's odds of making a successful jump from teen to adult. Throughout adolescence, give your child focused training for independent living. Many parents give children with ADHD a pass on expectations. They feel sorry for them, don't want to overwhelm them, or see enforcing expectations as too much work for too little gain. Don't set children up to fail by overloading them with agenda items, but focus your energy on the key skills of successful living and make them applicable to the child's daily life. Lythcott-Haims suggests the following:

1. **Dollars and sense.**

   There are many ways for children fresh out of school to go wrong financially. At the top of the list is to incur debt. Student loans, in particular, are seductive, as they offer deferred payment and let the borrower ignore exorbitant interest. While educational investment can pay off big, that's true only if your child actually finishes a degree in an area of study that leads to gainful employment. Young people also overspend on car loans and apartment costs. Daily dining out is a huge financial drain, which children don't realise because the bills come in small increments.

   Solution: From middle school on, parents should train children for smarter spending by starting them on strict budgets, dispensing a set amount of money each month to buy everything they need, from toothpaste to clothing, and letting them manage (mostly). This takes getting used to by both parties, and you'll have a few failures along the way, but it beats being an ATM parent, especially with children with ADHD. Beyond budgeting, I suggest giving children almost nothing for free, except on special occasions. Instead, offer children opportunities to earn money with work-like tasks. To teach credit management, loan your children money (no, really) at a fair market rate of interest. Begin with small loans and extend greater credit only when they are repaid. This can be done from a fairly young age and teaches them lifelong skills. 'My dad did this since I was 12. I'm now 45 and have had to access credit for many things in my life but have never defaulted on a loan. If I had, I wouldn't have gotten another one,' said a client of mine.

2. **Career ladders.**

   It's ridiculous to expect 18-year-olds to know what they want to do for the rest of their lives, yet parents keep asking, 'What do you want to be when you grow up?' Expect children to work as soon as they are able, even if they don't get paid initially. There are many volunteer opportunities in most communities, where younger teens can get simulated work experience. Some parents pay their children to volunteer as part of their financial arrangement, which I strongly encourage. While children should be students first, having no work expectation for them isn't a gift, it's a burden that will make their transition to adulthood harder and their career choice ill-informed.

   Solution. Talking about, and having your child study and experience, different careers as soon as you can get them interested. Think about what makes your child unique, particularly how ADHD may enhance some careers and not others, and help them think it through, too.

3. **Self-regulation.**

This can be the toughest transition of all. There are more self-care tasks than most children realise before moving out and taking them over. The first occurs when the alarm clock goes off each morning and your child hits snooze twenty-three times. At home the standard response is to wake the child up, which, if they aren't big on school attendance, may be necessary.

Solution. Move the responsibility from your shoulders to your child's, beginning with perhaps one day a week and working from there. It's usually better to have eighteen absentees a semester and one day of self-dysregulation a week than perfect attendance courtesy of the parent.

4. **Meal-planning.**

Feeding oneself is more complicated than children realise, particularly if they're used to food appearing magically on the dining room table or being handed out of a drive-through window.

What to do: Have your child run the kitchen one night a week beginning in middle school. If you can't do this without incentive, move some of your dining-out money over to your child's 'restaurant' and pay them to cook and serve dinner. Leave a tip if you think the service was good. This is more than an exercise in self-care and nutrition. A lot of children make their way for a few years in the food service industry, and this kind of practice can give them an edge when they are there.

5. **Medication and treatment.**

In our office we take teen preferences seriously in planning medication and therapy. If we can't reach an informed agreement, we won't see them – though that rarely happens. Aside from getting buy-in about the treatment plan and improving the clients' experience, we're training them to have a serious interest in and keen understanding of what we're doing and why we're doing it. They can take over when they're out on their own.

Solution: You can do the same thing by involving your child in the process of treatment with providers who have the same philosophy.

If you've gotten an accurate diagnosis, your child's transition to adulthood will be different than it is for people without ADHD. If you plan ahead and keep planning, that's all it will be – different, not impairing.

Gender, Sexuality and ADHD

In recent years, a spotlight has been shone on the topic of gender identity, a topic that has often been misunderstood, dismissed or ridiculed. Parenting in today's society means being aware of the issues surrounding gender identity and how these issues affect your child and family.

During adolescence and young adulthood, many issues of identity will be explored and investigated. These may include morals and values, beliefs around race, religious and cultural practices, career paths, and gender and sexuality. The challenges inherent in ADHD can give these issues an extra layer of complexity.

Gender identity has always been a huge factor in self-identity. Gender roles and expectations are deeply embedded in many people's consciousness. The first question asked to those expecting a child is often, 'Do you know if it's a boy or a girl?' Gender-reveal parties become more extravagant by the day. Sports and school rolls are separated by gender, with expectations of behaviour, dress and preferences attached to the separation. It is still not common to speak about or to others without the use of gendered pronouns. In the face of all of this, the notion of questioning the gender assigned to you at birth can be daunting to face, let alone announce to the world.

If your child approaches you with concerns about gender identity, it is important to listen with compassion and an open mind. Opening up the conversation has taken immense courage on your child's part, and their concerns about this matter should be treated with as much love, respect and support as every other challenge you have faced together as parent and child.

As with any other issue you have experienced with your child, it is vital to educate yourself so that you can offer balanced, steady guidance through this rocky area, while preserving your child's already fragile self-esteem. The language surrounding the issue is especially important to understand and use correctly.

The distinction between biological sex and gender is often misunderstood, and these terms may be used incorrectly.

Biological sex refers to the characteristics which classify an individual as female, male or intersex. These include chromosomal, hormonal, and anatomical characteristics. Sex is generally assigned at birth based on physiological characteristics, including genitalia and chromosome composition.

Gender is based on how the person identifies within the social constructs of norms, behaviours and roles of females and males.

Gender identity refers to the personal concept of oneself as male or female, or both, or neither. A person's gender identity may be the same as their assigned sex (cisgender) or differ from it (transgender).

Gender expression means the way a person communicates to the world their gender identification. This can include mannerisms and modes of dressing and speaking.

Sexual orientation relates to who a person is attracted to, emotionally and physically, and considers their own gender and that of the person they find attractive.

To have effective gender conversations with your child:

Listen to and acknowledge your child. Accept that your child is speaking their truth, even if it differs greatly from your experience. Allow them to express their feelings without interruptions, judgement or advice. Ask questions and validate their courage in starting the conversation. Above all, make them feel heard and understood.

Avoid gender-normative responses. It can be hard to accept that your child sees themselves differently from how you (and society) see them. Examine your own beliefs and values on gender and be open to understanding a different perspective. There is a great deal of literature available online regarding gender identity, which can help you relate to your child and allow them to feel comfortable in discussing their experiences with you. Ask about their preferred name and pronouns and how you can make changes to support their identity and be respectful of their privacy and decisions.

Guide your child through the minefield. Historically, intolerance towards gender differences has fostered offensive behaviour including name-calling, bullying and discrimination. However supportive and accepting your family is, these attitudes still prevail in many areas of society. Your child needs to be fortified against the reactions they may receive from intolerant members of society. Help them develop strategies to cope when they encounter offensive reactions from others, including safety plans to keep them out of dangerous situations. Practise appropriate responses, both verbal and behavioural, to others' reactions, while emphasising that the reaction says more about the other person than your child.

These situations can be especially difficult for ADHD children who have issues with emotional dysregulation or rejection sensitivity dysphoria. Processing emotions that feel overwhelming without overreacting is challenging, as is hearing criticism and condemnation without allowing it to further damage their self-esteem. These children will need additional support, understanding and kindness to develop resilience during this difficult time.

Get help. As always, take advantage of as many resources as possible to support your child, yourself and your family. There are many health-care providers who specialise in gender issues, as well as online and in-person support groups.

Dear Fathers,
Don't Let a Condition Your Son Didn't Ask for Define Your Relationship with them.
The last thing any father wants is to look back on his life and regret that he wasn't more
attuned to what his child needed when they were growing up. If your son has ADHD,
he doesn't need your criticisms or ridicule. He doesn't need 'tough love'. He needs
actual, unconditional love and understanding. It's not easy, but it's so important.
Ryan Wexelblatt, LCSW

If you were born in the 50s or 60s, you grew up at a time when ADHD was rarely diagnosed. Often, the guys in our grade who had (undiagnosed) ADHD were known for slinking into school high, reeking of pot. Other ones were shuttled into Special Ed classes, often with children who had much more significant challenges. Others didn't fit this mould – they could read books all day, but rarely socialised with anyone. Some of the lucky ones discovered vocational school or found a teacher who saw their strengths and helped them exploit them. ADHD has history. It has been around since the late 1700s, when it was first mentioned in a German medical textbook.

ADHD stems from a genetic mutation that sometimes is passed from parents to children. I can't tell you how many fathers have told me, 'I was just like him when I was his age.' Other fathers have shared with me that, based on their sons' behaviour, they're positive they have ADHD but were never diagnosed. There's a wide body of scientific evidence to prove ADHD exists, and it is genetic.

ADHD is more common today, but it is still not well understood by most educators and mental health professionals. People going into these fields learn very little about ADHD in their education and training. The only reason I can do the work I do is because I sought out education and training on my own. The majority of work I use is not from the mental health field, but from the speech-language pathology field.

So, what does it mean that ADHD is poorly understood by the people who work with our children? It means there's not a lot of effective help out there aside from medication. More importantly, it means that ADHD is often seen as a character flaw. Criticisms like 'lazy', 'unmotivated,' and 'he doesn't care about anything but video games' are often used to describe boys with ADHD.

I can't tell you how many times I've heard teachers make comments like 'He's smart; he just doesn't care.' This is a reflection of the teacher's frustration, which stems from their lack of education about how to support students with ADHD. It's important to know that intelligence has nothing to do with ADHD. You can't talk a child out of ADHD-related challenges by appealing to their intellect.

The bottom line is this: If you view ADHD as a character flaw in your son, there's a high likelihood it's going to negatively affect your relationship with him for many years to come.

The good news is that ADHD symptoms in children typically improve with brain maturation. There are many highly successful people who have learned to manage ADHD. There are also some who go through life struggling to sustain employment and social relationships. Unfortunately, some go down a dark path of drugs or alcohol as a way to self-medicate.

As your son's father, you need to make an important decision: Are you going to take a little bit of time to understand that the things your son does that annoy you or create stress in your house are not done intentionally? Are you going to allow yourself to understand that his brain development is lagging in certain areas, compared to other guys his age?

My unsolicited advice to you is this: You must take the time to educate yourself on the condition and focus on positive parenting. Watch some of my videos on the 'ADHD Dude' YouTube channel but, most importantly, don't let a condition your son didn't ask for define your relationship with him. ADHD is not his identity. It's not an excuse for disrespectful behaviour, but it is something that you can learn to help him deal with and that will help your relationship with him immensely.

Boys learn how to be men from their fathers and other male role models whom they choose to emulate. Think about your son being a father one day: Do you want to see him criticise your grandchildren or become frustrated with them? I think the last thing any father wants is to look back on his life and regret that he wasn't more attuned to what his children needed when they were growing up.

Let your son know that you're trying to learn what you can do to help him because, at the end of the day, that's what he needs most from you.

Your unconditional love and understanding, particularly when he's struggling the most, is what will help him become the type of man that you hope he'll become.

Glossary

Accommodations: Changes made to the learning environment curriculum in order to better serve children with special needs or learning differences. Accommodations can include but are not limited to test presentation, extended time, different testing locations and variation in the way material is presented and/or taught to students.

ADD: This refers to 'Attention Deficit Disorder', an older term for ADHD which some people still use, especially in reference to the presentation of ADHD that has less hyperactivity and is more characterised by inattention. This term has been replaced with the term 'ADHD' to include all presentations of this disorder.

ADHD: This refers to Attention-Deficit/Hyperactivity Disorder, the official name given this condition by the American Psychiatric Association. It is described in the *Diagnostic and Statistical Manual of Mental Disorders* as a persistent condition that impairs functioning or development, characterised by chronic inattention, hyperactivity, and often impulsivity.

ADHD Coach: A professional who is trained in both the field of coaching and ADHD who works primarily with adults and older teens to get past obstacles and reach their goals. Coaches often help those with ADHD with organisational and executive functioning challenges.

ADHD-Combined Type (ADHD-C): A subtype of ADHD characterised by both inattentive and hyperactive/impulsive symptoms of ADHD.

ADHD-Not Otherwise Specified (ADHD-NOS): A subtype of ADHD diagnosed when the inattention, hyperactivity and impulsivity symptoms are present, but the individual does not meet the full criteria for the other subtypes of ADHD.

ADHD-Predominantly Hyperactive-Impulsive (ADHD PH-I): A subtype of ADHD characterised by impulsivity and hyperactivity but lacking the symptoms of inattention.

ADHD-Predominantly Inattentive (ADHD-PI): A subtype of ADHD characterised by inattentive symptoms, but lacking hyperactivity and impulsivity symptoms.

Anxiety: Uneasiness of the mind, typically shown by apprehension, worry and fear about everyday situations. Anxiety can co-exist with ADHD.

Attentional Bias: Preferring to pay attention to certain objects, thoughts and activities that one finds interesting.

Behaviour Modification (or Behaviour Therapy): A type of treatment provided by a trained mental health professional that teaches clients how to identify the interconnection between thoughts, feelings and behaviours, and learn new skills that replace negative behaviours with positive ones.

Behavioural Contract: A simple positive-reinforcement contract between student and teacher, or between parent and child, that is designed to change behaviour. The contract explains the desired behaviour that will be increased and the reinforcement that will be earned. In addition, inappropriate behaviour is often listed, including the consequences for the behaviour.

Child Behaviour Checklist: A behavioural rating scale used by parents and teachers to evaluate emotional and behavioural problems in children.

CHADD – Children and Adults with Attention-Deficit/Hyperactivity Disorder: A non-profit organisation committed to helping people with ADHD, their families and the professionals who work with them.

Classroom Behaviour Management: Strategies and techniques used by teachers to manage the behaviour of students in the classroom and reduce classroom disruption.

Clinical Trial: Also called a research study, a clinical trial is designed to test an intervention, treatment or new approach. Clinical trials may compare a new treatment to a treatment that is already available.

Coexisting Conditions: When two or more mental health conditions are present in the same individual, they are said to be coexisting (also called co-occurring or co-morbid). For example, ADHD can co-exist with depression or anxiety.

Cognitive Restructuring: Changing self-defeating thought patterns brought about by earlier life experiences.

Comorbidity: Two or more disorders occurring in an individual at the same time.

Comprehensive Assessment: An evaluation process that takes into consideration any factors that contribute to an individual's current problems or functioning difficulties. These can include behaviours, education or employment skills, family history and relationships, emotional well-being, social skills, traumatic events and coexisting mental health conditions. Strengths and abilities are also assessed. The process forms the basis for a diagnosis and treatment plan.

Conduct Disorder: A group of behavioural and emotional problems in children and adolescents that can be exhibited as aggressive behaviour towards people and animals, destruction of property, lying, stealing, deceitfulness, and serious rule violations.

Daily Behaviour Report Card (DBRC): A daily method of communication between teachers and parents in which the behaviours of the child throughout the day are reported. The card can be adapted to develop behaviour goals, monitor the child's progress, or determine if behaviour interventions are working to improve the child's behaviour.

DSM-5 Diagnostic and Statistical Manual of Mental Disorders: This manual, written by the American Psychiatric Association, describes how mental health disorders are classified, including the symptoms used for diagnosis. It is used by various health care professionals and insurance companies across a wide range of settings to classify mental disorders for diagnosis and insurance purposes.

Distractibility: The inability to sustain attention on the task at hand so that it disrupts a person's concentration.

Dyslexia: A specific learning disability that impairs a person's ability to read. It is characterised by spelling challenges, word retrieval while speaking and a lack of fluency, causing reading to be slower and require much effort.

Executive Function (EF): Mental skills that allow us to control and coordinate other mental functions and abilities, such as planning or task completion. EF deficit is common in those with ADHD.

Functional Impairment Difficulties: These are life challenges which interfere with a person's ability to function in major life activities, including social situations, school, employment and in the community.

Hyperactivity: Having increased movement, impulsive actions, and a shorter attention span. A hyperactive person has constant activity and is easily distracted and impulsive. Other characteristics of hyperactive behaviour also include inability to concentrate, and aggressiveness.

Hyperfocus: A deep and intense mental concentration fixated on an activity, specific event or topic.

Impulsivity: Acting with little or no thought of the consequences or reacting rapidly without considering the negative consequences of the reaction.

Inattention: Failure to pay attention to a specified object or task.

Independent Educational Evaluation (IEE): An assessment conducted by a qualified examiner not employed by a school district to determine if a student may be eligible for special education. An IEE is conducted if parents disagree with a school district's assessment of their child's eligibility for special education.

Individualised Education Plan (IEP): A written document that describes the educational goals at school, and the methods of achieving these goals, for eligible children with disabilities. In Australia this is mandated by the *Disability Discrimination Act 1992* and the Disability Standards for Education This plan is based on the child's current level of performance.

Intervention: A structured process (or action) that has the effect of modifying an individual's behaviour, cognition, or emotional state.

Limited English Proficient (LEP): The term used by the federal government, most states, and local school districts to identify students whose difficulty in speaking, reading, writing, or understanding the English language will make it difficult to succeed in English-only classrooms.

Medication Holiday: A planned period of time, for medical or evaluation purposes, when prescribed medication therapy is temporarily discontinued. This should be undertaken only with the guidance of the prescribing medical practitioner.

Mental Health Therapist: A master's or doctoral level, licensed professional who is trained in assessment, diagnosis and treatment of mental health disorders. Most mental health therapists practise in areas of specialty, which can include ADHD and related disorders. They are trained in a broad range of therapies such as Cognitive-Behavioural, psychodynamic, marital, family, parent-child interaction, coaching, to name a few. They can include psychiatrists, psychologists, clinical social workers, professional counsellors, and marriage and family therapists.

Modification: Adjustments made to an assignment, test, or the general curriculum to meet the needs of a student when the expectations of the curriculum are beyond the student's ability. Modifications are written into the student's IEP.

Multimodal Treatment: ADHD in children often requires a comprehensive approach to treatment. This multimodal approach includes multiple interventions working together, tailored to the unique needs of the child, including parent training, medication and behavioural therapy.

Negative Self-Talk: Negative inner dialogue that brings out emotions such as guilt, fear, pessimism, anger, frustration, anxiety and depression. These thoughts often damage self-esteem and can appear in times of increased stress or emotional turmoil.

Neurobehavioural: Related to the relationship between the brain and behaviour.

Neurologist: A health care professional trained to diagnose and manage brain disorders.

Neuropsychologist: A psychologist trained in how the brain and the rest of the nervous system affect a person's behaviour and cognition. They are able to administer neuropsychological testing which aims to identify any challenges to full brain functioning, including identifying learning disabilities or the impact of illnesses or injuries to the brain.

Neurotransmitter: A chemical in the brain that functions as a messenger to transmit nerve impulses between nerve cells (neurons) within the nervous system.

Non-stimulant Medication: A medication that has been approved to treat ADHD – generally considered second-line medication – prescribed to those who have an incomplete response or no response to stimulants, cannot tolerate stimulants, or have certain coexisting psychiatric conditions.

Occupational Therapist: A licensed health care professional who provides therapy centred on sensory integration to address the physical, behavioural, and emotional effects of ADHD, and identifies goals to help the child succeed at school and at home.

Peer Rejection: When someone is purposely excluded from a social relationship or social interaction by peers.

Planned Ignoring: A behavioural intervention strategy in which one provides no attention to negative and maladaptive behaviour to reduce inappropriate behaviours.

Positive Behavioural Support (PBS): Rooted in research, PBS provides a systemic approach to decreasing problem behaviours and increasing socially acceptable behaviours in the individual and in the system, such as a school.

Prefrontal Cortex: The front part of the frontal lobe in the brain that plays a role in controlling attention, behaviour, judgment, and emotion.

Progress Monitoring: A practice to assess a student's academic performance, record performance data, and evaluate how well the student is responding to instruction as well as the effectiveness of the instruction.

Prosocial Behaviour: Positive actions to help others, motivated by a sense of empathy and caring, rather than for personal gain.

Psychologist: A licensed mental health professional trained in the study of behaviour, emotions and functioning. Psychologists are trained in psychological therapy, consultation and testing.

Psychoeducational Testing: An assessment process that includes tests, observations, and history taking to identify a student's cognitive strengths and challenges, in order to develop a plan for the student's success in the classroom.

Rebound Effect: The tendency in some medications (including some ADHD medications), when withdrawn from use, to lead to symptoms of greater severity than were present before the medication was initiated.

Response to Intervention (RTI): A multilevel prevention system used by schools to maximise student achievement and reduce behaviour problems. RTI is used to identify students at risk for learning failures, monitor student progress, provide evidence-based interventions, and adjust the interventions based on students' responsiveness.

Self-Regulation: Managing (regulating) one's own behaviour with appropriate behaviour and actions in order to attain one's goals.

Sensory Processing Disorder (SPD): Previously know as Sensory Integration Dysfunction, SPD is a condition in which the brain and nervous system are unable to correctly receive, organise and process information coming in from the senses, causing learning and behavioural problems.

Specific Learning Disability (SLD/LD): A disorder in the basic learning processes involved in understanding and using spoken or written language, that significantly interferes with a person's ability to listen, think, speak, read, write, spell, or do mathematics.

Speech or Language Impairment: A communication disorder including difficulties with articulation, stuttering, or a language impairment that adversely affects a person's educational performance.

Stimulant Medication: Medication that stimulate (increase) certain activity in the body's central nervous system, including the production and activity of neurotransmitters. Most medications approved for the treatment of ADHD are stimulant medications. When taken as prescribed, they generally help improve the symptoms of ADHD by promoting alertness, awareness, and the ability to focus.

Target Behaviour: A specific behaviour that has been chosen or 'targeted' either to increase in frequency (if it is a positive behaviour) or decrease in frequency (if it is a negative behaviour).

Token Economy System: A behaviour modification system in which a student earns tokens for exhibiting the desired behaviour. The tokens are exchanged at a later time for a reinforcer which is typically selected by the student.

Working Memory: A system in the brain that temporarily stores and processes the information needed for much more complex tasks such as reasoning, comprehension, and learning.

Notes

Notes

Notes

Notes

Notes

www.ingramcontent.com/pod-product-compliance
Lightning Source LLC
Chambersburg PA
CBHW041801280326
41926CB00103B/4767